BUREAUCRATIC
PROPAGANDA

BUREAUCRATIC PROPAGANDA

David L. Altheide
John M. Johnson
Arizona State University

Introduction by
Joseph R. Gusfield

Allyn and Bacon, Inc., Boston, London, Sydney, Toronto

For Tasha and Tod:
To help them see
a little more clearly

Library of Congress Cataloging in Publication Data

Altheide, David L
  Bureaucratic propaganda.

  Bibliography: p.
  Includes index
  1. Propaganda. 2. Bureaucracy. 3. Organization.
I. Johnson, John M., joint author. II. Title.
HM263.A669   301.15′4   79–11837
ISBN 0–205–06716–6

Printed in the United States of America

Contents

Preface

This study of official information has evolved with our changing interests, topics of study, and concern with bridging conceptual and methodological gaps between "micro" and "macro" levels of analysis. We are especially interested in showing the applicability of field studies to organizational and institutional analysis. Specifically, skills and techniques of individual impression-management are important at all levels of social life, including how members of an organization work to promote certain images of purpose and effectiveness.

We feel that a reconceptualization of propaganda that will include these crucial skills and procedures of impression-management can provide further insights into the role of various forms of symbolic communication in our lives. Moreover, our investigations into how official information is constructed and presented, and into the audiences it is intended for to achieve particular purposes, make it quite clear that any social scientist who accepts such reports as 'data' without being aware of the work that shaped them is likely to add to the mystique of legitimacy of these reports, as well as to obtain a highly distorted view of the organization.

Many people have provided important direct and indirect insights and support to our work. We are especially indebted to: Jack D. Douglas, Stanford Lyman, Joseph R. Gusfield, Peter Manning, Robert Snow, William Sanders, Paul Rasmussen, Gerald R. Deaver, and Danny Jorgensen.

A special thanks must be extended to the contribution of Arthur J. Vidich. The timely typing of the manuscript by Linda Jorgensen, and the heart-felt encouragement from Carla Altheide and Duane Altheide are greatly appreciated.

David L. Altheide
John M. Johnson

Introduction

Joseph R. Gusfield

I learned to drive an automobile comparatively late in life for an American—after twenty-five. When I was nineteen and in the U.S. Army, my division began a campaign to teach all men to drive an Army two-ton truck. I told the officer in charge that I didn't even know how to drive a car. It was no use. I was ordered into the cab of a truck and given the wheel. Promptly I drove the truck into a ditch. After this display of ignorance or stubborness, I was dismissed from the training session. My unit, and the entire division, reported that 100 percent of the men were now trained in driving a two-ton truck. Two years later, at another post, I was ordered to assume duties as an auxiliary truck driver. After all, my service record attested to the "fact" that I had been so trained. So was I vividly introduced to the discrepant worlds of "official facts" and "realities."

David Altheide and John Johnson have done a significant service to our understanding of the public world of fact and its relation to actualities. In using the concept of "propaganda" as a metaphor for the created world of organizational and official fact, they follow in recent sociological footsteps. They extend and enlarge the critical view now developing in contemporary sociology of official records as created and constructed events. They build on the work of phenomenological sociologists such as Aaron Cicourel, Jack Douglas, Harold Garfinkel, John Kitsuse and David Sudnow, who have studied psychiatric, legal, educational and suicide records. "*Propaganda*," wrote Harold Lasswell, "is the making of *deliberately* [Ital. mine, JG] *one-sided statements to a mass audience*." * What Altheide and Johnson demonstrate is how deliberation operates in the creation of much of official and public fact, not just in the special world of government public relations, military psychological warfare and commercial advertising.

We live in a world of symbols. The "society" and the real events outside of our immediate view must be reported to us and monitored. The

* Harold Lasswell, "Propaganda," *Encyclopedia Britannica*, v. 18. Chicago: Encyclopedia Britannica, Inc., 1965, p. 580.

keeping and transmission of records about what an organization does is a vast part of the public domain. In describing how newsrooms use records, how TV ratings are constructed and interpreted, how welfare agencies and naval units construct their records, how a religious movement counts "souls," readers of this book are given insight into the fragile nature of the public world.

It is not only the bureaucratic character of modern organization that requires keeping records. It is the political context of competition for scarce funds, for prestige and for continued political support that makes records-creation a self-serving activity. The development of the public as an arena of political and cultural activity has put a premium on rational discourse, as Alvin Gouldner points out in his book, *The Dialectic of Ideology and Technology.* As the court gave way to the newspapers and the cultural patron to the mass consumer, the audience of official actions was now diverse and multiple in its origins, interests and values. With the emergence of popular and participatory electorates, public accountability to voters, clients and consumers became the order of the day. Records are not only, or even chiefly, matters of internal orderly organization. They are performances for an audience, and rhetorical rather than scientific.

Altheide and Johnson point out that records have a dramaturgical significance. They present the person or the organization to spectators. The various Bureau of Labor Statistics indices of economic trends are not just matter-of-fact reports on the State of the Economy. They reflect the success or failure of an administration. They set off waves of response in business and financial circles. How they are constructed is then not without considerable consequence. In areas of economic development, planners are aware of the difference between setting goals high and spurring possible activity, or setting them low and making achievement of the plan more possible and thus more supportive of the incumbent government. Such considerations are behind the general skepticism about records, indices and stated goals that *Bureaucratic Propaganda* induces. This makes the reader eager to go beyond the summary statement or the single comprehensive statistic to the context and method by which the "fact" emerged.

From the standpoint of the audience of spectators, the organizational reporting of its activities builds up a version of social order. It presents a consistent world capable of being understood. Governments cannot tell their subjects that the economic realities are beyond official discovery, understanding or evaluation. So the Gross National Product, the amount of unemployment, the rate of productivity are expressed in "hard" figures as if their determination was exact and confidence in their "realness" can be assumed.

Scientific method often becomes a tool by which authority is made legitimate. The limitations, inexactitudes and necessary "fictions" used in obtaining conclusions are glossed over. The judgments used in obtaining data are ignored in the conclusions. What results is the sustained conception of an orderly world within which actions can be taken and defended on rational grounds. We cannot face the awesome possibility that the world may be significantly ruled by chance. "God does not play dice with the universe," Einstein is reported to have said.*

Another aspect of the social construction of records engages the chief concerns of Altheide and Johnson. This is the self-serving manner in which records are made and kept. At all levels of organizations, there is clear realization of the consequences of recording outcomes and of steps taken to insure rewarding rather than punishing results of monitoring and reporting. The instance of crime reports has long been discussed among criminologists. The stake of police in magnifying or minimizing reports is known. The use of discretion makes possible a variety of judgments. The nature of a charge or citation is by no means "given." For example, is a particular act to be construed as petty or grand larceny? That will depend on the monetary evaluation. Is an act a matter of assault or public drunkenness? Choice, self-interest and organizational interests are operative. Some years ago the U.S. Census was subject to considerable political pressures to define an area as an SMSA (Standard Metropolitan Statistical Area) or to increase the size of an SMSA from one category to another. Newspaper advertising rates were governed by the size of the circulation area and that was "pegged" to census categorization. The authority of records and statistical statements is not to be taken as an effort to ascertain a shiny, untouched and unscrubbed "reality."

Yet, Altheide and Johnson unduly minimize the limits to bureaucratic propaganda. A great deal of distrust exists among modern populations. Efforts to change behavior through such campaigns as anti-smoking and safety belt use are notoriously unsuccessful. The subtler systems of reality construction that the authors emphasize are not without suspicion. In the United States, as well as other modern societies, the search for the self-serving and self-interested character of official records is always a part of the scrutiny and doubt with which these populations greet governmental and corporate organizations. At this writing, the crisis of energy in America has been several years in the public eye yet still has not convinced many people of its reality. Whether fortunately or not, the American public is hardly a "pushover" for official rhetoric or records. The attitude of the 1940 Republican candidate for President is not untypical. Several years after the election, Wendell Willkie was confronted with a campaign speech of his that contradicted present testimony at a Congressional hearing. He waved the past speech aside with the phrase, "That's just campaign ora-

---

* I have examined the ways in which Science and public media construct a reality of order and exactness in the case of auto accidents, with particular reference to the role of alcohol in my forthcoming *The Illusion of Authority: Rhetoric, Ritual and Metaphor in Public Actions.*

tory." Just as we do not believe that the latest announced movie is *really* "the greatest ever made," so the skepticism that Altheide and Johnson want to engender is not wholly absent from daily life.

Much of this is evident in the recent revolt against experts. The criticism of the medical and academic professions is especially noteworthy. To see the vested interests in one or another version of reality is a way of taking the authority of professional knowledge with at least several grains of salty doubt. Increasing demands for client participation and forms of control strike at the legitimacy of professional authority and the right of professionals to assess and define the reality of their fields.

But the problem of how publics can relate to expertise and bureaucratic organizations remains. Altheide and Johnson have done much to heighten the realization of just how subtle are the ways in which the process of creating the world does operate. But the ability of the consumer, the client, the citizen to get behind and beyond the facades of lies, damn lies and statistics is still limited. If the public world is a facade, reflexively produced for the benefit of its progenitors, how is the individual to find his or her way in it? The authors recognize the problem but there it remains. Can these two worlds—the one official and suspect and the other actual but unknown—be bridged? Using the metaphor of propaganda helps to begin construction of that bridge. It washes away the assumption that deliberate construction of fact is only found in certain select areas. *Bureaucratic Propaganda* calls attention to the pervasiveness of its process and the subtlety of its results.

BUREAUCRATIC
PROPAGANDA

1

Propaganda
and Everyday Life

INTRODUCTION

We live in the midst of an information explosion. Many of our ideas about problems, issues, and the possibilities for the future are tied to the information we receive about them, and so it is crucial to understand how this information is derived and whether it is valid. We are especially concerned about information the public receives from the mass media and about the sources that provide media industries with the daily barrage of facts, figures, and interpretations. All this information contributes to people's sense of social order by supporting taken-for-granted standards and criteria of legitimacy.

Any person or organization who wants to be accepted and treated as legitimate will appear to be complying with preferred standards of knowledge and reality. Erving Goffman (1959) and others (cf. Lyman and Scott, 1970) have shown how people appear to be "who" their audiences expect them to be. These scholars enjoin us to view social life as a "drama" in the process of unfolding. They also say that anticipation-inspired-performances promote social rituals, routines, and rules that provide a sense of order and reality, which can also be the basis for charging that anyone not complying with such "rules" may be incompetent. But, as Goffman (1959) and others also note, a lot of "work" must take place to secure the presentation of self so that a performance does not become discredited and the performer redefined as illegitimate or as an undeserving outsider. We find similar work required with organizational self-presentations, or accounts. Therefore, we can use "propaganda" as a useful concept for clarifying how a major contributor to social order—the organizational form—survives through the appearance of legitimacy.

PROPAGANDA IN PERSPECTIVE

Propaganda, as a social scientific concept, has not been well understood. We will not systematically review the immense literature on this topic, because others have already done so (cf. Lee, 1952; Smith, 1968). Nor will we fault the scholars who have contributed to this knowledge; their focus was different than ours. We do suggest that a broader perspective on the essential meaning of propaganda shows it to have profound implications for current theory and research on our understanding of legitimacy, modernization, bureaucracy and formal organization, official information, and mass communication (cf. Bensman and Lilienfeld, 1973). We believe that propaganda, like all social phenomena, is not unique to one era or sphere of social life—although it has been treated as though it were. We also will argue that the historical context in which the original interest in propaganda as a phenomenon emerged has not been sufficiently analyzed. We hope to clarify this historical context and to note the important ties with legitimacy, modernization, bureaucracy and formal organizations, official information, and mass communications. Each of these topics now comprise specialities—and in some cases subdisciplines—within disciplines, and none, with the exception of mass communications, deals with "propaganda" in any systematic way. One result has been the failure to treat propaganda as a unique form of communication, rather than a heuristic concept useful in unravelling the interplay between appearance and reality.

Our aim is to extend the dramaturgical framework—the view that social order is accomplished through prescribed and institutionalized performances—to organizational analysis. This will be done by emphasizing two aspects of organizational activity: (1) what the members of the organization understand to be the practical significance of certain information for a particular audience; (2) the actual procedures used in constructing official reports to reflect what the audience expects from any "legitimate" organization, and the discrepancies between this official view and what many members know to be the truth. Just as students of organizations have long recognized the necessity for individual workers to appear to have adopted the organization's perspective for the sake of upward mobility, the necessity of convincing the public and other relevant audiences in the "external environment" that the organization is legitimate is also regarded as necessary. As Robert Presthus (1978: 256) notes:

> Legitimacy constraints also emanate from the environment. Any legitimacy an organization has been able to generate constitutes an asset in manipulating the environment.

Within the dramaturgical framework individuals and organizations can be conceptually compared in terms of impression management; but there are some important differences. Most significant is the medium of communication through which information is shared. In the case of individuals, the medium may involve speech, body language, eye contact, physical proximity, clothing, smell, and other aspects of personal style (cf. Lyman and Scott, 1970). These media may be manipulated by the actor in order to accomplish a particular impression with an audience in a situation. With organizations, on the other hand, official reports are the major medium of communication used when addressing audiences external to the organization.

This basic difference is very important for assessing the validity of information we receive. Consider individual interaction as an example. If someone is telling us something that we find hard to believe, we almost instinctively become more attuned to the person's body posture and eye contact. If either indicate that the person is nervous or somehow seems uncertain—maybe even guilty—about what we are being told, then we are less likely to accept the information at face value. The point is simply that in interpersonal communication we have more than one source of information, and with increased experience, we become more skilled in comparing one with the other. We are also aware of the significance of the situation in which the information is communicated. Anyone who has ever been involved in dating and courtship realizes that the words "I love you" mean one thing in a passionate embrace when two people barely know one another, but they may mean something quite different at another place and time. Anyone who takes these words literally without qualifying them is likely to learn a very painful lesson. Such knowledge comes with experience.

The techniques we have for assessing and comparing varieties of interpersonal information are usually unavailable in the case of official information generated by organizations. We have only the documents being read or shown or interpreted, and we seldom have the inside knowledge available to check on them; we must simply take someone's word for it. To do so implies that dramaturgical management is irrelevant for organizations, and that public knowledge about them is completely valid. As we will show in the following chapters, this naïve view has been legitimated by cultural myths and clever performances.

In addition to the differences in kind of information available to us about individual and organizational performance, there is a difference in complexity. Individuals may at times be torn between alternatives, but at a given time they do make unequivocal assertions. Despite the arguments by some psychoanalysts about what a person really intended, or really wanted to do, we can nevertheless say that an individual did act in a certain way at a certain time and place. However, this is not so true with organizations because, as outsiders, we do not see the myriad of conflicts and perspectives that occur within; we only get the public relations and front-work side of an organization.

What images these fronts will convey depend on the impressions believed to be desired for a particular audience. For example, during the oil embargo of 1973 and the overall curtailment of natural gas during the following two years, many institutions and organizations gave their unqualified endorsement of conservation and cited specific adjustments being made to "do their part" in winning the energy war. All pronouncements were intended for public consumption via the mass media in order to validate institutional legitimacy. Moreover, opportunities for such responses help promote the public belief that organizations are real entities, uniform in scope and purpose, rather than comprised of groups and divisions that frequently disagree. Conflicts abound, as do major conflicts that feature long and bitter battles over resources, respect, and control. This is more true in large corporations made up of dozens of departments that often compete for symbols, materials, and financial rewards. But such splits are seldom communicated to outsiders through official information. Indeed, often the only way we learn about the exact nature of this small-scale warfare is through disgruntled "insiders" who "leak" information to the press and other mediators. Thus, there are multiple realities within organizations, but official reports generally convey only one reality. Presthus's (1978: 119) cumulative research experience in organizations leads him to observe: ·

> Internal differences of interest and opinion are muffled in an effort to present a public image of a discipline and unity that will enhance the organization's authority and its competitive chances. Dissent and criticism are repressed or confined within the organization. . . . The common requirement that speeches and publications be cleared through a 'public-information' agency is germane. Unfavorable reports can easily be dismissed as irresponsible or unauthorized, the implication being that the organization's elites are its only responsible spokesmen. These are the priests who represent the organization before the public, interpret its catechism, and explain away any disparity between its high ideas of service and its routine behavior.

This book is about the gap between organizational image and reality, the reasons this gap exists, and the implications it has had—and will continue to have—for our lives. We have selected propaganda as a useful concept for examining the nature of dramaturgical management through official information. But current formulations of propaganda, and especially the connotations of the term, need to be spelled out so that a broader application of the core meaning of propaganda can be applied to official information as a mode of institutionalized legitimacy. Consider Qualter's (1962) definition of propaganda:

> The deliberate attempt by some individual or group to form, control, or alter the attitudes of other groups by the use of the instruments

of communication, with the intention that in any given situation the reaction of those so influenced will be that desired by the propagandist.

Stated differently, if some interested party wants to influence and manipulate a particular group of people via communication to that party's own advantage, then how the party does this is called *propaganda*.

For now, it is important to emphasize why anyone would want to influence or manipulate another with propaganda, because this suggests that propaganda involves interaction between a communicator and a target audience. The definitions each has of the other will have a bearing on the form and content of propaganda, as well as on whether a serious attempt is made to manipulate the audience.

Our reformulation of propaganda will be apparent in the following pages; for now we can simply distinguish it from its "traditional" connotation, and refer to it as *bureaucratic propaganda: Any report produced by an organization for evaluation and other practical purposes that is targeted for individuals, committees, or publics who are unaware of its promotive character and the editing processes that shaped the report.*

Readers accustomed to the traditional connotations of propaganda may find our usage strange; this is to be expected since the historical tendency to associate propaganda with some forms of communication and not others has itself been a product of "bureaucratic propaganda." Specifically, and as the remainder of this chapter will show, students of propaganda have focused on governments' efforts to manipulate a mass of people through the mass media (cf. McQuail, 1969); others have examined advertising. However, there are surprisingly few investigations of official information from other spheres of social life, and particularly those claiming to be "efficient," "rational," and "scientific." In light of the dominance of certain interpretations of propaganda, we will put propaganda in perspective in order to show how current limited usage of the term developed in social science and restricted its conceptual application to certain kinds of official information.

The Emergence of Propaganda

The first appearance of propaganda has been traced to the Greek city-states about 500 B.C. with the codification of the "rhetoric" that was promoted by Plato and Aristotle. These "tricks" of logic were deduced in part from the actual practice of successful lawyers, demogogues, and politicians (Smith, 1968).

One of the first people to use knowledge for more than debate and intellectual one-upsmanship was Niccolò Machiavelli (1469–1527). He may also have been the first to market his manipulative skills for a professional career. His discourses describe how to maintain a kingdom, placate the masses, and in general, use knowledge to present desired appearances. For example, when considering whether or not a prince should keep his word, Machiavelli wrote (1963: 62–63):

> How praiseworthy it is that a prince keeps his word and governs by candor instead of craft, everyone knows. Yet the experience of our own time shows that those princes who had little regard for their word and had the craftiness to turn men's minds have accomplished great things and, in the end, have overcome those who governed their actions by their pledges. . . . It follows, then, that a wise prince cannot and should not keep his pledge when it is against his interest to do so and when his reasons for making the pledge are no longer operative. . . . *Therefore a prince will not actually need to have all the qualities previously mentioned, but he must surely seem to have them* [italics ours]. Indeed, I would go so far as to say that having them all and always conforming to them would be harmful, while appearing to have them would be useful.

Machiavelli's skill in using information for practical purposes was institutionalized and accepted as common sense by officials and bureaucrats within two centuries.

Skill in "tricky logic" has always had a practical nature, but modern usage of propaganda as a deliberate way to influence people appears to have evolved out of a religious order in 1622. The Propaganda of the Congregatio de Propaganda Fide (Congregation for Propagation of the Faith), a standing committee of the cardinals in charge of missionary activities, expressed a holy commitment to "spread the word" rather than specific strategies (Smith, 1968).

In each of these cases, note that the nature and form of propaganda was influenced by the audience to be addressed and the purpose to be served. One does not win an argument with scholars through emotional appeals; other tactics must be used. The cardinals could not propagate their faith if they did not speak in the language and appeal to the cultural symbols shared by the faithless.

It was the emergence of "public opinion" as a legitimate and essential political fact of life that pushed propaganda beyond mere rhetoric and sacred incantations. Until the idea of the public was recognized as a relevant audience to be communicated with, there was no need to develop sophisticated techniques for manipulation; rulers simply did what they and their supporters deemed necessary. Indeed, symbolic legitimacy was not always essential for authority; power was often enough. Henri Pirenne (1956: 150) provides an apt example of the direct role of power in creating order and dominance during the tenth century in Europe:

How could the political power have remained centralized in the hands
of the king at a time when the people were entering en masse into
the cadres of the great estates, into dependency on the seigneurs?
Political power was bound to follow effective power, and to crystallize
itself, so to speak, around those who really possessed that power The
protection of human beings is not merely the primordial function of
the State: it is also the origin of the state. Now the king no longer
protected his subjects; the magnates protected them. It was therefore necessary and beneficial that they should dismember the State
to their own advantage. They certainly had public opinion—or shall
we say, the sentiment of the peoples—on their side. Nowhere do we
see that the 'little man' attempted to save the monarchy. He no
longer knew what monarchy was.

In short, when the social and economic conditions are compatible with
absolute power, then legitimacy is relatively clear-cut.

But when social and economic conditions changed to the extent that
a government relied on the symbolic support of the people, as was true
with republics and democracies, then public opinion came into existence.
According to one student of the development of public opinion, Hans
Speier (1950: 376), public opinion will exist when a unique "right" is
granted a significant portion of extragovernmental persons:

In its most attenuated form this right asserts itself as the expectation
that the government will publicly reveal and explain its decisions in
order to enable people outside the government to think and talk
about these decisions, or to put it in terms of democratic amenities,
in order to assure "the success" of the government's policy.

If a government denies the relevance of the citizens' voice, or if enough
information is not made available to the citizens, then public opinion does
not exist.

People in power had always been aware of the potential for revolts
and the necessity to keep abreast of public sentiments, but the right of
the masses to play a more direct role did not occur until ideas and conditions changed. Speier (1950) and Palmer (1936) agree that even though
the term *public opinion* was first used in the eighteenth century and did
not become a part of political theory until the nineteenth century, the
impetus for the fundamental change involved the Protestant Reformation
and the Renaissance, both of which resulted in widespread discussions
about competing beliefs, ideas, and opinions about the role of the common man in government. Speier (1950: 379) argues that the final changes
involved basic institutional processes, which led to the restriction of absolutist rule and contributed to the rise of public opinion. Among these
changes were:

1. Gains in economic power of the middle class.
2. The gradual spread of literacy and the growth of a broad reading public, without mediation of priests.
3. Relatedly, the growth of secular literature and libraries.
4. The change of musical life and public concerts.
5. Coffee houses and salons where intellectuals could meet.

Such changes, of course, affected the middle class more than others, and not everyone was "really" involved in promoting public opinion as a political force, but the idea had been spawned and was beginning to have effects.

Public opinion as sentiment became a symbolic reality when government officials openly began considering it in making their decisions. The term was first used following the French Revolution by Louis XVI's finance minister, Jacques Necker, who sought to bolster confidence in persons investing in the Paris money market. That these people mattered to the financial stability of France, and had therefore forged a significant relationship with the government, is also noted by Rehberg's (1809: 58) claim that the government felt compelled to answer:

Necker's publication of fiscal statements was done to:

> calm the public which began to distrust the administration of finances and feared that the income of the treasury could not offer any security to the capital and interests of its creditors. (Speier, 1950: 379).

The significance of public opinion for future government involvements was not clear at this time, although at least one contemporary of Necker's saw trouble ahead. At the end of the ancien régime, Count Vergennes (Speier, 1950: 385) wrote in a confidential report to the king:

> If Necker's public opinion were to gain ascendency, Your Majesty would have to be prepared to see those command who otherwise object and to see those obey who otherwise command.

Some enlightenment thinkers felt the government should play a role in what could euphemistically be termed *adult education.*

> The people should be brought to develop their patriotic virtues by way of exaltation over public celebration in which they were to participate—an idea—one might say, which was realized in both the institutionalized public celebration of the French Revolution and in the Nuremberg festives of the Nazi's and in May Day celebrations (Speier, 1950: 383).

But the Nazi's time had not yet arrived; first would come decades of official and intellectual vacillation on the true significance and role of public opinion for the social order, including the question of what should be done about it. Even though propaganda procedures on behalf of the government had not yet been institutionalized, some officials attempted to gain mileage by fueling public sentiment:

> The art of arousing public opinion became nevertheless a valued skill during the nineteenth century even of statesmen like Bismarck, who failed to respect public opinion, remained indifferent to its moral claims, and made no attempt to raise its level of competence (Speier, 1950: 385).

But this was an exception, at least in the nineteenth century. Many government people believed that public opinion could provide a useful direction for the conduct of both domestic and foreign affairs. As Speier (1950: 386) notes:

> If war did occur, government by public opinion would enter therein in the conviction that the national interests they defended were the interests of enlightened mankind. . . . According to the theory of public opinion, it is the function of government in foreign affairs to make the world safe for the rule of public opinion.

Such claims became a moral foundation for pursuing policies suggested by government officials:

> Once the importance of public opinion was discovered as a new factor in international relations, it became tempting on moral as well as on expediential grounds to utilize it (Speier, 1950: 384).

The firm grounding of this noble ideal in the enlightenment tradition and generations of democratic promoters did not protect it from the awesome forces of World War I. Not only did these events suggest that public opinion may be misdirected, but they also led many critics to argue that the public could be duped by clever propagandists. Intellectuals like Walter Lippmann (1922; 1925) passionately placed the entire issue of the nature and role of "public opinion" in perspective:

> The public is not, as I see it, a fixed body of individuals. It is merely those persons who are interested in an affair and can affect it only by supporting or opposing the actors (1925: 77).

And,

> We may be sure that any body of farmers, business men, trade unionists will always call themselves the public if they can. . . .

> No ordinary bystander is equipped to analyze the propaganda by which a private interest seeks to associate itself with the disinterested public (1925: 133).

In short, the widespread belief in, and support of, public opinion rendered it vulnerable to symbolic manipulation by those who wanted to appear legitimate; public opinion was itself subject to propaganda. This realization led Lippmann (1922: 103) to conclude:

> It is the thesis of this book that the members of the public, who are the spectators of action, cannot successfully intervene in a controversy on the merits of the case. They must judge externally, and they can act only by supporting one of the interests directly involved.

Such insights make it apparent that the criteria and significance of legitimacy in a particular historical period are inextricably tied to information control. The agent who can manipulate sacred symbols, but avoid detection, is capable of appearing legitimate, and therefore, of becoming more forceful in defining and maintaining the public view of social order.

The brief historical context of the emergence of propaganda shows that the relevant audience—the public—had only recently come into existence. The main source of potentially corrupting and manipulative messages was the government, especially in times of crisis (cf. Lasswell, 1927), such as World War I. Indeed, journalists and intellectuals joined their respective government forces to capture the "public mind." This was done because it was believed that the majority of people were vulnerable to slick emotional appeals by the enemy. For this reason our own government fed its citizens propaganda to counter any images set forth by foreign powers. And our enemies did the same (cf. Irwin, 1936).

The engulfment of intellectuals and scholars by World War I had two effects pertinent to this discussion: First, many social scientists became involved in the study of propaganda via the mass media, including investigations into more effective ways to dupe the enemy citizens. Second, the funding of research and the emergence of an extensive literature involving the government as the source of propaganda messages led to the continuing focus on this aspect of propaganda and discouraged further extensions of the concept to other spheres of social life. The net effect has been to remove propaganda from other arenas in which images of legitimacy can be manipulated for self-serving purposes.

The influence of historical context on the study of propaganda is best illustrated by showing how the "traditional" view of propaganda needs to be further elaborated if it is to apply to the strategic use of official information by virtually all formal organizations in the United States and throughout the Western World. We refer to this more inclusive use as "bureaucratic propaganda."

FROM TRADITIONAL TO BUREAUCRATIC
PROPAGANDA

We want to emphasize that propaganda is a powerful force in contemporary society and that it has become institutionalized primarily
through organizational reports. But the empirical and theoretical tradition
that shaped the conceptual development of propaganda has tended to exclude the more conventional and "rational" domains of social life. Indeed,
many critics of irrational acts and beliefs, including Jeremy Bentham and a
host of social scientists, argued that rational approaches can be relied on
for guidance. All of these people have overlooked how even the most
"rational" approaches and methods to issues and problems can be used
and misunderstood.

By way of introduction to our framework for recasting propaganda,
it is useful to see the role of organizational propaganda (bureaucratic
propaganda) within a propaganda agency—the United States Information
Agency (USIA). Leo Bogart's (1976) study was completed in 1954 but
was not officially released until 1973. Interviews with agency personnel
show how the avowed purpose of the USIA to "sell America to the
world," especially to those countries most susceptible to Communist influence, was stymied by practical considerations involving congressional
approval, funding, selecting men and women for various jobs, and resolving disputes about the best way to convince their operatives and legislative
overseers that they were doing a good job. As one operator put it,

> So much of our program is geared to gaining Congressional favor
> that we aim more than 50 percent of it on what effect it is going
> to have on Congress and less than 50 percent on what effect it is
> going to have on people overseas (Bogart, 1976: 27).*

Part of this effort at casting their official reports to insure future funding
was "to maintain the appearance at all times of fairness," partly because
some scrutinizers did not understand that "you cannot fight black shirts
and brown shirts and red shirts with stuffed shirts . . . idealists who don't
believe in hitting below the belt." USIA operators also had to convince
their audiences overseas that they were being fair.

> We have to maintain the appearance at all times of fairness. We
> are news reporters and a reporter does not go out and get just one
> side of the thing. If you are telling a story, you want to be telling

---

* Bogart, Leo. *Premises for Propaganda: The United States Information Agency's
Operating Assumptions in the Cold War.* New York: Free Press, 1976. Reprinted with
permission.

a comprehensive story, even though it's slanted in the sense that you show us in a favorable light (Bogart, 1976: 134).*

In short, this effort to achieve international propaganda (or traditional [political] propaganda) was dependent on successful bureaucratic propaganda. The latter supported the former. Those outside the organization who did not realize what was going on and did not see through the organizational propaganda were led to believe that our international propaganda effort was sound, effective, and well-coordinated. For example, Congressmen were not likely to learn from the USIA's annual report about internal squabbles and conflicts between policy makers and the field operators. Thus, many legislators and millions of taxpayers were officially led to believe that the United States was pursuing a well-coordinated and systematic propaganda effort when in fact various departments and officials were battling over scarce funds, prestige, and approval from superiors.

The traditional definition of propaganda as the deliberate attempt to alter attitudes through communication may have been adequate at an earlier time in our history when the most obvious efforts to define reality through manipulation were occurring. This was especially true during and following World War I. Indeed, the distorted messages that many nations have engaged in during our various "hot" and "cold" wars helped focus public and social-scientific attention on the awesome potential of such communications. All indications are that major world powers still promote domestic and international propaganda for their own purposes. Anyone who lived through the Vietnam conflict period is well aware that governmental and military censorship and control of public information did not end when allied troops pushed Hitler and Goebbels to suicide. Governments still do lie to the public, and through their influence and political perogatives have been able to affect what the public knows and believes (Bagdakian, 1974). However, and as we shall argue in more detail, the experience and sophistication of the American public and other industrialized peoples are making such governmental pronouncements less credible. For example, the Watergate episode has clearly damaged American political leadership. But this brand of propaganda is far less crucial in influencing public opinion and spurring people to take action than are the official and "scientific" reports we have termed bureaucratic propaganda. The President of the United States, for example, need not convince Americans that there is a crime problem; reports of police, FBI, and other agencies are routinely carried by the news media, and these are convincing.

In order to see the role of propaganda within modern organizations, we must first conceptually refine what the essentials of propaganda are

* Bogart, Leo. *Premises for Propaganda: The United States Information Agency's Operating Assumptions in the Cold War.* New York: Free Press, 1976. Reprinted with permission.

and note relevant similarities and differences between our expanded application and that traditionally associated with the term. Examining the definitions of Qualter (1962) noted earlier, and also Lippmann (1922), Goebbels (1948), Ellul (1965), Lasswell (1927), Smith (1968), and the fifty or so definitions offered by Childs (1965) shows that four common elements are implicit in propaganda: (1) target, (2) medium, (3) purpose, and (4) truth. Contrasting how "traditional" use of propaganda differs from our formulation of official information generated for organizational purposes, or "bureaucratic propaganda," is an important step toward a more systematic understanding of the role and use of official communications in contemporary life.

1. Target

Traditional Propaganda. Practitioners and theorists agree that the target of propaganda is a mass audience (cf. Merton, 1946). Hitler's brilliant propagandist Goebbels, stated:

> It is crowds rather than isolated individuals that may be induced to run the risk of death to secure the triumph of a creed or an idea, that may be fired for enthusiasm for glory and honor. . . (Neumann, 1942: 125).

Goebbels had little respect for his audience.

> If today an educated person says: "That is too primitive for me," then I counter: "You name me a world view which does not do this to set the masses in motion. . . . I can only advise him to listen to the parson in Hinterupfing. He speaks that way too, so that his provincials understand him, and his words are not at all on the level of a sermon which the Pope might deliver in Saint Peter's" (Baird, 1974: 18).

Ellul's (1965: 6) insightful comments about propaganda are also committed to a mass audience.

> For propaganda to address itself to the individual, in his isolation, apart from the crowd, is impossible. The individual is of no interest to the propagandist . . . to win men over one takes much too long . . . to create certain convictions in an isolated individual is much too difficult. Propaganda ceases where simple dialogue begins.

As noted earlier, the focus on a mass audience in traditional propaganda grew out of the experience of World War I and the prevailing theories of social order. Social science was committed to the doctrine that technology and urbanization had stripped away the stabilizing influences of family, religion, and friends. According to this view, millions of isolated individuals were the result; they were believed to be susceptible to a variety of stimuli that could drive them one way and then another (De Fleur, 1970: 112–117). The mass media, and especially newspapers and radio, were capable of communicating with the members of a mass society, and thereby came to be very influential. As World War I dragged on thousands of miles away from home, it became apparent that the mass media could be used to manipulate the public to support the war effort and to degrade the enemy with carefully selected atrocity stories. Following the war, many persons who had cooperated in this deception became concerned about the power of such propaganda over a mass society and began studying it. Thus, the link between government, the mass, and propaganda was established and has been a central feature of propaganda analysis ever since. This emphasis has persisted despite studies that show that America is less a mass society than a conglomerate of conflicting interest groups (cf. Katz and Lazarsfeld, 1955; Freidson, 1953; Gusfield, 1963).

Bureaucratic Propaganda. The target for bureaucratic propaganda is often an individual, group, or specific segment of the population. Unlike traditional propaganda, which focused on the mass audience to gain their support, bureaucratic propaganda may aim at influentials and interest groups involved in specific decision making.

We find that even the government, the traditional source of propaganda, is now more attuned to the newer forms of information control and uses them quite effectively to justify budget appropriations and to appear decisive. A decision by President Carter in January, 1977, to increase the strength of NATO forces in Europe raised some questions about what "increase" means, in light of the uncertainty about the approximate size of NATO troop and support strength. A writer for United Press International put it this way:

> Depending on what forces are counted and other variables, analysts estimate the number of NATO combat aircraft at 1,800 to 3,460 and Warsaw Pact aircraft at 2,500 to 3,680. . . . The report (Congressional Budget Office) says some analysts question the entire concept of comparing numbers of people, weapons and units, calling them "bean counts" with little meaning. Using such criteria . . . France and Britain should have easily defeated Germany in 1940 (Arizona *Republic*, Jan. 8, 1978).

It is easy to recognize that such qualifications are never made when officials are making their case for increased military spending. Carter's 1979 budget requested a ten billion dollar increase for the Defense Department, most of which would go to strengthen NATO. The increase was said to provide for "prudent growth" in the contributions to United States ground and air forces, committed to defending Western Europe, which was claimed to require an annual three percent increase to offset increased defense spending by the Soviets (Phoenix *Gazette,* Jan. 23, 1978).

It is the strategy of the organizational propagandist wittingly or unwittingly to cultivate the assumptions and "knowledge" of these targets for personal gain. In this sense, these propagandists understand the essential and strategic use of information in the context of our rational and bureaucratically based society. Most decisions helpful to an organization's survival, continued public and governmental support, and general legitimacy involve selected people. This fact, plus the array of conflicting ethnic groups and subsocieties within our nation's borders, actually make it unwise to appeal to the mass audience; Americans will agree on very little. This pluralism makes it essential to pick and choose the correct target for each situation and purpose.

This does not mean that the mass audience is irrelevant for bureaucratic propaganda. The public belief in consensus government and the concomitant symbolic necessity to achieve legitimacy when possible urge practitioners of information control to obtain public approval. Such approval is seldom given, but is inferred from the lack of massive protest following publication of a decision or action paved with bureaucratic propaganda. "Modern princes" seldom consult the public when more practical and expeditious means are available, although the public may be used as part of a strategy to support an individual or program (cf. Wise, 1973). President Johnson did this with his Vietnam policy; President Nixon did this with Vietnam and Watergate; President Ford did this with the Mayaguez incident. In each case, claims were made that the public is "behind me" and the number of telegrams received would be cited in support. The effect was actually to define for the public what the issues were and what position should be taken. This strategy did not always work, as indicated by Johnson's, and then Nixon's, Vietnam strategy, and Nixon's resignation over the Watergate incident. But these defeats were produced less by public outrage and their understanding of the issue than by opponents who were able to foster other public definitions of the "facts" and provide other interpretations about what the respective events meant to social order, public confidence, and our form of government (cf. Altheide, 1976; Vidich, 1975). In brief, the effort to promote the myth that public approval matters in many areas of everyday life is now a strategic element for contemporary users of propaganda.

2. Medium

Traditional Propaganda. The early efforts to manipulate the "mass society" relied on the mass media. This was the most direct way of manipulating public opinion. The most famous effort to control the media in modern times was Hitler's domination of press, theatre, film, and radio. This control, plus dramatic mass rallies, enabled his assistant, Goebbels, to repeat mythical themes of German invincibility, Jewish inferiority, and the eternal rightness of the Third Reich (Baird, 1974). The significance of this media control for running the Nazi government was well understood by Goebbels:

> By sealing them off hermetically from the outside world and by reiterating its empty phrases about salvation, universal happiness, and so on, has succeeded in bamboozling the peasants and workers into believing that this state of affairs constitutes paradise on earth. One can arrive at independent judgment only by means of comparison. Here such possibilities of comparison are totally lacking (Riess, 1948: 104).

The apparent German success, combined with American efforts in both World Wars, led researchers further to emphasize the power of the mass media and its importance for propaganda. What was overlooked, however, was the variable significance of diverse media for different audiences at different times. The possibility that other media may have even greater significance in promoting power and programs seems never to have been raised. Goebbels was aware that the important media change with historical and social conditions: "What the press has been for the nineteenth century, radio will be for the twentieth century (Riess, 1948: 105)." Just as Goebbels geared his propaganda efforts to radio and his other favorite media (Hardy, 1967; Zeman, 1973), politicians and others who specialize in presenting visual images over television strive to strike a responsive chord in viewers. The idea is to get people to react and not necessarily think (T. Schwartz, 1975). There is no doubt that the mass media continue to play an important part in propaganda efforts, but other media must not be overlooked.

Bureaucratic Propaganda.   Organizations use a variety of media in their propaganda work. The more obvious efforts of public relations specialists, advertisements, and financial and other bribes are minor compared to how the official reports are constructed and used. The public may never see these projects or annual reports. Perhaps only a congressional committee or some citizen's group will use these accounts as "evidence" for some program or action. The report, and the context in which it is used, such as a hearing or committee meeting, are relevant media for bureaucratic propaganda. For example, Tad Szulc's (1976: 13) description of the ongoing battle between the Pentagon and the CIA for control of American intelligence led members of each agency to fashion their reports primarily for self-serving reasons. This was especially important for Congressional funding.

> What existed, then, was a collection of intelligence fiefdoms, all auton-
> omous in such matters as drawing up their secret budgets for con-
> gressional authorization. For the most part, Congress did not know
> what it was approving because requested intelligence funds were
> concealed in other budgetary line items.

The skillful placement of information in an effort to reduce its digres-
sive impact may also be considered a kind of medium. Any situation in
which information is presented, assessed, and decisions rendered should
not be overlooked as an important medium susceptible to manipulation
and distortion through official reports. The results, findings, and recommendations of these "media" may find their way to newsrooms and then
be disseminated via the mass media. But what the mass media do with
these reports depends on their organizational needs and not on direct
manipulation by government and other organizations. This does not mean
that reporters or their superiors are never influenced by these interests,
but rather that ideological autonomy is a characteristic of news organizations in the United States and most Western European nations. The absence of overt ideological pressure does not guarantee that other systematic
distortions will not infect news messages. As we point out in chapter 2,
the news process creates its own perspective for looking at events. This is
why the news media are a medium in their own right. They do not merely
select and refine organizational reports and other sources of information;
they also construct priorities and emphases in fulfilling their own practical
requirements. The upshot is that the organizations that provide official
reports to fulfill their interests may rely on reporters, who know little
about the substance of the report, to present the sanctioned image to the
public. But the reporter is also constrained in his or her work by fulfilling
the requirements of newswork. Both parties are involved in the propaganda process, and the medium each uses must be understood.

3. Purpose

Traditional Propaganda. As traditionally viewed, propaganda is the
deliberate attempt to alter attitudes to make them correspond to those of
the propagandist. Propaganda can also reinforce deeply held cultural beliefs. Baird (1974: 4) found the myth of Aryan superiority to be dominant
in his study of Nazi propaganda. The Nazis used their control of the mass
media to repeat and reinforce anti-Semitic themes already in vogue. As
Goebbels argued,

> A government must make propagandistic preparations in order to draw the people on its side. . . . Public enlightenment is essentially passive; propaganda is active. . . . We are determined to work on the masses until they have fallen to us [Riess, 1948: 101).

The Nazis could do this because they could exert a great deal of pressure on the mass media "in the National interest." However, as access to the mass media has become more of a problem, and as the number and array of media outlets have increased, such control is more and more difficult. But propaganda has not disappeared; it has just changed. The purpose of propaganda is closely bound with the resources one commands; if the media are necessary to capture the national mind, but if they are not readily available, then that purpose will not be fulfilled. The same is true of any purpose: one must work within practical limitations. This is what contemporary propagandists have done.

Bureaucratic Propaganda.   The purpose of modern propaganda is to maintain the legitimacy of an organization and its activities. The practical and day-to-day aspects of organizations are well understood by their workers, but all actions are symbolically changed when placed in the context of an official report. These accounts, subject to evaluation by superiors, other officials, and organizations, are constructed to reflect what an organization is presumed to do and how well it does it. In hoping to satisfy evaluators and thereby legitimize the organization's activities and purpose, official reports have inadvertently presented contrived, managed, and essentially decontextualized pictures of their respective portions of social life. Thus, the overriding purpose of bureaucratic propaganda is not to dupe everyone, but it is intended to convince relevant persons. However, as these reports claim to be "objective" assessments of a task, and are then disseminated to the public via the mass media, their purpose changes. What was once only part of culture is now shaping culture. For example, police crime statistics are no longer merely one way of organizationally accounting for the kind and amount of certain types of work done by individuals as a way of justifying expenditures and salaries; crime statistics are now regarded as "objective" indicators of the amount of crime in our society and the threat it poses to all our safety unless the tide is turned.

Bureaucratic propaganda is less a feature of the mass society, mass media, and government domination, than it is the widespread belief in science, rationality, and objectivity. These topics will be examined in more detail later in this chapter, but for now it must be emphasized that the subtle power of propaganda lies in its behind-the-scenes power to influence decisions and define reality. We have already noted how the use of such media as official reports and "objective" studies can directly influence decisions that in turn can indirectly affect the public domain. Simply stated, the purpose of most official information is to maintain the positions and interests represented by officials who sponsor and sanction the information. That organizations are committed to their own survival should lead us to anticipate numerous self-serving actions, including attempts to define reality through the resources they command. As noted previously, this is what Ellul (1965: 15) refers to as "sociological" propaganda, or the meaningful context for many individual decisions and beliefs. Without intending the cumulative effects on what amounts to an ongoing structuring of culture, people as workers in organizations can promote myths and incorrect assessments of social situations just by doing their jobs. Consider official reports.

Reports may be constructed in order to obtain further funding, promote organizational careers, assign responsibility for a particular act to an "enemy," and in general "cover your ass" from revelation before a sanctioning body. The USIA became very adept at this during the cold war. Bogart (1976: 11 ff.) found that even though field operators did not think strong anti-communist messages would be effective, pressures from the rampaging forces of Joseph McCarthy forced USIA personnel strategically to emphasize the "communist menace." The aim was not merely to provide another ideological orientation through such programs as Voice of America, but to "prove to the boys on the Hill that we are good Americans." The impact of this pressure was described by one operator:

> We seem to blow with every wind that comes from the Hill. . . .
> Every Tom, Dick, and Harry with an axe to grind on the Hill can
> swashbuckle through the thing and pull things out of context and set
> that part of the program . . . off in an entirely new direction that
> may be partly at variance with what the upper echelons of the Agency
> have decided is right and proper and may also cause us to lose con-
> siderable credibility overseas (Bogart, 1976: 28).*

Even though USIA policy became "warped by having to justify everything in terms of fighting communism," the organization continued to operate; the meaning of the work just changed.

> A great deal of our activity is designed to show our effectiveness,
> particularly in terms that can be explained before a congressman
> (Bogart, 1976: 28). †

The impact of altering activities and official reports "to not tread on congressional toes" was to emphasize the accounting procedures over the pre-

---

* Bogart, Leo. *Premises for Propaganda: The United States Information Agency's Operating Assumptions in the Cold War.* New York: Free Press, 1976. Reprinted with permission.
  † Ibid.

sumed goal of international propaganda. Thus, the image that the USIA was an effective "propaganda machine" was itself a piece of organizational propaganda.

A more recent example involves efforts to curtail the flow of illegal "heavy" narcotics into American cities. The Drug Enforcement Administration, (DEA), was created in 1973 to combat this aspect of the drug problem. Like most organizations, a great deal of effort was made to legitimize itself before appropriate funding bodies. This could be done by spectacular news coverage for big "busts" and by making many arrests. But unlike most official reports that are accepted by other officials and organizations, a Senate subcommittee critically scrutinized the DEA's activities. They concluded:

> Although DEA has presented statistics to demonstrate considerable numbers of arrests of violators and seizures of illicit drugs, the ability of higher echelon dealers and financiers to bring illicit drugs into the United States had not been effectively deterred (Arizona *Republic,* July 18, 1976).

Focusing on arrests enables agents to quantify their worth and demonstrate their effectiveness to superiors who can be instrumental in furthering their careers. Most importantly, however, such statistics promote the organization by establishing with other agencies, as well as with the public, that "something is being done about the problem." The strategy of feeding the public information was demonstrated when another article dealing with drug enforcement appeared on the same page of the newspaper as the previous quotation. The emphasis on statistics is evident.

> The U.S. Customs Service reported . . . that drug seizure in Arizona for fiscal 1975–76 totalled $51.2 million . . . 4.6 pounds of heroin with a street value of $1.6 million was seized in 1975–76 . . . 7.1 pounds of heroin was seized in the state in 1974–75. In addition, 153,629 pounds of marijuana was seized . . . [with] a street price of $49.4 million.

The USIA and DEA were not alone in recognizing the practical side of organizational survival. All indications are that such piece-meal deception, covering up, and further distortions lay behind our tragic Vietnam policy; officials who made original estimates of enemy troop strength had a lot at stake in those figures being believed, especially when plans of operation had been put into effect based on them. To change the numbers could amount to changing generals. The case of Lt. William Calley, convicted of slaughtering Vietnamese women and children in the hamlet of My Lai, appears to have happened in a similar way. Many officers knew about the task, had cleared it, sanctioned it, and had taken part in similar operations.

But it was to their advantage and the public image of the military to pin it on one man; guilt was assigned and the image was maintained. In each case information was created for the purpose at hand, which, if not understood by outside evaluators, could be construed as ineptness, deceit, and fraud. As our case studies indicate, such an interpretation is far too simplistic. Although intentional deception and fraud does occur in organizations, the major part of bureaucratic propaganda is a result of responsible and honest persons following procedures, but always mindful of the practical side of their task. This leads us to the significance of truth and falsity in propaganda.

4. Truth

Traditional Propaganda. Propaganda is a tactic in the ongoing struggle to use the idea of truth for strategic purposes. There would be little reason to promote propaganda efforts if the audience were not presumed to seek knowledge; propaganda is simply a contrived and artful way of presenting some facts and interpretations as though they were truthful. Propagandists like Goebbels knew that what people regarded as the truth was a result of familiarity. Thus, truth for all practical purposes could be established by repeating views of reality. As Goebbels observed (Riess, 1948: 101):

> There ought to be nothing mystifying about propaganda. We openly admit that we want to influence the people.

Convincing the people that something was true made the influencing a bit easier.

If Machiavelli can be considered the forerunner of propaganda, then Goebbels and his boss, Hitler, qualify as more recent experts. Both men believed that people would more easily believe a "big lie" than many smaller lies. Their tactic, now widely adopted by public relations specialists, marketers, advertisers, and other media practitioners who abound in government and industry, was to pick a theme and repeat it again and again. However, if the people were too aware that the messages they received were inconsistent with their own experience, then the message might have been identified as propaganda and then disbelieved. Even the awesome fear and repression of the Nazis could not prevent thousands of German citizens from turning to other sources of information. More than fifteen hundred Germans had been sentenced to concentration camps and jails for listening to "enemy lies," especially the British radio reports, but others continued to listen.

> Goebbels' monoply on news was shattered. Slowly, but inexorably foreign news reports began to circulate in Germany, although most people were still suspicious of foreign sources. Gradually the discrepancy between official and 'unofficial' news became more and more flagrant and resulted in peculiar, sometimes hilarious, situations (Riess, 1948: 179).

Goebbels did not want this to happen. He felt that information channels must retain their credibility for maximum effectiveness in shaping public opinion. Indeed, Baird (1974: 32) reports that Goebbels was angered by Hitler's abuse of "legitimate information channels."

> Because of Hitler's misuse of this traditionally respected medium of information, the communique gradually lost its credibility until by 1945 it had become little more than a sounding board for Hitler's last-ditch fanaticism.

Successful governmental propagandists have realized that people cannot be constantly lied to or the messages will boomerang and do more harm than good. Goebbels was brilliantly aware of the importance of using the facts to promote the Nazi cause. He did not always lie to the audience, but would distort the facts enough to present the favorable images he wanted through interpretation and juxtaposition. Thus, a good deal of Nazi "propaganda" was correct; events did happen in ways that were usually implicitly alluded to. The truth of Nazi propaganda was verified by Alexander George's (1959) study of the accuracy of inferences made from Nazi propaganda regarding military plans. By comparing reports made during the war with interviews and captured documents obtained after the war, George found that 85 percent of the messages contained accurate statements. The importance of maintaining credibility in order to delude more subtly has also been understood by the United States Information Agency (USIA) during the cold war. According to one USIA operator:

> It's an excellent medium in which to expound our foreign policy to foreign audiences without these audiences knowing that the U.S. government is doing it. It does not stamp it as a propaganda medium as long as people think it's private enterprise and not a government operation (Bogart, 1976: 116).*

Bureaucratic Propaganda.   Propagandists use correct facts and plausible interpretations in fulfilling their purposes. We have seen several ex-

---

* Bogart, Leo. *Premises for Propaganda: The United States Information Agency's Operating Assumptions in the Cold War.* New York: Free Press, 1976. Reprinted with permission.

amples of how political propagandists managed their messages. The success of the Nazi program unwittingly established the connection between propaganda, politics, and the mass media. What has been overlooked is the essential aspect of propaganda—the practical use of information. It is still worthwhile to scrutinize explicitly political messages for propaganda, and less obvious political purposes also must be scrutinized for the strategic use of information.

The practical use of truth is characteristic of most organizations in our modern age. They have found the cultural values of science and objectivity to be very useful in presenting information about their efficiency and overall necessity to the whole society. Virtually none of the reports presented in statistical summaries include statements about how the reports were actually compiled, and why one interpretation rather than another was used in making sense of what the officials claim to be "facts." Instead, what now occurs with greater frequency is systematic distortion of everyday reality in order to present official reports that present the organization and its members in favorable terms. It is massive public relations (PR) gone wild.

Bureaucratic propaganda uses truth for organizational goals. This is done by presenting managed and often contrived reports as though they were done "scientifically" and therefore depict "objective" truth (cf. Wheeler, 1976). The idea is to make the reports appear to be scientific, when in fact they are not.

Police and FBI statistics are one example of this systematic distortion. Police and FBI statistics are notorious for being not readily comparable from one city, state, and region to another and also for distorting the nature of crime in American life. Local police officials who provide the data for these national assessments are aware that high crime rates are political issues, which they can tap for larger budgets to acquire more officers, facilities, and equipment.

For example, in 1974 Phoenix, Arizona, claimed the highest crime rate in the United States. This "intolerable situation" enabled the police department to obtain large federal grants to employ more personnel and purchase sophisticated equipment, including two helicopters. Of course, most of this new hardware was used for traffic control and not burglary detection and robbery prevention. This was reasonable since the Chief of Police eventually conceded that Phoenix counted some incidents as "crimes" that other cities disregarded, such as fifty-cent burglaries. The organizational benefits that can follow high crime rates also help explain why major cities do not officially cut crime to the point of reducing their budget. To the contrary, the statistics usually show crime increasing disproportionately to population growth; and if there is a slight decrease, it is attributed to the increased number of police officers who can continue to curb the rising criminal menace if only they can be given more money.

The logic of crime prevention works both ways. In certain cases, a city's reputation may be damaged by having too much crime. At that point it is predictable that significant gains will be made in crime prevention. This has happened in Washington, D.C. The figures generated by the police department showed a 33 percent reduction in crime between 1970 and 1975. Such successful record keeping prompted the Police Chief to state that Washington "is one of the safest cities in the nation. By 1978, it will be the safest city."

Much of the information that constitutes the more basic inaccuracies is derived from crime and theft reports by various organizations and businesses. Their figures on losses are presented quantitatively as "proof" and "facts" about the extent of the problem, along with public reminders that all such losses will be passed on through price increases. Thus, the public realizes that "crime affects us all" and thereby supports even greater efforts to increase police activities and provide these agents of control with even more power, at the demise of all our civil liberties.

In more specific terms, shoplifting is reported by businesses to be an annual multi-million—if not billion—dollar loss. This has prompted law enforcement bodies and state legislatures to enact tough sentencing for a first offense on even the smallest item. Individual cases may be dispensed with a warning, fine, or even a six-month jail term in some states. Efforts have been made to strengthen the laws in recent years as shoplifting rates continue to climb. But how are estimates of the extent of shoplifting arrived at? Who provides the data? Very few shoplifters are caught, and all indications are that the majority of persons who do get caught are teenagers looking for a challenge. The extent of shoplifting that is done is never directly observed, but is *inferred* from the amount of merchandise lost, or what business people refer to as "shrinkage," unaccounted for items. Since businesses have had so much "shrinkage" in recent years, it is presumed that shoplifters are at work. However, there is some evidence that the majority of the lost items may have been stolen by employees who, in the words of one expert, "know the scene, and know how security operates." One student reported having direct knowledge of some $6,000 worth of items removed from a retail store during the course of one year.

Many of these transactions involved members of management, who would also report and help prosecute shoplifters trying to steal small items. In at least a few cases of which we are aware, these managers actively directed such pilferage (cf. Altheide, *et al.*, 1978). But this was never reported to the police. Thus, this store's claims to having a "shoplifting problem" were a partial justification and smokescreen to keep supervisors and law enforcement people from scrutinizing the day-to-day affairs of employee activity that permits blatant theft.

Only a few studies are now available on this topic, but we believe that employee theft is rampant throughout the society and greatly surpasses the loss of material from all shoplifters, "professionals" included (cf. Altheide, *et al.*, 1978). More research must be done, but for the moment we can at least gain some perspective on the kind of information left out of police reports about crime, including appeals to state legislatures for more money and people to crack down and enforce shoplifting ordinances. Without an awareness of the organizational routines that promote and mask employee theft—and blame it disproportionately on would-be-shoplifters—the official and public understanding of business crime in particular, and of crime and justice in general, cannot be understood. Adding the work context and the situations in which reports are compiled helps clarify what is really going on in this store, and undoubtedly, many others as well.

In sum, students of propaganda have assumed that the government is the significant definer of reality and that other organizational accounts are less salient for our lives. Although this may have been true during World War I and possibly through World War II, massive social, political, economic, and industrial changes have blurred the traditional distinctions between the interests and methods of government and other organizations. First, governments find it increasingly difficult to control the citizens' views and behavior, particularly when the populace becomes more educated. Second, many organizations today openly compete with the government for public support and for access to information. Indeed, the official information of both government and various businesses often conflict. The current energy situation is a good example. Spokespersons for the American Gas Association (AGA) argue that higher prices are necessary in order to pay for further gas exploration since the known supply peaked in 1967. If these figures are correct, then the United States would run out of domestic supplies of natural gas by the end of this century. However, the only source for these data is the gas producers themselves, and efforts to check on the validity of these estimates have not been encouraging. For example, in 1976 an investigation by a committee headed by Rep. John Moss of California, found that the largest gas producing companies virtually dominated the procedures for estimating gas reserves. The gas companies selected geologists to conduct the studies and instructed these hired hands to provide "whatever estimates their companies wanted them to give." (Miller, 1977: 16). Indeed, one geologist told the Moss committee that the company he worked for actually drew up his estimates for him. The problems with using such data for realistic energy projections are evident.

Third, governments in general, and especially those in the Western world, must rely on the assistance and support of organizations, especially large corporations that deal in international markets and often play a part in foreign policy and balance-of-trade problems. Finally, governments increasingly depend on organizations to regulate themselves, including appointing "industry officials" to staff regulatory bodies.

In short, the power of government has increased substantially, but the dependence on extragovernmental organizations for ideas, support, and legitimacy has also grown. Such significant structural interdependencies are another reason that traditional notions of propaganda must be updated if social science is to benefit from expanding knowledge about the role of official communication in sustaining widespread notions of legitimacy.

Now that the theoretical shortcomings of traditional usages of propaganda have been presented and the necessity to expand its conceptual application has been shown, the rise of the institutional context that sanctioned and legitimated the use of bureaucratically created information will be examined.

THE RISE OF ORGANIZATIONS AND OFFICIAL INFORMATION

Bureaucratic propaganda has gradually surpassed other forms of deception as the Western world has become more orderly and rational (cf. Presthus, 1978: 44–84). We refer to the establishment of rational procedures as an institutional approach to legitimacy. As more people have become more educated, established procedures for efficiency and control have infused our cultural stock of knowledge. All this has taken several hundred years to achieve. The preeminence accorded the belief in, and appearance of, rational coordination as the height of legitimacy is more recent and has been accompanied by the establishment of bureaucracy as the major organizational form. What will be emphasized or presented as legitimate depends on the criteria of legitimacy that the target audience takes for granted. For example, publics base support or disapproval for social protest on background knowledge and beliefs about the salience of the issue, groups involved, and tactics employed (Altheide and Gilmore, 1972; Turner, 1969). What the public(s) expect and honor as legitimate may change with historical events, region of a country, and individual leaders. For example, political machines were largely accepted in Chicago, New York, and other large urban centers. The favoritism, nepotism, and political payoffs were a way of life because they appeared to work for the officials and many of their constituents. In these cases, officials had little justifying to do; accounts were not called for. However, when criteria of legitimacy change, usually at the hands of other interest groups, what was previously taken-for-granted as "the way things are" suddenly needs explaining. Even though political factions do play a big part in creating the appropriate scenarios for moral indignation and the withdrawal of symbolic support, Scott (1972) has shown that the social and economic basis for the establishment and persistence of political machines often transcends individual power groups. Thus, it is possible for machines to flourish in any social milieu, but it is not likely that they will do so. This kind of practical legitimacy, when viewed from the perspective of the relevant audiences, further suggests that criteria of legitimacy appear in interaction between leaders and followers, but that expectations and opportunities are also influenced by broader social and economic contexts (cf. Vidich, forthcoming).

The most thorough study of the social and economic dimensions of legitimacy is found in Max Weber's work (1968). In general, his comparative study of social change showed property ownership and control to be an important contributor to change in other social institutions. Specifically, Weber saw three forms of authority and legitimacy as indicative of corresponding differences in social structure: charismatic, traditional, and legal-rational types emerged from a particular historical and cultural epoch, and each in turn produced other social effects. Thus, whole societies could be characterized as being predominantly one or the other, and the consequences of this ordering scheme could be historically and sociologically studied to ferret out the impact on industrialization, religiosity, and readiness for adaptation and change. The brilliance of conceptually relating something intangible like a religious belief to something tangible like manufactured goods is seen in Weber's (1958) analysis of the Protestant Ethic and the Spirit of Capitalism. Briefly stated, he argued that widespread acceptance of a traditionally based explanation and justification of a deity-determined social order led people to engage in activities to demonstrate their pre-selection for eternal rewards. Much of this activity to assure acceptance in the other world, according to Weber, was based on transforming lives and making profits on a rational basis in this world. Thus, capitalism grew and was legitimated by a religious and moral belief; economic rationality and efficiency became taken-for-granted criteria of legitimacy in this world long after the other-worldly foundations disappeared.

The establishment of rational-legal administration and organization in the Western world was indispensible to an expanding industrialization, grounded in capital and expert management. The idea of "organization" came to be identified with rationality and it took the form of *bureaucracy* as the key administrative apparatus. Bendix (1968: 341) has aptly summarized the essentials.

> The persons who occupy positions of authority are not personal rulers, but superiors who temporarily occupy an office by virtue of which they possess limited authority. The work of these officials is done on a continuous basis under supervision on the basis of documents. As a result the officials are characterized by the following attributes: they are personally free and appointed to their position on the basis of contracts their loyalty is enlisted on the basis of the faithful execution of their official duties; their appointment and job placement

depend on their technical qualifications; their administrative work is a full-time occupation; their work is rewarded by a regular salary and by prospects of regular advancement in a lifetime career.

As Bendix (1968: 344 ff.) and other interpreters of Weber (see Collins, 1975; Roth, 1968) have noted, the commitment to abstract norms and the depersonalization of authority promote continuity and stability within the organization.

The practical side of bureaucracy became more important as bureaucrats and officials heralded the rational accounts as reality itself. This was especially true during the eighteenth and nineteenth centuries, when "science," "rationality," and positivist notions of objectivity became wedded to bureaucratic organizations. Positivists believed that reality existed independently of the perceiver, or the bureaucrat. Some scholars—and most notable among sociologists, Emile Durkheim (1951)—even claimed that individual reality could be understood by mimicking the techniques of the natural sciences actually to "measure" the objective "facts." This style of science and the faith in rational and rule-guided behavior provided a new way of seeing social life that was compatible with bureaucratic procedures. Facts could now be objectively mustered to answer a variety of questions, including the moral condition of a society and the costs and benefits of social change. Most importantly, officials who were responsible for answering such questions could rationally show the efficiency of their own enterprise—organized work. This belief in the absolute categorization of things in nature was part of a calculative attitude that, according to Douglas (1971: 59–60) was

> fundamental to the development of the *rational policy orientation* of officials and rulers that made official information the means of 'testting' and 'proving' the effectiveness of official policies. Just as the calculation of the return in relation to the investment (i.e., profit) was so fundamental to the 'spirit of capitalism,' so was the calculation of *effects* of official action relative to the policy-determined *practices* (i.e., effectiveness) so fundamental to the development of all official information. Just as the *Werkmeister* in the German asylum in 1622 established a work plan for the inmates, kept records on the work, and determined by checking those records at the end of each week whether that plan had been carried out, so did the officials check on each other (and the rulers checked on them all) by examining the official records, normally through an annual report, a practice which continues to this day.*

The reports, and especially the quantified accounts, became significant not only for "proving" the existance of certain conditions but also for documenting an organization's effectiveness.

* Douglas, Jack D. *American Social Order*. New York: Free Press, 1971. Reprinted with permission.

As Jack Douglas (1971) has argued, the advent of bureaucracy and the widespread use of "numbers" or statistics to document categories of events enabled officials to speak authoritatively of their responsibilities and to provide proof to both superiors and subordinates that certain tasks were being accomplished. This was especially true of the church and later of police forces in the nineteenth century, which were charged with keeping order.

> We have here, then, the beginnings of the *bureaucracies of official morality*. From their very beginnings in the early seventeenth century they were dedicated to the ideas of 'rational control' of their charges by means of 'rational' procedures. From the very beginning they, like all official organizations, were *responsible* to the political rulers. Unlike officials of an earlier day, the growing size and complexity of Western societies made it very difficult for rulers to check directly on their operations. For this reason the rulers believed that some form of *accounting information* was necessary. That is, they needed some form of information which could be *legally and morally sanctioned* as the basis for *judgments* of the work of officials, and which could, therefore, be used to decide whether officials were doing their jobs morally and legally, how funds should be allocated to produce the desired results, and so on (Douglas, 1971: 52).*

Not only did bureaucracies report on moral phenomena, but the legitimacy of this information also became a morally sanctionable phenomenon in its own right. The "bottom line" on reports was what counted, and often the figures and official findings from previous reports became the standard for future reports and, by implication, a model to be followed by other officials.

The explicit political use of bureaucratically generated information that we have briefly noted does not account for the common-sense foundation for today's widespread use and acceptance of bureaucratic propaganda throughout our society; the major reason for the rapid growth of this form of knowledge was the success of the bureaucratic form.

Weber's analysis of rational coordination, both as an ideal type and as a historical trend, drew attention to the structural basis of modern organizations, although how these structures would interact with people in varying environmental contexts was not explicated. More recent studies of organizations (cf. Dalton, 1959; Homans, 1950) show that there is a large gap between the formal prescriptions and the informal activities of workers (see especially Collins, 1975: 285–346). Further reflection and research on the relationship between organizational rules (including bureaucratic ideals) and daily occurrences raised important questions about the internal and external environments within which organizations are realized on a daily basis. The major internal "variables" have included work groups, cliques, divisional and departmental competitiveness, conflicting career

---

* Douglas, Jack D. *American Social Order*. New York: Free Press, 1971. Reprinted with permission.

paths, and ineffective channels of communication. Each variable has been regarded as an actual or potential "barrier" to achieving more rational and efficient coordination, which in turn was presumed to be essential in promoting the goals and therefore the success of the organization. Most importantly, legitimacy was to follow success; thus, survival had its own rewards.

The significance of external environments for organizations has not received the same attention as the internal one, even though the environmental context for any social activity has been sociologically acclaimed as (usually) *the most important factor.* As scholars have turned their attention to this issue, it has been revealed that successful organizations become legitimate to the extent that they adopt and mirror certain standards, rules, procedures, and myths that many organizations of a like kind share (Meyer and Rowan, 1977). Moreover, researchers have shown that attempting to "look good" as a "real organization" may be more important than the quality of products turned out and the efficiency with which this is done. Stated differently, the environmental context, the arena in which legitimacy and recognition is bestowed, can reap greater rewards than mere careful and conscientious work. One important myth to realize, according to Meyer and Rowan (1975: 344–345), is rationality.

> The impact of such rationalized institutional elements on organizations and organizing situations is enormous. These rules define new organizing situations, redefine existing ones, and specify the means for coping rationally with each. They enable, and often require, participants to organize along prescribed lines. . . . Thus, the myths built into rationalized institutional elements create the necessity, the opportunity, and the impulse to organize rationally, over and above pressures in this direction created by the need to manage proximate relational networks.

The implication of this insight is that organizations search the institutional realm for prevailing beliefs and taken-for-granted standards about what everyone knows to be true of a viable organization. As Meyer and Rowan (1977: 348) observe:

> Rivals must then compete both in social networks or markets and in contexts of institutional rules which are defined by extant organizations. In this fashion, given organizational forms perpetuate themselves by becoming institutionalized rules.

By adopting the institutional trappings, procedures, and language, an organization demonstrates its competence and good faith; or, in the words of Meyer and Rowan (1975: 349),

The organization becomes, in a word, legitimate and it uses its legitimacy to strengthen its support and secure its survival.

The significance of this perspective for our conception of bureaucratic propaganda can now be stated.

The emergence of bureaucratic propaganda in the form of official information is linked conceptually and historically to the versions of legitimacy offered by Weber and contemporary students of organizations. Recall that Weber saw rational coordination as one aspect of increased secularization and industrialization. The bureaucratic logic of set procedures and routines to be carried out by a person in an office would grow and flourish, he thought, because of its efficiency and continuity; the form would remain after individual occupants came and went. And in the process of the increasing bureaucratization, the world would be further transformed and reality changed:

> The Puritan wanted to work in a calling; we are forced to do so. For when asceticism was carried out to monastic cells into everyday life, and began to dominate worldly morality, it did its part in building the tremendous cosmos of the modern economic order. This order is now bound to the technical and economic conditions of machine production which today determine the lives of all the individuals who are born into this mechanism (Weber, 1958: 181).

The recent focus on organizational environments emphasized that appearances count as much as if not more than actual efficiency and productivity. What matters is the appearance of legitimacy, and this is achieved by reaffirming the socially constructed reality shared by others (cf. Berger and Luckmann, 1966). It is the role of bureaucratic propaganda in the guise of official information that creates the impression that the organization is complying with institutional expectations. Stated differently, official information contributes to the construction of reality, but it can also be used as a model of legitimacy for other organizations to emulate. This is because official information is the main connection between organizational insiders and outsiders. Such linkages become more important, as we shall see later, when the news media broadcast certain images to the public, which in turn expects to find the specific elements in other organizations. Thus, official information promotes and reinforces at the same time.

The widespread acceptance of rational coordination as a means to an end led to greater attention to dramatizing and presenting rationality with official reports. Since most people (the outsiders) had little contact with the routines of the insiders and also lacked the requisite internal information to know exactly why and how (and therefore, what) actually went on within an organization, greater attention was given to presenting the public and other audiences with information that would be convincing. In other words, the audience was presumed to believe in rationality and efficiency as legitimate; what remained was to make certain that the reports reflected such beliefs. Thus, rational procedures came to be focused on in reports that made massive operations appear to be run by rules and tried-and-tested procedures. In this context, there was no place for failures, waste, inefficiency, or in general, any data that could be construed as contrary to the organization's stated goals.

With the international acceptance of industrialization (Vidich, forthcoming), the prevalence of this bureaucratic standard now cuts across national and ideological boundaries. Bendix's (1968: 335–351) analysis of rationality in Western and Eastern Europe shows how the drive to produce legitimate looking reports operates in the Soviet Union. While emphasizing that totalitarian regimes such as the Soviet Union do not have a background of stable expectations and legal and administrative rationality and noting that the ethic of production and the control of the Party often clash, Bendix (1968: 349) emphasizes the practical resolution through official reports:

> Where some success has been achieved, more success may be possible, and it is the responsibility of the Party in this system to test continually whether this 'more' can be achieved. . . . Moreover, the Party authorities are well aware of evasions and collusive practices at the operational level . . . the official viewpoint of the regime is to consider all evasions or collusions as evidence of slack which may be taken up by additional pressure. The Party jargon reflects this orientation by speaking of 'still further successes' which proper political agitation will make possible, thus asserting at the same time that the Party is eminently successful but that its functionaries can still do much more in tapping the underutilized resources of the country and the hallowed initiative of the masses.

The pressure to manage production dramaturgically leads the managers and the Party watchdogs to engage in periodic collusion and to perpetuate illegal practices in an effort to satisfy their respective audiences' criteria of legitimacy. However, Bendix (1968: 349) stresses that

> illegal practices are condoned only where they lead to successful performance in terms of the official criteria, and that the collusion which makes such practices possible disintegrates quickly with the first signs of impending failure.

Bendix's sound theoretical insight that such conflicts negate the optimum rationality more likely to operate in the West does not erase the significant point for the present analysis: the appearance of rationality consistent with the prevailing official standard of legitimacy is routinely accomplished. Indeed, we shall argue in the following chapters that the appearance of rationality is more important in modern bureaucracies than "what really happens." It is only the former that the public and other audiences are often familiar with.

In most cases we must depend on the respective organization's or agency's collection, interpretation, and presentation of data. Such presentation or "packaging" is increasingly important and has become a valued skill in its own right, especially when official information is an organization's only product. This is particularly true since the rapid rise of the service and administrative occupations and agencies that followed industrialization. It is one thing to produce automobiles, but it is another to produce welfare "eligibility records"; the former are tangible and can be more easily checked than can the latter, but the imprecise nature of "eligibility" work affords more opportunities for influencing official reports. As Meyer and Rowan (1977: 350–351) note, the organizations have few external evaluations to rely on and resort to vague and institutional ceremonies. For example, with service departments,

> it is utterly unclear what is being produced that has clear or definable value in terms of its contribution to the organizational product. . . . Ceremonial criteria of worth and ceremonially derived production functions are useful to organizations: they legitimate organizations with internal participants, stockholders, the public, and the state. . . . They demonstrate socially the fitness of an organization.

When official reports are regarded as representative of the "organization as a whole," the diverse activities, motivations, factions and conflicts that surround any organization are overlooked. This is especially important when many of the diverse purposes play a part in shaping the report. This practice has promoted the notion that organizations exist independently of their members (cf. Collins, 1975: 300).

In view of how official reports may be read as a reflection of an organization's membership, it comes as no surprise that individual members seek to give the impression that the organization—and by implication, the workers—are doing what they are presumed to do. Collins (1975: 308) nicely states the unanticipated result of such organizational surveillance:

> The more emphasis on control by inspecting outcomes, the greater the emphasis upon controlling the situations of inspection and the form of the records.

The upshot was that records had implications for individual careers and collective futures, an understanding that encouraged officials and their subordinates to use two or more sets of records: one was for the inspection of other officials and organizations and one was for private use, for insiders only.

Several examples illustrate this practical use of official information. Educational researchers have shown that school teachers keep their own "unofficial" records for assessing student performance and potential, especially when their assessments are inconsistent with the more public and officially recognized aptitude tests (Cicourel and Kitsuse, 1963: 49–75). The practical way out of what is not a dilemma for seasoned educators is to place greater emphasis on a student's past grades and recommendations of former teachers. Thus, the evaluators' assessments of student ability enabled some students who did well on standardized tests to be placed in "low ability" groupings while others who were placed in "high ability" groupings did not do as well on the standardized examinations.

The use of information for organizational reasons is also illustrated in Julius Roth's (1963) study of a tuberculosis sanitarium. The work of physicians and nurses who treat patients is more closely tied to efficiently processing patients than it is their individual medical symptoms. Most patients were not allowed some treatments until others had been performed, physiological tests indicated progress, and set waiting periods between each step had elapsed. However, a nurse who worked there and contracted TB was treated, cured, and released in one-fourth of the time it took other patients. The difference was not due to her superior condition but rather to her different circumstances: she was a nurse who needed to be back at work. Thus, one patient could be treated more promptly on the basis of her medical condition, but not everyone. Nevertheless, the schedule of the typical "patient's career" came to be established via official reports as the necessary procedure.

Sam Adams's (1975) account of how Pentagon officials used fictitious estimates of the size of the enemy in the Vietnam conflict also illustrates the practical interest in official information. When Adams was assigned to investigate the Viet Cong, he found in the CIA's own files strong evidence that the then public announcement that the enemy numbered 270,000 was understated by no fewer than 400,000. When Adams noted this discrepancy in a number of organizational memos, he was at first ignored and then told to not make trouble. His superiors explained that the war was being waged on the official but incorrect figures and to change them now would be politically inexpedient. It took the Tet offensive and the loss of more than 6,000 American lives to enemy troops that did not officially exist to nudge Adams's superiors into changing their numbers.

As these examples illustrate, the utility of information has great political and social consequences. This is especially true during our time of "democratic feudalism," whereby organizations and other groups throughout society compete, often in open conflict, for recognition, support, and symbolic legitimacy. The moral differences endemic to such seething pluralism came to be resolved through a combination of moral entrepreneurship in the form of challenging another's humanity and social responsibility and also through scientific-rational claims. The latter took the form of "objective" appraisals of, for example, degrees of social disorganization, lack of proper socialization, and in general, "scientific" confirmation that certain behavior was deviant, wrong, and harmful to society (cf. Davis, 1975). Examples of this mixture of moralizing and scientific pontificating can be found with poverty, alcohol, race, marijuana and some drugs, crime, suicide, divorce, sex, and child abuse. Even though the emphasis of most such work was on eradicating or solving such problems, the moral dimension was gilded with a veneer of "scientific objectivity," which was more acceptable to an increasingly urban, secular, and sophisticated society.

As the number of organizations increased, especially in government, competition for scarce resources grew, and the need to show "objectively" the kind of job that was being done encouraged officials to present their work in the most favorable light. Just as Michels's (1949) study of organizations showed that those who control information also influence what the members think problems and issues are (and thereby maintain control) research in modern organizations, such as police departments, the Pentagon, big business, and a host of government agencies, reveals how they use information in the form of official reports as a "front" to present public images of issues, problems, and efficiency (Douglas and Johnson, 1977). In the case of police departments, for example, crime categories and statistics are used to show "objectively" that "crime waves," exist and that the society can be saved only by pouring more money and resources into police departments. Similar arguments were used by the Pentagon in "objectively" citing body counts of enemy soldiers to prove our government's success in Vietnam. Just as research has shown many of the "crime wave" scares to be organizational fictions for practical purposes, revelations about the ad hoc procedures for determining how large the enemy was, how many were killed, and whether the war was being won have made it painfully apparent that these official reports reflect the practical and self-interested concerns of the members of an organization more than they do the nature of crime and war.

Much the same is true of other areas of life that more people already understand to be somehow grounded in arbitrary and selfish interests. Taxes are one example. Anyone who has ever undergone a tax audit or delved beyond the standard instructions and exemptions that accompany the Internal Revenue Service's 1040 forms realizes that most tax laws are created for businesses rather than individual citizens. Even though one may not know all the details that go into an oil depletion allowance for one of the major oil companies, many people would think that "it all has something to do with politics," regardless of the official reason, the statistics, and expert testimony. And they would be correct! What must be done, however, is to expand this understanding of official information and make it more explicit to include other areas of daily life such as crime statistics, social problems, and efficiency rates, and all the other criteria used to justify a variety of organizations and programs. Until such reports are understood, and perhaps challenged and seen as an organizational product with practical consequences, we will not gain better awareness of social life and our problems. This is especially true of social scientists who too readily use official reports for their own research. Douglas's (1971: 78) advice seems sound:

> If sociologists are to fulfill their purpose of creating scientific knowledge of social phenomena, such as moral phenomena, then they must remain free of all the basic assumptions of official information, the implicit goals of such information, and of the organizations which create it. They must, instead, construct their own information about the phenomena, controlling the methods used to get the observations on which such information is ultimately based. . . . If we cannot or do not remain as true to the phenomena as possible, then we can only do pseudoscience which can be used to control human beings; but not make them freer.*

A big step in obtaining a better understanding of social life is to reassess the nature of organizations, information, and propaganda in our lives.

RESEARCH PERSPECTIVE AND
THE PLAN OF THIS BOOK

The remaining chapters further document and elaborate the place of bureaucratic propaganda in our society today. We report ethnographic materials obtained from a variety of organizations during the last decade. The general purpose of each of these studies was to obtain first-hand observations and understandings about how individual members of the respective organizations conceived of and used information in fulfilling their tasks as well as in promoting their activities to "outsiders" such as officials, committees, and the public. Our materials show that many of these workers were oriented to such practical concerns as maintaining friendships, promoting individual careers, "covering their asses," getting back at real and potential enemies, and above all, maintaining appearances of competence and legitimacy for their superiors, who, in turn, engaged in elaborate dramaturgical management for relevant outsiders. In brief, then, the organization existed mainly for outsider appearances, while the experienced insiders continued to encounter and resolve the myriad of situated and routine problems that seldom were publicly acknowledged, and therefore, unknown to most people.

* Douglas, Jack D. *American Social Order.* New York: Free Press, 1971. Reprinted with permission.

A key element in unravelling these newer forms of propaganda and in showing their relationship to the growth of organizations and bureaucracy is the communication process. By communication we mean the selection, interpretation, transmission, and receiving of information. Unlike mechanical models of communication that emphasize technical and deterministic properties, our interest in communication focuses on the process of sharing subjective meanings of actors, and how the definitions and understandings of one person are influenced by what is relevant for a particular purpose in a specific situation. If another person does not share similar subjective meanings and does not take for granted what the other does, then communication is incomplete and true intersubjective understanding does not exist (cf. Schutz, 1967).

Central to this theoretical orientation is the presumption that the context of all action, including communicative acts, is itself part of the communication process. Stated differently, what is not explicitly noted is often implicitly understood; if two parties do not have the same stock of knowledge, then one actor must be more detailed and more specific in any effort to achieve optimum communication with another. By the same token, if two actors share backgrounds and stocks of knowledge, then detailed meanings can be conveyed with physical gestures, such as a nod, a sigh, or a giggle.

The significance of context and shared understanding and meanings has a number of practical dimensions already revealed by researchers. Douglas (1967) has shown that coroners' definitions of a corpse as a suicide or an accidental death are based on many unexamined assumptions about what the deceased must have intended, must have been feeling, and a belief that certain physical evidence "clearly" demonstrates mastery of firearms, drugs, or even natural gas. Other researchers have also found that the meanings of life and death are often tied to a number of individual circumstances and can therefore not properly be treated as "real variables" with an objective meaning independent of the particular context (Jacobs, 1967). Indeed, lay people, like coroners, tend to supply their own contextual information in order to make sense. Essentially the same point has been made by Garfinkel's (1967) studies of psychiatric records and transsexuality. Studies of educational testing and evaluation clearly show that the perspective of the testers is often significantly different from the students in regard to the definition, recognition, and interpretation of an item as a question, an answer, or as something irrelevant. For example, Cicourel, *et al.* (1975) found that children interpret picture-word association tests from their own experience of what a particular drawing looks like and what a correct answer is. Thus, some students, when presented with a drawing that the test-maker intended to be seen as an "elephant," actually saw "Dumbo" and answered the question accordingly, albeit incorrectly from the adult-test-maker-evaluator perspective. Thus, the power to define the appropriate context, (such as, this is a "test") is closely tied to correctness and adequacy (for example, elephant is correct, but Dumbo is wrong).

As we discuss later in more detail, the establishment of rules to guide human action within specific settings such as organizations was presumed to define the context adequately and therefore to serve as a guide to what would be done in specific situations. But, as many studies have shown, few situations are exactly alike and therefore actors must interpret rules and/or must negotiate between their peers and superiors what rules will apply in particular cases. Studies of police work provide some of the best examples of the problematic interpretation and use of rules.

Cicourel (1968), Bittner (1967), and Manning (1977) present the contextual reasons that police officers must interpret constitutional, state, and police regulations differently in various circumstances. Nevertheless, it is important for these officers to appear to be complying with the expectations of their superiors, peers, other police organizations, and the public. Of course, not all parties expect the same thing; to this extent, the police continually play to different audiences with diverse standards of professionalism and competence. As Manning (1977: 51) observes in his study of drug enforcement:

> The facts about investigations are not shared between organizational segments, yet one level is required to make investigations and to justify them, while another level has responsibility for the evaluation of the success of these investigations. Patterned ambiguities concerning the term, 'major violators,' and the basis on which accounts will be accepted by supervisory officers maintain the appearance of consensus between segments, while allowing the uncertain and often fruitless job of enforcement to proceed.

The appearance of complying with the rules has a similar effect on organizational survival as the adequate presentation of self in everyday life has on social survival (cf. Goffman, 1959). In both cases (individual and organizational) fronts are erected to legitimate selves and action irrespective of what one really thinks or feels and irrespective of what the organization really is or is not doing. In the case of individuals, people may use the rules of legitimate appearance to rob and plunder (cf. Altheide, 1975). In the case of organizations, practical ways of "doing the job" may actually contradict the ideological justifications for the existence of the organization in the first place. Thus, Manning and Redlinger (1977) and a host of other investigators show that the police engage in many illegal acts in preventing specific illegalities by "criminals." The FBI and CIA spy on citizens, illegally bug telephones, and harass people in order to prevent other crimes from occurring, and the Attorney General of the United States may cooperate in the systematic obstruction of justice by his subordinates who are acting in the best interests of "national security." Too many accounts of similar activities are available to dismiss this phenomenon as "exceptional," "due to corrupt individuals," and the like. Rather, it is part of the organizational mandate to survive as an individual and to promote the organizational goals and public image (cf. Douglas and Johnson, 1977). Essential to the process of organizational survival is the faithful production of information and evidence that gives the appearance of legitimacy. As Manning (1977: 58) notes:

> Organizational knowledge, for example, is not simply filed for general use, but is differentially distributed. The power to conceal and differentially reveal information relevant to investigations lies in the administration after the fact and prospectively in the hands of investigators. . . . Other bases of authority maintain the control of the higher segments, but information control and the power to conceal are tokens of the power system of the organization and come to bear in some instances.

Thus, skillful accounting is crucial to maintaining the "reality" of the organization for the members who already share a good deal of "inside information." But the editing becomes even greater when information and images are presented to "outsiders," the members of the relevant audience. Again, we need not look to the various factions involved in "organized crime"; we need only look to the practices of the police forces designed to protect us all from law violators.

> To maintain the power derived from the dependent uncertainty of those below them in the organizational hierarchy, officials fabricate information (both for the public and for other investigators), and conceal information they possess. They do this to protect themselves from those above them, and typically above and outside the immediate unit (Manning, 1977: 58).

   Communication of information within an organization differs in important ways from information available to external audiences. In all cases, if the information is accepted, it defines that portion of reality for the person who accepts it. In the case of insiders, they realize that some information is for "public consumption" and should be seen as mere "public relations." Information useful for insiders will be more situation-specific and will be scrutinized for consistency with facts, considerations, and nuances with which the organizational member is familiar. This is why it is difficult, although not impossible, to fool very many insiders for any length of time.
   But there is more to communication than explicitly formulating messages aimed at a target audience. Recalling our earlier discussion of the

background expectations and stocks of knowledge of both the sender and the receiver leads us to consider whether the receiver is merely "passive" or plays a more direct role in the definition and content of the information he or she is obtaining. This issue becomes more important when it is noted that most of the information we receive seems familiar; we already know something about it and often feel competent to evaluate it. In short, what the audience takes for granted and accepts as legitimate can also become a basis for exploitation by skilled communicators. The foundation for commonly accepted, but nevertheless mythical "knowledge" has been described by Ellul (1965).

One big problem facing technological societies, according to Ellul, is the manipulative effect of "sociological propaganda," or the established cultural meanings and taken-for-granted understandings about reality. With technology, Ellul notes, modern society has become consumer oriented. This has opened up great opportunities for advertisers of commodities, ideas, traditions, futures, and explanations. The mass media have added layer on layer of sociological propaganda so that today culture is largely an artifact of a consciousness imbedded in technology and materialism. The net effect of this institutionalized bombardment by the mass media is a universal but unacknowledged deception. Reality becomes a spiral built on the "four great sociological presuppositions of the modern world": material wealth, success, progress, and the goodness of mankind. Once this foundation is established in sociological propaganda, then specific problems, priorities, and principles may arise that are politically meaningful. But a social context must exist for political propaganda to work.

> Sociological propaganda can be compared to plowing; direct propaganda to sowing; you cannot do the one without doing the other first (Ellul, 1965: 15).

Ellul cogently shows how "culture gone wild" can create symbolic environments that people cannot break through or control. In this sense, Ellul would agree with Simmel that "culture is tragedy"; the creations of culture—the values, beliefs, and mass media—take over and dominate other cultural forms.

The work of Edelman (1964; 1971), a political scientist, provides an excellent example of how the public faith in governmental regulation is returned in kind with rhetoric that promotes the cultural myth of "government as serving the 'people's' interests."

> Administrative agencies are to be understood as economic and political instruments of the parties they regulate and benefit, not of a reified 'society,' 'general will,' or 'public interest.' At the same time they perform this instrumental function, they perform an equally important

expressive function for the polity as a whole: to create and sustain an impression that induces acquiescence of the public in the face of private tactics that might otherwise be expected to produce resentment, protest, and resistance (1964: 56).

Public acquiescence is obtained by playing to sacred cultural themes that themselves come to symbolize reality (cf. Calhoun, 1957). Indeed, the themes are repeated both in ritual and in everyday language; astute politicians listen and then replay these themes to their audiences, but in a more eloquent way.

> The magical associations permeating language are important for political behavior because they lend authoritativeness to conventional perceptions and value premises and make it difficult or impossible to perceive alternative possibilities (Edelman, 1964: 121).

The net effect, according to Edelman, is to inhibit citizens from seeing that their own reifications of cultural myths are the major impediments to social change, including governmental performance. To this extent, Edelman is in essential agreement with Ellul that the taken-for-granted foundations of legitimacy are institutionalized in both language and politics.

Our conception of bureaucratic propaganda benefits from Edelman's and Ellul's analyses, but there are several important differences. First, Ellul does not distinguish between propaganda and the rest of culture. We do not see the two as entirely synonymous; bureaucratic propaganda is an important part of culture that *can* have the impact on culture that Ellul claims. Second, and more important, Ellul does not establish how a particular culture is defined, promoted, and maintained. This seems to be a prior question, and we believe the answer rests in official information. As reality definers, organizations that construct and then present essentially self-serving messages are significant shapers of modern life. They help establish what Ellul termed "sociological propaganda." But how this is done, and what the alternatives may be, are left unanswered by Ellul's work.

Edelman's focus on symbolism and politics does provide useful insights into how everyday speech and metaphors simultaneously support established routines and implicitly delegitimize any alternatives. Overlooked in his analysis, however, are other sources of legitimacy, other operative standards of reality maintenance. Moreover, the version of official information discussed by Edelman may change with governments and the coming to power of new social and economic interest groups, but other nongovernmental forms of legitimacy would remain and be supported by all who rely on official information.

In brief, then, it is not enough to see culture as "bad faith" or scholarly to ferret out the impact of myth and symbolism on our lives. These efforts need to be integrated with a broader perspective on the relationship between the communication process, organizational theory and research, official information, and propaganda. Drawing on the materials noted above leads us to propose that bureaucratic propaganda is a synthesis of each of the above. We contend that the effect of this new form of propaganda is to present the myth that "rational procedures" can be trusted to convey adequately the reality and meaning experienced by the members of an organization to "outsiders" who do not share the same frame of reference and who do not regard the information in an instrumental way. As we shall argue in some detail, the role of government has changed and grown appreciably, but in the process, it has become more like an organization and has also adopted the rational-bureaucratic-efficient model of accounting to the public. All this has changed the character and significance of propaganda.

In sum, then, scholars have recognized the role of information in promoting both individual and collective self-interest. Machiavelli and Goebbels—and their historical benefactors such as the USIA—appreciated the use of strategic information. Ellul recognized the pervasiveness of information distortion in modern life, which led him to see a good deal of the entire Western culture as decadent. What has been missing from these analyses is an appreciation of the role of bureaucratic propaganda in promoting the image of the organizational form as rational and efficient, and the significance of this for prevailing standards of legitimacy.

In clarifying how the concern with external legitimacy informs internal organizational routines, we also address the "micro" or specific and detailed views that are both a product and a producer of the "macro" or larger institutional myths regarding rationality, objectivity, and official information. We believe that this approach is a useful way to put the internal activities in the context of the historically developed mandate to appear rational and thereby to link conceptually public beliefs and understandings about specific activities and aspects of social life with the broader historical picture. The examples we include also show the usefulness of 'micro' studies for validating and clarifying 'macro' developments. Moreover, the juxtaposition of case studies when conceptually unified shows them to be more similar than different as scenarios for the enactment of institutional images of legitimacy.

Even though all official information greatly distorts what actually occurs within an organization, the goals of an organization will shape the nature of the official information. Each of the following chapters illustrates the use of official information for somewhat distinct purposes. For example, chapter 2, "Propaganda and the News," emphasizes how the organized character of television news promotes an internal structure that depends on official information generated by other organizations. Indeed, the mass media remain the most significant link between the institutional impression management of the government and new forms of bureaucratic propaganda. Chapter 3 focuses on program ratings that influence all television programming, including news. The materials show how arbitrary the use and interpretation of much "measures" are, even though managers insist that they are objective and scientific. Chapters 4 and 5 show how the welfare-state generated welfare bureaucracy strives to look objective and efficient on paper in order to continue doing what state, regional, and departmental feudal lords desire. These materials show how the form of bureaucratic reporting can easily accomplish dramaturgical management for both the clients and the workers. The world's largest evangelical organization is examined in chapter 6. The Billy Graham Evangelical Association's (BGEA) innovative way of bureaucratically counting newly won souls serves to promote the public image that this group is fulfilling a basic human need. Chapters 7 and 8 turn to the life-and-death consequences of playing war with numbers. Chapter 7 illustrates how military preparedness can be rationally programmed and objectively proven, when in fact the people involved realize the ritualistic aspect of it all, especially the officers whose careers may rise or fall on the official information their subordinates come up with. Chapter 8 shows the same logic at work in Vietnam via objective reports such as "body counts" and "air strikes." The concluding chapter will suggest further applications of an understanding of bureaucratic propaganda for our lives.

2

Propaganda
and the News

Propaganda has always depended on the use of various media. Orators, poets, pamphleteers, movie makers, organizational spokespersons, journalists, and others have (either wittingly or unwittingly) adapted their message formation and delivery to fit changing technological, political and social needs (cf. Fathi, 1978). The rise of electronic media has led to the perfectability of propaganda and, as noted in chapter 1, prompted more subtle and persuasive techniques.

Among the more innovative developments for effective propaganda use was the establishment of news organizations devoted to disseminating a myriad of public information on a daily basis. Even though journalists usually attempted to avoid being part of a propaganda effort (and they often succeeded), historical events, such as wars, and pressures from many governments occasionally led to compromising the ethics of neutrality and objectivity.

In this chapter, the historical relationship between government and news agencies will be discussed as a form of what we have termed *traditional propaganda*. We also stress how the size and complexity of news organizations have tended to diminish the control of government over content; government now depends on the news media. Moreover, the organizational demands of administering news on a daily basis, especially in television news, have generated complex and restricting organizational formats, time schedules, and commercial priorities that provide a bureaucratic context for many other organizations to supply self-serving information. News organizations have come to rely on such messages as institutionalized news sources, which in turn are influenced by the practical demands of generating newscasts and publishing newspapers on a daily basis. Taken together, the sources and the organizational imperatives lead most news agents, especially television reporters, to approach their information with a *news perspective: the view that any event can be summarily presented in an interesting and visually exciting way with a beginning, middle, and end, and that this can be accomplished within a few hours.* This perspective fundamentally distorts events by *decontextualizing* them from the complex situations and meanings that surround them and then *recontextualizing* them within the practical context of the newscast. Thus, the context of the original message is important, but so is the context and work involved in shaping that message to meet practical demands.

As we argued in chapter 1, much of the information derived from the various news sources is not emotional or filled with value-laden terms and ideologically sounding goals. To the contrary, it is increasingly presented as "factual" and even as "scientific," even though it is all carefully edited before reaching the newsrooms. The nature and impact of the subtle but nevertheless very evident shift from government control to a self-sustaining organizational environment for generating public information will be presented as a crucial context for the new forms of propaganda that have largely gone unnoticed.

Organized news has always served a practical purpose, but over the last hundred years the purpose has changed. Ideally, of course, news agencies serve to inform the public of significant events, people, and even trends. But what the events, people, and trends would be was influenced by the history and organization of newswork. The most general shift in the nature and significance of news in the United States has been from a small, almost exclusive circulation concerned only with matters of commerce to a preoccupation with attracting a mass audience in order to make money.

Throughout most of the eighteenth century, newsletters focused on shipping schedules and bills of lading. The dominant audience was the businessman. There was no daily newspaper until the 1780s. No big circulation sheets existed before the 1830s, when Benjamin Day (1833) and Gordon Bennett (1835) more fully utilized expanding technology to produce daily newspapers for the public.

Unlike their predecessors and many of their contemporaries, Day and Bennett did not restrict their coverage to commerce, prominent citizens, and editorials and opinion. They broadened the coverage of news to include events involving "common people," as well as spectacular and "sensational" stories about the dark side of wealthy and famous people. This coverage often involved scandal. Such a focus permitted these publishers to sell their papers to the public as a whole and also to sell advertising space. The people bought the sensationalism and the advertisers paid for reaching a certain number of people. This was why circulation became very important: more money would come in from direct sales, but more importantly, advertisers could be asked to pay more to reach a larger audience. This evolution of the newspaper changed its purpose; no longer was it aimed at a small wealthy class of people, but rather it was now targeted for a mass market. Not surprisingly, this new purpose (to make money) greatly influenced news content.

Before the advent of mass circulation newspapers, the emphases of newssheets were on shipping reports and political action. Political interests often sponsored these newsletters in order to promote their own causes. The flames of the American Revolution were fanned with pamphlets as well as newspapers. During this period, editorial opinion was what news was all about, and this trend continued until the "mass circulation liars" drove the pamphleteers out of business. Editorial opinion did not disappear, nor did the political purpose of the news, but they were mitigated in order to build sales. As Hughes (1940: 16) noted:

> What the advertiser bought was circulation, and his money paid the costs of publishing the paper. Sales of the newspapers to readers barely paid for the ink and newsprint paper. But to make advertising space worth paying for, there must be wide circulation. The circulation liar was an inevitable phenomenon in a period when, to survive, it was necessary to boast. Circulation was achieved through the news columns.

Concern with profits grew concomitantly with news interest. The crowning point of this era of zealous commercialism occurred in the 1890s with "yellow journalism," spawned to promote the Spanish-American War in an effort to increase circulation. The change from political opinion to news stories also expanded the character and the power of the press. As Will Irwin (1936: 79) observed:

> The trial-and-error experiment in the great American laboratory was discovering that the press had a real and vital power. It did not reside in the editorial page. It did not even consist wholly in the occasionally dramatic exposé of a private citizen, a politician or a corporation. The long steady education which the editor was giving his readers through his selection of local and world news, through the point of view he instilled into the authors of his local news stories, through the kind of news he chose to 'play up' on his front page or to 'play down' under a single head inside, through his very headlines—in this lay the real power of the press over a modern world.

The necessity and impact of information being used to promote points of view and courses of action led to an inevitable connection between news and propaganda.

The suggestion that news can be seen as a type of propaganda is not new. It was originally made by Will Irwin in 1936 in his much neglected book, *Propaganda and the News*. Irwin, a journalist, traces the emergence of propaganda from the time of Caesar to the end of World War I and the beginnings of public relations, government press agents, and the entire stock of "publicity" positions that now pervade our lives. As the public grew more sophisticated, the newspaper editorial lost much of its clout; but an editor could still influence opinions. This was the beginning of the change in the nature of propaganda, but it was in the German innovations of World War I that the press became more directly tied to shaping opinion and action.

> . . . in the prewar sense [propaganda] meant simply the means by which one spread his opinions. In the modern sense it means a traffic in half-lies or selfish or dishonest ends (Irwin, 1936: 222).

The Germans selectively picked events for publication in order to shape the image of America held by German citizens. They would, for example, omit the more cultured and "dignified" news and play up the gang wars, racial tensions, and lynchings. They were trying to make "psychological preparation" for war. Here were the beginnings of a strategy that was later perfected by Hitler and Goebbels. Most importantly, this strategy led Americans and the other Allies to realize that they too had to "fight for the hearts and minds" of their supporters as well as fighting their enemies. Many prestigious journalists joined the Allied effort, including H. G. Wells, Arnold Bennet, and Rudyard Kipling. Irwin (1936: 155) nicely summarizes the impact:

> Taught by Germany, which had in turn learned the trade from the United States, the Allied propagandists applied all the tricks, ruses, and devices of the expert publicity agent. In these conditions the news was slanted almost automatically. If a writer turned out a proportionate story of conditions at the Allied fronts, the censors deleted all passages implying the exercise of critical instinct; glory alone remained. The propaganda departments planted and manufactured news.

World War I convinced many military and other government officials that a war of information and propaganda was as important as one of bullets (Bartlett, 1940). By World War II, elaborate techniques and procedures for enhancing public support and for demoralizing the enemy had been developed by social scientists and other patriots (Lerner, 1951; Lee, 1952). The success of most of these procedures is questionable, but the establishment of such an institution is a fact (Katz, *et al.*, 1954). A central part of the propaganda effort was directed toward editing and often explicitly constructing information that would be presented as news. The reliance of reporters on government support and assistance, along with a widespread interest in winning the war, made the interests of the journalists and officials more compatible. Indeed, many of the well-known journalists of this era, such as Ernie Pyle and Edward R. Murrow, seldom questioned government sources and were generally regarded as necessary morale boosters for the troops as well as for readers and listeners back home. Murrow's popularity prompted government officials to offer him a post with the United States Information Agency (USIA), the official propaganda network of the United States. Many journalists worked with this agency throughout the Cold War period, using their journalistic credibility and contacts to promote government interests at home as well as abroad (Bogart, 1976). The significant point about these developments is that news agents were now originating as well as reporting events. Problems occasionally arose when other government officials and editors were unaware of the USIA-inspired role in selected news reports. For this reason, the CIA today maintains a secret coordinating panel to prevent United States officials from being duped by their own propaganda! (Arizona *Republic,* Jan. 18, 1976).

As the USIA experience suggests, the character of news-government relationships was greatly influenced by all the hot and cold wars that have been waged during the past sixty years. Government officials and journalists were presumed to share the same values and commitments to national policy and the growing institutionalization of such news sources as press conferences and "off the cuff" interviews led to an increasing reliance of one for the other. In brief, their interests merged, and when there were occasional rumblings of disagreement, the threat of government censorship or even banishment was ever present. The extreme case occurred during the McCarthy era, when journalists and even actors who had little involvement in editing news reports were chastised and even blackballed through government pressures. It is not so surprising or noble that Edward R. Murrow's reporting of McCarthy's tactics and perspectives finally led to the politician's demise. What is surprising is that Murrow's efforts were largely a singular event in a context of widely supported political and journalistic repression. That such repression was able to be sustained further indicates the long-term alliance between the press and the government.

The sharing of essential perspectives by government leaders, editors, and individual reporters continued during several other wars and "national crises" because of a great ambivalence by the latter of openly disagreeing with the awesome positions and responsibility represented by the former and also because of the increasing necessity to be on good terms with government officials who could provide newsworthy tidbits of information; if inside dope was withheld because a reporter was persona non grata, then the journalist could be replaced in order to keep up with the competition. Thus, hanging onto one's job as well as "doing a good job" by getting "inside" information encouraged reporters to play up to news sources and respect their wishes.

The role of the press in perverting public information about more recent wars, including the Cold War, has been well documented by Aronson (1970). After noting that the rise of the wire services and syndicated columnists who wrote for a chain of newspapers eventually resulted in standardized editorials and coverage of national issues, Aronson (1970: 19–20) assessed the impact on the nation:

> Such a [national news network] has its positive aspects in bringing into some areas a broadened news diet that nourishes the parochial wastelands, but it also tends to ensure that all persons will be similarly influenced by the news and commentary they absorb daily. It follows that they will tend to think alike, and their thinking will be encouraged to support the 'national interest.'

Such "support" was then shown in the reporting about the genesis, nature, and aftermath of Korea, Vietnam, the Bay of Pigs fiasco, the emergent national definitions about Iron Curtain countries, and the widespread chill of Communism that sparked the Cold War and ultimately produced an arms build-up that the world is still trying to dismantle. The government's influence on selected journalists can best be described as awesome. United Press's Robert C. Miller told a group of journalists in 1952 about the kind of reportage coming out of Korea (Aronson, 1970: 122–123).

> There are certain facts and stories from Korea that editors and publishers printed which were pure fabrication. You didn't know that when you printed them. Many of us who sent the stories knew they were false, but we had to write them because they were official releases from responsible military headquarters, and were released for publication even though the people responsible knew they were untrue.

Much the same was true with reporting about the Vietnam conflict, although the widespread use of television coverage did make a significant change. Nevertheless, the relationship between government officials and editors and reporters kept the "facts" within the proper government channels (cf. Epstein, 1973; Braestrup, 1978). Halberstam's (1978: 94 ff.) analysis of the impact of Henry Luce's editorial direction of *Time* magazine on material related to the war is instructive, especially since television networks often look to the national news magazine to "legitimate" topics for coverage (Batscha, 1975: 123). *Time* did not begin any kind of critical reporting about the conflict in Vietnam until late in 1967, even though reporters like Charles Mohr were aware of the corruption and ineffectiveness of the puppet government in Vietnam. But no one took his views seriously; it was as though he either never fully understood what a Luce-controlled magazine would emphasize, or he simply had too much integrity. Indeed, Mohr, like a few other journalists who were critical of the war, were taken to task by their superiors, often through the magazines and newspapers they worked for. As Halberstam (1978: 125) notes:

> Luce had always understood that information was power and, unlike other publishers, was not bashful about savaging other publications and journalists. The magazine strengthened its own vision by denouncing other visions. Throughout the Vietnam War, *Time* did most of its heavy-duty assault through the press section, attacking anyone critical of the war, praising anyone who liked it. It was a powerful weapon, and it was frequently and often brutally employed.

How powerful politicians and other people of influence seek to manipulate publics via the mass media has also been noted with regard to drugs (Epstein, 1977), Watergate (Altheide, 1976; Schorr, 1977), foreign policy (Batscha, 1975), and crime (Cohen and Young, 1973). But the role of the media organization in the process of creating, selecting, and presenting public information has not been as clearly understood (Tunstall, 1977). This is especially true with television (Tuchman, 1974, 1978; Burns, 1977).

> If senators—and even Presidents—routinely allowed their speeches to be quoted before being made, it was because . . . the news media were the real audience. If congressional committees devoted almost as much of their secret sessions to scenarios of how to publicize their work as they gave to doing the work, it was because they considered their product largely futile if it didn't get on the evening news (Schorr, 1977: 181).*

Our studies of the mass media as well as the reports by dozens of other social scientists and journalists indicate that media organizations are no longer subservient to government interests and have increasingly come to influence governmental decisions (Rivers, 1965; 1970). The events of Watergate and the aftermath of Vietnam, as well as the nature of media-hyped presidential campaigns, make it apparent that leaders depend on these disseminators of public information for legitimacy (cf. Schandler, 1977). Former CBS correspondent Daniel Schorr (1977: 294) observes:

> The reality that television presents, however imperfect, has become . . . the only important reality. Because television is the arbiter of the significant, little can succeed without its blessing. Proposals, pro-

*From CLEARING THE AIR by Daniel Schorr. Copyright © 1977 by Daniel Schorr. Reprinted by permission of the publisher, Houghton Mifflin Company.

grams, grievances, issues and candidates need to be legitimized by
the 'tube' or they cannot gain votes, popular support and money.*

Indeed, the demise of Senator Eagleton as a vice-presidential candidate in
1972, Nixon's resignation from the nation's highest office, and President
Carter's urging to have his friend Bert Lance resign from a cabinet office
after being negatively portrayed in the mass media further suggests that
politicians need media support and cannot long endure a hostile press (cf.
Altheide, 1976; 1977).

The growing ability of the national media to define significant issues
and personalities (cf. Shaw and McCombs, 1977) requires careful examination of the organization and perspective that now informs all news,
and especially television news. Once this is done we will better understand
how the mass media have become the key definers and legitimizers in our
society, and in the process, have become the major source of bureaucratic
propaganda (cf. Bensman and Lilienfeld, 1973: 213 ff.).

THE PURPOSE AND CONTEXT

The remainder of this chapter focuses on how television news is organized, on the effects on the selected news sources, as well as on how reporters construct the reports they glean from them (cf. Tuchman 1969;
1976, 1978; Roshco, 1973). Materials are drawn from various studies, including more than one year of participation and involvement in a network
affiliate station, Channel B in Western City (pseudonym); from all facets
of the news process of the major networks at the National Political Con-
ventions in 1972; from a network owned-and-operated station in California;
and from periods of observation with news personnel in Washington and
Arizona. In addition to these materials, selected studies of network and
especially foreign affairs news will be drawn on to broaden the scope of
application and understanding.

Television did not become commercially viable until around 1950. Its
rapid growth and popularity is attested to by its spread: today, more than
96 percent of American homes have at least one television set, and nearly
half of the homes have two or more sets. This phenomenal increase has
created tremendous demands on the television industry to improve the
technology of television in order to transmit clear and sharp pictures and
to provide more air time to sell to advertisers. At the same time, larger
audiences could be attracted to deliver to sponsors only if they watched
the programs that were offered. This was especially true when competing
stations vied for the same market, or segment of the population. Competi-

tion for high ratings, or official estimates of the size and character of the viewing audience, led to programming rampages aimed at pulling in the "numbers" essential for successful television business. A technical director detailed the significance of good ratings:

> The big problem we have now in news is ratings and that's taking everything. The point is we have to bring up our ratings and how we're going to do it, we don't know yet. . . . If we had good ratings now the newsroom could call the shots at the station . . . ratings continue to be the primary concern of the news director and literally everybody in the newsroom . . . news is our biggest money loser now.

In general, the purpose of television (to make money) influenced the kind of messages that would be presented (mostly entertainment) in order to "capture" an audience that was viewed as unintelligent and susceptible to program manipulation.

As a veteran reporter explained:

> If we can spark his interest, if I can start off with a flashy lead that will at least keep him there chewing his TV dinner and sipping his beer, till the next bigger news story, we will have succeeded.

Television news bears the mark of this logic, which, when combined with a largely unreflective journalism, promotes propaganda as news. Today more than 65 million Americans watch the news on one of the three major networks. Even more people watch an additional half hour or hour of news on one of more than 700 commercial stations. Surveys show that people trust television news more than other news sources (Roper, 1971). Indeed, many researchers now regard television news as the most influential shaper of public focus and opinion. In order to understand the character of television news, it is essential to clarify how news is viewed by the people who work on it and to note the effect this view has on how news is defined, how events are selected for coverage, and how events are presented.

The interest in capturing the largest share of the ratings in order to build revenue has important consequences for how and what is presented as news. "Visuals" become more important and can promote a kind of misleading interpretation. Former CBS newsman Daniel Schorr (1977: 92) explains:

> Trying to do newspaper-style reporting in a visual medium, seeking to transmit facts with the tools of fantasy, entailed compromises. One had to bend scripts to fit around sometimes barely relevant films. Trying to cram in more information than time permitted, I tended to read too fast and was frequently admonished to sacrifice a few facts

for a less breathless pace. I chafed at the straight-jacket of the conventional TV news story—a brief introduction voiced over silent film, a snippet of somebody speaking and a brief conclusion. The format left me with the feeling that I had merely 'teased up' a story that remained to be told.*

Robert Batscha's (1975: 219) study of foreign affairs broadcasting raises further questions about the impact of visuals on adequate presentation.

Who greets the President as he descends from his plane in Moscow gives little knowledge about the ideological differences that separates these two nations; nor does it give more than a superficial, often misinformed impression of the intricacies of international diplomacy. . . . Most foreign affairs occur out of reach of the camera lens, either in the minds of men or behind closed doors, and the event often represents only the outward tip of the iceberg of diplomacy and relations among governments.†

Moreover, the interest in entertaining visuals entails giving high priority to bulky equipment that may further limit understanding. As Batscha (1975: 78) notes:

The cumbersomeness of these tools has prompted many critics to conclude that the function of the television correspondent has changed . . . they say, he finds himself preoccupied with the logistical problems of photographing the story, of "getting the picture"; and the reporting aspect, including the search for news and the surfacing of important stories, becomes secondary.‡

Schorr (1977: 18–19) argues that the impact of visual priority on the public definition of events can be decisive in influencing future action.

Watergate, in the early days before the 1972 election, was a classic example of a story in search of pictures. Time and time again, to meet the needs of various news shows and specials, I took our cameras through the sixth-floor office to show where the door had been taped, where the suspects had been captured. . . . It was hard to remember when the site became the symbol, but it was the stand-up that did it.§

* From CLEARING THE AIR by Daniel Schorr. Copyright © 1977 by Daniel Schorr. Reprinted by permission of the publisher, Houghton Mifflin Company.

† From FOREIGN AFFAIRS NEWS AND THE BROADCAST JOURNALIST by Robert M. Batscha. Copyright (©) 1975 by Praeger Publishers, Inc. Reprinted by permission of Holt, Rinehart and Winston.

‡ Ibid.

§ From CLEARING THE AIR by Daniel Schorr.

In terms of the visual medium's impact on who has access to the network's definition of news, Schorr (1977: 17) agrees with other researchers (Altheide, 1976; Epstein, 1973) that access can be won through pictures.

> Denying 'picture opportunities' becomes the objective of those wishing to keep a story out of the public eye—almost literally—and creating such opportunities becomes the need of those who want the story told. In that sense, television becomes not merely the witness to a contest, but the arena for the contest, and perhaps the arbiter.*

In brief, the emphases on ratings and on providing entertaining and visually exciting newscasts become the organizational rationale for evaluating newswork. To have good ratings means that everything is being done "right," whereas ratings lower than the competition's imply the opposite. However, since individual news stories are not "rated," but only the newscasts, the people in charge of coordinating the overall operation become more important—and also more vulnerable—to the rating logic. This is particularly true of producers, who arrange the entire newscast, and of the assignment editors, who select events to be covered. In local stations, a news director is in charge of the entire operation and may be blamed for low ratings, although his primary function at Channel B and most other stations is to promote public relations with the community and especially with important business groups. By the same token, the news director in local operations is often a conduit to the newsroom for opinions of local politicians. On the whole, however, the news director has less daily impact on the day-to-day operation of news than does the producer.

A producer's job influences what is defined as newsworthy and what quality work is. A successful producer, including the "field" producer who accompanies network crews to actual story assignments, is able to evaluate an assignment in terms of its potential for visual entertainment. He knows that superiors in New York will be evaluating the work he sends on in certain ways. Not surprisingly, most producers reflect the same tastes and opinions about the news as do their superiors (Batscha, 1975: 81). As these "gatekeepers" encourage the reporters subordinate to them to do "good work," the latter quickly acquire the organizational perspective on what constitutes good news. For example, producers claim that the public is uninterested in foreign affairs news. Any reports about this topic must be couched in certain ways.

> These criteria are made clear to the correspondent as he gathers his story. He must communicate to an audience that is in the 'middle,' of which the attention span is limited, and which does not always have the necessary background to comprehend the whole story. . . .

* From CLEARING THE AIR by Daniel Schorr. Copyright © 1977 by Daniel Schorr. Reprinted by permission of the publisher, Houghton Mifflin Company.

It should conform to the subjects and ideas that the viewers can readily comprehend, given their existing frames of reference (Batscha, 1975: 220–221).*

The best way to insure that the viewers understand "one major idea" is to portray stereotypes as reality. Correspondents learn that New York has predefined notions about what is relevant to their audience, and this in turn promotes stereotypes—for example, Germany is associated with German beer festivals. One result is that the producer rather than the reporter on the scene often defines, selects, and interprets what is important about an event. As one correspondent said:

> It's deeply demoralizing. There is a deliberate shelving of a reporter's input into a story, and the producer has been elevated into a super editor and genius in everything. To get a piece on the evening news, I never speak to the managing editor . . . I talk with the producers here and those in New York. . . . They control, run, dominate, shape the content of the evening news. Somebody has to control the shape of the evening news. But the reporter who knows the story should control content, but he doesn't (Batscha, 1975: 122–123).†

Putting the show together in an appealing way requires that the producer conceive of each segment as part of a whole. This requires "segmenting" the show into various parts, each segment being separated by a punctuation mark—a commercial. The aim is to lead "the audience through the news so that their distracted minds do not have to make sharp twists and turns to follow what is going on" (Batscha, 1975: 11–12).

The impact of organizational forms of what is presented as news is suggested by the "segmenting" noted above. The routine way of doing this, of coordinating the newscast, is defined by the format, the presentational parameter within which the news lives.

Channel B's format included world and national news, local news, sports, and the weather report. These items, plus an occasional "comment" and "perspective" comprised the newscast. Of course, commercials were interspersed throughout. Once the format was set (and it changed several times in an attempt to raise the ratings) the task was to fill in the "show order," or the order in which news items would appear. A modified "show order" for Monday, January 31, 1972 is presented in Table I.

The producer's main responsibility is to make certain there is enough material to fill the one hour newscast. The format is a useful guideline for the producer and the assignment editor, or "desk." For example, this show

TABLE I. *A Show Order*

SUBJECT	LENGTH	
1. Open	:30	(e.g., "This is the Channel B early news.")
2. Headline Tease	:30	
3. World and National	3:30	
4. Tease	:07	(e.g., "More on this in a moment.")
commercial	:30	
commercial	:30	
commercial	:30	
5. Film story A	2:00	
6. Live Item	:30	
7. Film Story B	1:00	
8. Live Items	:45	
9. Tease	:07	
commercial	:30	
commercial	:30	
commercial	:30	
commercial	:10	
10. Tease	:10	(e.g., "And now we'll find out why bread costs so much.")
11. Agc. and Stox	4:00	
12. Live Items	:45	
13. Tease	:07	
commercial	:30	
commercial	:30	
commercial	:30	
commercial	:10	
14. Live Items	:45	
15. "Perspective" Toss	:10	(e.g., "Doug Smith has some thoughts on this.")
16. "Perspective"	3:00	
17. Tease	:07	
commercial	:30	
commercial	:30	
commercial	:30	
commercial	:10	
18. Sports One	3:00	
commercial	:30	
commercial	:10	
commercial	:60	
19. Sports Two	2:00	
commercial	:30	

TABLE I. (*Cont.*)

SUBJECT	LENGTH	
commercial	:30	
commercial	:30	
20. Film Story C	:30	
21. Film Story D	1:50	
22. Film Story E	:30	
23. Film Story F	1:30	
24. Film Story G	:30	
25. Tease	:07	
commercial	:30	
commercial	:30	
commercial	:30	
26. Film Story H	1:30	
27. Live Items	:30	
28. Film Story I	2:00	
29. Live Items	:30	
30. Tease	:07	
commercial	:30	
commercial	:30	
commercial	:30	
31. Live Item	:30	
32. Weather Toss	:07	(e.g., "In a moment we'll find out if tomorrow is a good day for a picnic.")
33. Weather, National	2:00	
commercial	:60	
34. Weather, Local	2:00	
35. Close	:30	(e.g., "Thanks for being with us; Bill will return with more Channel B news at 11:00.")

order indicates that eleven minutes are accounted for by commercials; another two minutes are required for "teases" and "tosses"; the sports and weather are allotted five and four minutes respectively. The format also calls for a standard 3:30 for "world and national news." This totals to nearly twenty-six minutes of news. The remaining thirty to thirty-five minutes will be filled with local film stories, the "perspective," "live items," and video packages provided by the network.

If the local news is particularly slow the wire services can always be counted on for "live items" to be read (without film) by the anchorman.

If the producer decides that there are holes to fill, he always has a stack of wire copy that can be rewritten to standard lengths, usually from 20 to 45 seconds. The number of live items varies from two to ten, depending on how much time needs to be filled.

Another way to fill holes is the network News Program Service (NPS) video "feed," which provides monthly "features" or less timely stories each day at 3:00 p.m. This filler enables affiliate stations to cover any time surpluses, as when the scheduled news is lacking several minutes. Such lacks will commonly occur if an anchorman reads too fast (faster than three seconds per line of copy) or if one or more stories have to be scrapped because tape machines or projectors malfunction. For these reasons NPS is often a life saver. By the same token, this news source is relied on when other news is not forthcoming. This was more true of the noon news since film crews generally did not have time to cover local stories, process film, and have it ready for the noon show. Consequently, film stories are at a premium and the time is often filled with NPS features.

In order to insure having enough film stories available, selected pieces are stacked nearby. At any time the producer may rush in from the booth and ask a writer, "What have you got?" Several alternatives will be suggested and the producer will then choose one, such as seminaries advertising in *Playboy* to attract recruits. In this way packaging the news show becomes routinized.

The format provides predictability and order to the newscast in order to promote ratings. It also provides, short, snappy, and visual stories rather than good public information. Indeed, the journalists who are the "leg men" for organizational imperatives often feel constrained. As one foreign correspondent said,

> We are so preoccupied with the daily news developments and putting it on film in the shortest period of time that we have little opportunity to give perspective or an overview of what happened today, this week or during the month (Batscha, 1975: 88).°

Batscha's (1975: 223–225) conclusion of the constraints of scheduling and format on news content applies to both network and local news:

> Because the broadcast format promotes simplicity, capsulation, and stereotyping, the individual's map lacks certain facets of the overall picture. Stories on complex ideas, long-term trends, and economics do not often receive air time. . . . The demand for simplicity and conciseness and the need for the visually interesting story results not only in the potential danger of presentational bias and stereotyping,

but in the words of a news magazine's advertisement, in creating a public that is 'overnewsed and underinformed.' *

What the public is underinformed about, however, are not the official images presented by a myriad of organizations; to the contrary, the practical dimensions of newswork discussed thus far create a ripe solution for bureaucratic imagery to grow and for fronts to be maintained. That is what institutionalized news sources do for public information.

NEWS SOURCES

The format helps shape the show and suggests the priorities of scheduling short, concise reports for the fast-moving pace believed to be essential in entertaining the audience. But where the content comes from to fill in the format requires still more work and more organization. This is the "desk's" job.

The person on the desk knows that five to ten local film stories lasting from 1:00 to 2:30 each will be required to fill the local portion of the newscast. Having enough news is as much a problem for him as it is for the producer.

The daily potential crisis of not having enough news to fill the show influences the news process in several ways. Even though news will ideally be new, organizational considerations preclude too much newness. A series of deadlines require careful scheduling in order to have enough news for the 5:00 P.M. newscast. It takes approximately forty-five minutes to process film; another fifteen to thirty minutes to do a marginally good job of editing; driving to and from stories may add another thirty minutes; and, of course, there is the time required to cover the news event. The upshot of these practical contingencies is that most news events must be known about hours (and usually days) before the newscast.

Solving the problem of having enough news has established a handful of news sources that account for at least 90 percent of news reports. Assignment editors and other "gatekeepers" routinely rely on predictable sources in order to schedule news coverage (cf. Epstein, 1973: 142). The major sources include: press releases, the wire services, newspapers, various radio monitors (such as police and fire), and the NPS service noted previously. Table II presents an overview of the sources for the stories contained in the show order presented in Table I.

Eight of eleven stories presented on the evening newscast (Monday, January 31, 1972) were known about on the previous Friday (January 28, 1972) (not counting "world and national"). The desk's "future file," (a

*From FOREIGN AFFAIRS NEWS AND THE BROADCAST JOURNALIST by Robert M. Batscha. Copyright © 1975 by Praeger Publishers, Inc. Reprinted by permission of Holt, Rinehart and Winston.

TABLE II. *News Items and News Sources*

	SOURCE	TOPIC	ON NEWS?	NO. ON "SHOW ORDER"
1.	Personal	"Perspective"	yes	15
2.	Wire	Bus. & Agr. Report	yes	11**
3.	*	Blimp Feature	no	——
4.	*	Clothespin Feature	***	——*
5.	Press rel.	Prof. Growth Day	no	——
6.	Several	Film Story H	yes	26
7.	Press rel.	Feature	no	——
8.	Press rel.	Film Story G	yes	24
9.	Press rel.	Film Story I	yes	28
10.	Press rel.	Film Story B	yes	7
11.	Press rel.	Film Story E	yes	22
12.	Press rel.	Film Story F	yes	23

* I was unable to learn the exact source, but a press release is probable.
** These stories were filmed on Friday, Jan. 28, 1972.
*** This story appeared on the News, Feb. 1, 1972.

depository for potential news stories) contained thirteen press releases, three newspaper clippings, a few "live items," and several notes. From these sources the desk drew up the "beat sheet" or tentative news schedule for Monday's news. Table II illustrates the importance of what is included in the beat sheet for future news. The source, item, and whether or not it was on Monday's news reflects such prescheduling. The importance of certain news sources that facilitate scheduled coverage extends to the amount and nature of news. For example, the news varies by time of day (evenings are slow), day of the week (weekends are slow), and month of the year (summers are slow). The nature of news is also affected. For example, more press conferences are held during the week day. These fluctuations in news can be directly traced to the dominant sources of news. The relationship between the two can be illustrated with radio monitors and press releases.

Radio Monitors

Six radio monitors hang in Channel B's Newsroom and adorn most news operations. Included are monitors for police, sheriff, fire, and the highway patrol. These are the main source for "spot news," or unplanned, "breaking," and more spectacular news, such as homicides, suicides, burglaries, and fires. Each day's newscast has one or two of these stories, which are learned about by certain police code designations. For example, a robbery is a "211," burglary is "459," homicide is a "187." There are nearly 100 additional codes that are usually not recognized since they are not considered newsworthy (for example, illegal parking is a "586"). Some of the codes that news agents use as part of their own radio communication with the station include, "10–19" (return to station), "10–7" (out of service), and "code 7" (eating).

Even though these codes represent a small portion of the ever-present radio clatter, they tend to be disproportionately selected and presented as dramatic stories involving police. Spot news stories are not broadcast with the intention of presenting such views, but rather because they are deemed newsworthy, vis-à-vis other available news stories. Spot news represents the drama, suddenness, and "on-the-spot" news coverage with which newsmen associate news. Also, spot news is convenient, especially on evenings and weekends and is commonly "all that is available." As one reporter explained, "Night news is a little different than day news; . . . there is a lot more crime."

There is likely to be more crime news in the evenings and weekends for several reasons. First, the radio monitors are less audible during the day than on evenings and especially weekends. The importance of being able to hear this news source, especially when several sources clatter for attention, cannot be too strongly emphasized. One evening while riding with a cameraman and a reporter, a call for an ambulance ("11–41") came over the police monitor. The cameraman correctly remarked that "they probably wouldn't even hear it at the station," and therefore would not dispatch anyone to the scene.

A second reason that monitors are more relied on for evening and weekend news is the absence of an assignment editor. (Of course, this is not true at all stations.) One reason for his absence is that there are few weekend news sources that permit scheduled coverage; little occurs that the desk may learn about from press releases, newspaper clippings, and the like. Also, since less time is available for the newscast (one-half hour at 5:00 and 11:00) there is less need to search diligently for news. Consequently, more police-related stories are likely to appear on weekends. However, this news source only supplements the more organized and scheduled pieces derived from press releases, which permit news to be planned and scheduled.

Press Releases

Networks derive most of their news from the wire services (Epstein, 1973: 142), but local affiliate stations like Channel B obtain 75 percent of their stories from press releases. Most wire-service reports are either too close to the deadline for the newscast or too far from the station to be covered. One advantage of using press releases for local news operations is that they permit the assignment editor to plan tomorrow's or even next week's coverage (cf. Batscha, 1975: 123 ff.). By selecting from the dozens of press releases that are put out daily by various organizations, the "desk" decides which show the most promise for good news stories. Unlike the police monitors, which occasionally produce exciting chase scenes, press releases are more likely to involve press conferences or interviews, which are referred to by newsworkers as "talking heads." One cameraman explained why not many stories were being covered one afternoon.

> *C.M.:* Those son-of-a-bitches aren't getting any press release, they don't know what to do otherwise. . . . They depend so much on those damn press releases coming in there and telling them, you know, to go here and do this, that they have developed no outside sources for news.

The reason for this lack of "outside sources of news" is that they are unreliable and cannot be counted on days in advance to facilitate scheduling crews in order to "fill the show." Moreover, although "tips" may lead to exclusive investigative reports and exposes, they also may fall through. More importantly, the time and expense it may take to pursue such leads can detract from more efficiently using personnel to "fill the show," and that is what they are hired for.

It must be emphasized that news routines are symbiotically compatible with the purposes or organizations that provide potential news information. For example, a Public Affairs officer in the Navy explained how he handled his ship's premature departure from a fire zone that was ordered by the captain, who claimed to have seen an enemy commando swimming toward the vessel:

> I went ahead and wrote up all of the news releases on it, two copies to the, well, practically to everyone in the world, the full shot. . . . *Since we'd broken off a mission, our primary mission over there, we really had to do a job in the releases.* The whole thing was completely gundecked in my opinion (see chapter 8).

One consequence of relying on organizationally produced sources of information is to exclude people who are not affiliated with such enterprises from participating in newsworthy events (Goldenberg, 1975). This has led some persons to develop their own "press releases" to obtain public attention. One political activist explained how his group sought to bring public pressure against repressive actions by the local Sheriff's department against hitchhikers.

> With the Sheriff we couldn't go before the County Board of Super-
> visors because the Sheriff is an elected official; . . . all we could do is
> go to him and he gave me a rap of about 45 minutes [that their
> hitch-hiking policy is a good thing] . . . *so there was nothing we
> could do except put out a [news] release.* So I called up the station
> and talked to a reporter. . . . We always follow up on the [tips] and
> a lot of the things that we do happen to be newsworthy . . . like
> trying to stop the appointment of the Police Chief. That made head-
> lines for about three days.

Just as business people and bureaucrats promote their activities by passing on artfully constructed information to the news agencies, so, too, do
the "outsiders" view news in terms of its utility, such as having a "newsworthy event" like a demonstration. The utility of news is evident in the
words of one activist's description of a meeting in which a "staged demonstration" was discussed.

> The chair wanted to know if we should have a demonstration at all
> or rather the hearings would generate their own publicity . . . a
> reporter on one of the newspapers . . . mentioned that it would
> be very hard to get more than just normal publicity out of this
> thing . . . if something dramatic wasn't done *because the news media
> doesn't normally pay attention to the normal happenings!* Someone
> determines what's news and most of the time your stuff will end
> up in the waste basket and there's just no way of getting it across.
> . . . The news desk or manager have [sic] very concrete concepts
> of what news is and this does not include the minority community.
> They're not news unless they're opposed to the structure, and then
> they're news. . . . The general tenor of the meeting was that the
> mass media is there only when there is something that is objectionable.

Goldenberg's (1975: 28–29) study of four activist groups showed essentially the same practical understanding about press coverage.

> The more a group's political goals deviate from prevailing social
> norms, the more likely the group is to gain access to the press, other
> things being equal. . . . Leaders found they could attract attention
> from all three newspapers for nearly any demonstration—particularly
> if there were arrests—while reporters would not come to meetings
> and would not necessarily listen to their point of view during and after
> meetings with the welfare commissioner.

These examples suggest that the news organization relies on certain news
sources in order to fill the newscast, whereas members of certain organizations rely on the news to "inform" the public and usually to promote cer-

tain images. One never hears of an organization submitting a press release acknowledging a failure of its mission.

The self-serving nature of most information obtained from press releases, or even from wire services that had an origin in official pronouncements, is often geared to using the news reporters as an extension of corporate or official policy. This relationship between the media and the sources is more troublesome since television, even more than the press, requires cooperation in order to obtain the all-important direct quote and other pertinent visual detail noted above. As Batscha (1975: 32–33) notes:

> At the same time that correspondents almost uniformly respond that they 'hate to be used,' they also recognize the desire of government officials to manage the news and propagandize their policies and the frequency with which they succeed . . . because it tends to cover more stories with fewer words than newspaper, [television] is often more subject to 'use' by officials.*

When time pressures and the preoccupation with finding something entertaining lead the journalist to rely on a few sources to augment what may be a superficial understanding, "the correspondent is too often the victim or unwillful transmitter of the policy-makers' propaganda" (Batscha, 1975: 60). One example is how McGovern's aides, pollster Pat Caddell and campaign manager Frank Mankiewicz, distorted their boss's ability to win the blue collar vote in certain precincts during the 1972 primaries.

> If McGovern did well in two out of three of the Slavic districts we had pre-selected, you can be damn sure that we didn't tell them [the press] about the third. . . . We didn't do it but we could have made it all up—the ethnic and class make-up, even the results! No one ever checked up on us. We were doing the reporters' work for them (Wheeler, 1976: 192).†

Newscasts transmit to the public many of the decontextualized and incomplete reports that are originally learned about through press releases, but the organization of newswork contributes its ingredient to the distorted messages presumed to reflect real events. We are referring to the logic of the news perspective in transforming an event into an abbreviated, but entertaining, report with a beginning, middle, and end. Any news source that understands this organizational mandate and whose members are

*From FOREIGN AFFAIRS NEWS AND THE BROADCAST JOURNALIST by Robert M. Batscha. Copyright © 1975 by Praeger Publishers, Inc. Reprinted by permission of Holt, Rinehart and Winston.

† From Michael Wheeler, LIES, DAMN LIES, AND STATISTICS. Liveright Publishing Corp., New York, 1976. Reprinted by permission.

skilled in formulating messages compatible with this perspective is more likely to be used. Not surprisingly, this is why more and more bureaucracies and organizations employ people who are skilled condensers and simplifiers of reality. And if a source, such as a press release, becomes "old hat" among the journalists who periodically do get suspicious of the self-serving nature of these sources, new approaches to promoting image may be used. "Leaks" represent one organizational innovation, especially as employed by the Nixon administration.

> In the Nixon White House, the leak was the subject of a twofold obsession. The unauthorized leak would cause President Nixon—and hence his lieutenants—to fly into fury, launching investigations, ordering wiretaps, seeking court injunctions against publications. . . . At the same time, leaking was a cottage industry in the White House. Dozens of memoranda of the Watergate period routinely advised the planting of specific stories with friendly columnists like Victor Lasky and Evans and Novak. In a nasty twist to the leaking industry, subcontractors were commissioned to supply material to be leaked. The White House 'Plumbers,' so designated because they were supposed to plug leaks, also had the mission of filling the reservoir for other leaks. . . . It is possible that Watergate itself was the initial stage of a leak project—seeking material from Lawrence O'Brien's files and phone conversations that could be disseminated to his and the Democrats' disadvantage (Schorr, 1977: 180).*

By the same token, any source that is not disposed to simplicity and cut-and-dried perspectives on problems and issues is to be avoided. This is particularly true of the "academic," who, according to one correspondent, "has his passion and that's all he sees" (Batscha, 1975: 125). A network vice president put it this way in explaining why an academic's notion of more complex truth was largely incompatible with the organizational version preferred by television journalism:

> Look, during the President's trip we had a panel of six academic experts on China sitting around a table and discussing China and the implications of the trip for an hour on the air. They couldn't agree on anything. By the end of the hour you forgot what the issues were. Now, our correspondent over there can spend a day or two talking to people and asking questions and so on and get at the truth of what's happening. That's why we send a correspondent and keep the expert in the New York studio (Batscha, 1975: 126).†

The implications of this view are not only that certain news sources are preferred (which often promotes bureaucratic propaganda) but also that the nature of media work itself generates a simplistic way of ordering reality to suit its own needs. Media work is also bureaucratically endowed with an intolerance for less-than-utilitarian knowledge; it must fit the television format. The important thing about getting concise knowledge about the China trip, for example, is that it meets the time and "air" requirements better than more elaborate, yet probably more accurate, assessments. Another correspondent pushed the point even further by explaining her hesitancy to call on academics for consultation about matters that she may not be highly informed about:

> Academics give you too much and more than you want to know. They'll also give you political interpretations. It is rare to find the academic whom you can phone and get concise facts (Batscha, 1975: 126.) *

Yet another example of the same point was experienced by one of the authors who has appeared on television several times during the last several years. After the latest "live" interview with the anchorman about the subject of this book, the author was complimented with, "You're quite good; you've done this before haven't you?" The skill alluded to was the rapidity and conciseness of responses to rapid-fire questions, rather than the depth of explanation necessary to understand fully the complex interchanges between bureaucratic propaganda, modern organizations, and the mass media. Thus, reality is edited for a bureaucratic purpose.

Events are selected from a handful of sources in order to fill the show. This is the quantitative side of news. But the "desk" selects from among the dozens of press releases, newspaper clippings, and so forth the events that seem the most promising or that have the most potential as news stories. In short, he is always asking, "What can we do with it?" That is the reporter's job.

THE ANGLE AND EVIDENCE

Just as the military personnel, welfare·workers, and evangelical counselors to be discussed in later chapters have their practical orientation to the world, so does the reporter. A television journalist's task is to find something newsworthy in events that have been selected for scheduling and other practical reasons. A reporter explained:

* From FOREIGN AFFAIRS NEWS AND THE BROADCAST JOURNALIST by Robert M. Batscha. Copyright © 1975 by Praeger Publishers, Inc. Reprinted by permission of Holt, Rinehart, and Winston.

> I realize that the people I do work with are expecting a certain thing, so what I do is I try to read what other people are looking for and that's what I give them. . . .

The organizational interest in scheduling and predicting future news coverage, plus the format that calls for a half dozen short and entertaining reports, create a problem for reporters. It is partially solved by predefining what is important about an event and then using this as the basis for a story. Two major reasons for this development, of course, are the advent of tighter formats and the expanded role of the producer discussed earlier. A foreign correspondent reflected on this trend.

> In the old days (the 1950s) you went from Suez to Kenya just gathering background materials for a story. Today, before the team goes out on the scene, they have a clear idea of what they want. The role of the correspondent has been diminished. There is more help whether he wants it or not (Batscha, 1975: 80).*

The reporter constructs something newsworthy about an event with an "angle." The "angle" facilitates placing unique occurrences in a broader context and, in a sense, rendering "meaning by association." The relevance of the "angle" is suggested in this reporter's comment.

> *Rep:* We go out and we cover a story and we can say John Blow held up a bank at 4th and Market St. and escaped with $14,000, police are continuing the investigation . . . blah! Whereas, a bank robber, you know, a bank robber robbed a bank at 3rd and A St.; this is the 14th time this bank has been robbed; the teller who handed the money over was Mrs. so and so who comes from another job at such and such, a place where she had been robbed 4 times; her reaction to this robbery was that it was unique in that she noticed this or that, you know; *you make a story, you get hold of the basic foundation and you build.*

Institutionalized angles like conflict are the most commonly used, but other meaningful contexts are available. Angles may originate in recent national developments, local happenings, and other concerns. An example of national developments' providing a context for the local side of the story was the release of the President's Commission report on marijuana. An interview with an expert on drug use was the obvious angle for the story. Channel B's coverage of an airplane hijacking was

*From FOREIGN AFFAIRS NEWS AND THE BROADCAST JOURNALIST by Robert M. Batscha. Copyright © 1975 by Praeger Publishers, Inc. Reprinted by permission of Holt, Rinehart and Winston.

also made more meaningful by the broader national experience with this problem. Another example of a national angle was put forth when a national political convention threatened to invade Western City. As Channel B's news director said on one telecast, "Security has become the name of the convention game in the wake of the last National Democratic Convention."

The local scene can also present appropriate angles. An investigative report on border corruption was repeatedly updated by Channel B. More examples include stories about the good side of young people in contrast to the "rash of demonstrations and unlawful behavior." If it were not for the latter, the former would have been less meaningful to the newsmen who covered these stories. As one newsman explained about a story on volunteers clipping "coupons" for a local charity,

> *Rep:* We have had a good deal of inquiry about the good news, you know, and so this could fall in that category—young kids who are involved in something other than protests, and narcotics, and all that.

Still another source of angles is the newscast itself. A reporter covered a story on an alternative theory of creation set forth by a religious group. Even though he emphasized that the group's position was somewhere between Darwin and the biblical view, the reporter was instructed by the producer to include something about Bibles (although none were mentioned during the interview) because the "lead" to the next story was about "welfare cheaters swearing on a stack of Bibles." The concern to make the stories fit together thus became the angle for the story.

All of these angles are grounded in the reporter's sense of shared experience with fellow workers. Stated another way, particular events are related to a broader context, and it is the meaning of this wider framework that makes the story. While covering a demonstration at a university, a cameraman was asked what was the most newsworthy aspect. He replied,

> You mean, out of the whole thing? The flag coming down. The other stuff, I wouldn't have bothered. You know, I mean that's the school's business, but on the other hand, people have a right—they pay taxes— to know what's going on in their schools.

The topical angle of demonstration was suggested with a story on weaving. The reporter explained:

> They've already given me one lead because they call this a spin in, which is another demonstration. However, it is different than the type we normally are accustomed to.

One story without an angle was an assignment to do 2½ minutes on the local waterworks. The newsmen knew that since the story was assigned at 3:00 P.M. the intent was "to fill a hole" in the producer's show. Nevertheless, the reporter insisted that there was just "a bunch of double-talk in that script," and that "there was no new information." His problem was, "what do you say about water?" The story could have been more interesting had there been a rash of sickness attributed to water. However, since no such context was available, it had to stand on its own, and in the reporter's opinion, it didn't stand very well. Discovering and using angles for a framework through which to present the content of the story is one thing, but it is still not apparent how the content is used. We now turn to this question.

Reporters select and present the content as evidence of the angle. The angle is the framework to which specific content will be nailed in order to tell a story. The important point is that the story is simply the format or medium through which a definition of an event—the angle—is presented. This means that the story is already pretty well set before the reporters and cameramen leave the station, although they must be certain to not commit the mistake of "misconstruing" the story by letting the framework survive at the demise—and contradiction—of the content. A story on proposed alternatives to achieve more school integration illustrates the utility of the angle for content. As we left the station the reporter was asked,

> **Author:** What the hell are you going to do?
> **Rep:** Just barely give a background as to what these alternatives are; explain the story over [film] of kids, bless their little hearts, who have no say in the matter whatsoever, caught in the game of politics between their parents and the school board.

Thus, newsworkers seek evidence that supports the story line.

Which angle will be used depends in part on the reporter's knowledge, experience, and beliefs about the nature of events. Journalists become accustomed to "types" of stories; that is, events that can be treated in particular ways. If this cannot be done, then the event may be discarded or at least, distorted. Gaye Tuchman (1976) has noted that newspersons learn forms or types of stories that can be conveniently imposed on various assignments. Although most events can be molded to suit the reporter's preconceptions about "what is interesting," some cannot. Tuchman (1976: 97) gives an example about a reporter's inability to come up with "the story" about a women's movement meeting:

> There were a lot of interesting things going on, but I couldn't nail things down. There was formless talk. I could see things changing,

but it was hard to put my finger on it and say to the metropolitan desk, "This is what's happening."

In this context, what is presented "as happening" may be less a feature of the meanings of the event to the people involved than it is a definition of a situation that has emerged for practical and organizational reasons. Similarly, Rosengren, *et al.*, (1978) and his colleagues showed that journalists' beliefs about the impact on the audience of fictitious radio messages about an accident at a nuclear power plant led them to greatly exaggerate the nature and extent of citizen reactions. An important question to ask in this light is: Which angles or stories are usually used, and where do they come from? Moreover, if an angle is available to use, on which occasion will it be used? Both questions suggest that journalistic interpretation of events has both a historical dimension as well as a political one whereby a reporter may select one "typical" definition for an event rather than another one. Most astonishing is how journalists become blinded to the organizational influence on how they approach events. They forget that they are working from a perspective (the news perspective) and that all reality may not easily be grasped by it. Only on rare occasions do journalists become aware of this point of view, usually when they fall victim to it. This recently happened to C. L. Sulzberger of the *New York Times* when he was questioned by Carl Bernstein (1977: 55–67), a Pulitzer Prize winner from the *Washington Post* for his Watergate investigations, about Sulzberger's connections with the CIA. Sulzberger felt he was unfairly maligned (Phoenix *Gazette*, Dec. 27, 1977). Daniel Schorr, formerly of CBS news, became aware of the impact of predefining what is important and pursuing angles. As Schorr (1977: 226) reflected on his encounters with reporters who questioned him about his leaking of the Pike report, he observed:

> Fully aware of the irony of viewing the press for the first time from the other side of the barricade, I nevertheless shared the resentments of many who had been in the spotlight before me. . . . I began to understand what politicians and public policy advocates meant when they accused the press of being negative and trivial, oriented more to gossip than to issues.*

The practical consequences of angles can systematically distort events. The widespread acceptance of certain claims to be newsworthy has led newsworkers to rely on official sources of information, and in turn, to take for granted many of the angles and stories that now accompany such information. Sam Adams (1975) found this to be a major factor

---

in perpetuating United States involvement in Vietnam; official reports systematically underreported the size of the enemy strength. More recent reports indicate that it is not uncommon for our Central Intelligence Agency to plant false stories in foreign newspapers. However, the CIA must then act to make sure that "our side" knows the reports are false, and should not be taken seriously (Arizona *Republic*, Jan. 18, 1976). Another example concerns welfare fraud in Phoenix, Arizona. The title to one article indicated that only "13 possible frauds found out of 75,000 welfare files" (Arizona *Republic*, May 30, 1976). Students who work for the State Department of Economic Security have shown in unpublished research papers that fraud is quite prevalent and that it is actually promoted by career interests of supervisors who do not want to upset "the way things are done" by rocking the bureaucratic boat.

Still another example of the emergence of a new story line is "Watergate." What started out as a burglary attempt at the Democratic National Headquarters in 1972 became a central ingredient in the cauldron that eventually claimed President Richard Nixon and many of his aides. The news media played a significant part in this process, especially in how it promoted the theme that the Nixon administration was "the most corrupt in history." The effect was to encapsulate many unrelated events such as political spying, abuse of presidential priviliges regarding the Internal Revenue Service, the FBI, and the CIA under the term "Watergate." Thus Watergate came to symbolize the newly discovered, but actually very prevalent, use of official power (cf. Altheide, 1976 for further discussion). Most significantly, however, was how Watergate came to take on an objective meaning; it became a new potential story. Not long after the events involving the now infamous White House crew of former President Nixon, newsworkers all over the country would suggest that there were "other Watergates" in local, state, and even national arenas. They were sought out; potential victims were hounded by judiciary personnel, and usually by the press. This was true of former Senator Gurney of Florida, who was tried twice on the charge of improper handling of campaign contributions. He was acquitted, but came to suffer political and financial ruin; another casualty of the Watergate story.

Suitable stories come and go, but while they are with us, those who report on events from these angles tend to overlook how it all got started; they forget that all stories have origins. Watergate again serves as an example. A recent poll of newspaper editors and radio-television news directors rated the Watergate scandal and the resignation of President Nixon as the eighth all-time story in American history! It was topped only by the American Revolution, the drafting of the Constitution, the Civil War, World War II, the American moon landings, the development of the atom bomb, and the Great Depression. It triumphed over such events as the assassinations of Presidents Lincoln and Kennedy, the New

Deal, World War I, the Korean War, and the massive immigration during the nineteenth century. Even though it may seem odd that anyone could seriously place more importance on Watergate than on World War I, such distortions are more plausible when understood from the news standpoint: Watergate took on a symbolic life of its own before, during, and after Nixon's resignation; it became a way of making sense out of a number of complex events, and most importantly, helped journalists do their work (Koreagate, Lancegate, and so on).

This does not mean, however, that all official reports and statements are met with suspicion. To the contrary, most documents, "evidence," congressional reports, and the like are still reported by the news media as though they are real, objective, and are not the product of negotiations, power struggles, and both intentional and unintentional distortions. Only in rare instances will the "facts" be challenged, and only then if there is already available another story line—for example, why believe "the most corrupt administration in history?"

The reluctance of the news media to regard seriously the context and purposes that underlie the reports they receive promotes an official smoke screen. This is true with explicit public relations efforts to promote certain programs, and it is also true of reports couched in "scientific" terminology in an effort to make them look objective. An example of the former is the massive effort of the Atomic Energy Commission and various power companies to promote nuclear power plants as the "only sensible new energy source." Their strategy involved feeding news agencies simplified reports about the "exemplary safety record" of nuclear power and offering as evidence lists of hundreds of "scientists" and "engineers," most of whom had never worked with nuclear power and had certainly not systematically evaluated the social and economic costs and benefits. Further, power companies in Arizona, California, Washington, Oregon, Ohio, and Colorado stressed that electric costs would rise if nuclear power were not adopted. These "facts," along with promises of "thousands of jobs" led voters to defeat nuclear referendums in these states. What was not mentioned in these reports (and what few news agencies systematically investigated) were the number of "accidents" that had occurred in various nuclear plants, including partial and near meltdowns. Also neglected was the systematic analysis of the problem of nuclear waste, its destructive potential, and the burden this could impose on future generations. But the item that was most often neglected was the short life span of each power plant, of around thirty-five years. The astronomical costs of building replacement plants would surely mean ever-higher rates for customers as the social and health risks mounted. All these "objective" and "impartial" news reports, plus the cascade of advertisements throughout the mass media about the advantages and merits of nuclear power, achieved the purposes of the AEC and the respective power companies. But regardless of the respective sides in this important issue, the most important point to be made is that the public's decision was made on grossly incomplete information, and these messages were carried to them by the news messengers that many people have come to rely on. Such unreflective fulfillment of vested interests, especially in the face of its potentially catastrophic consequences, is but a more sophisticated form of propaganda.

NEWS AS PROPAGANDA

We have stressed throughout these pages that news reports propagandize by failing to describe the organizational considerations that influence any official report. The tendency of most news organizations, and especially local television stations, is to accept these reports and then "do a story" about the relevant events. News agencies are also organizations in their own right and provide their own practical solutions to the work of "getting out the news." The practices also influence what is selected as news and how it is reported. In each case the broader and meaningful contexts that surround specific events and subsequent reports are not included. This leads to distortion.

The message becomes more muddled when the public is unaware of the process by which messages are constructed. Just as governments throughout history have avoided close scrutiny and heatedly resist criticism, the news media have also grown very suspicious of outsiders. Researchers continue to have a difficult time gaining access to these organizations in order to study how the process works. This is especially true in Britain (cf. Beharrell, *et al.*, 1976; Tracey, 1977). One reason for this concern is that media organizations, like all bureaucracies, are always more and less than meets the public eye. Daniel Schorr (1977) discovered this when he suggested in a speech that CBS was soft-pedaling Nixon's wrongs because they feared a Presidential attack. He was chastised and told in a memo to check with his superiors in the future before embarking on further speaking expeditions:

> We expect you in each instance in the future to obtain written permission for lecture, and other non-CBS activities. . . . In the matter of public speaking appearances, we shall require texts of your proposed remarks before such written permission will be granted (1977: 117–118).*

When Schorr was finally dismissed because of his involvement in leaking the Pike report to the *Village Voice*, CBS denied that he had been fired.

---

* From CLEARING THE AIR by Daniel Schorr. Copyright © 1977 by Daniel Schorr. Reprinted by permission of the publisher, Houghton Mifflin Company.

When fellow employees questioned what had happened, CBS issued public relations statements to the effect that he had temporarily been relieved of his duties to work on a controversy over reporters' rights. As Schorr (1977: 280) ended his CBS connection, we read:

> Paraphrasing Walt Kelly's *Pogo*, I had found the story, and, in part, it was *us*. In probing into sensitive areas of government, I had raised problems inside CBS. It had been self-delusion to believe that one could practice old-fashioned no-holds-barred investigative reporting of the government while representing an organization that felt vulnerable to government pressures, its proprietor ambivalent about his conflicting commitments.*

News, then, is a vehicle for self-serving organizational accounts, but it also changes the meaning of these claims by calling them "news" and giving them the appearance of legitimacy and authenticity (cf. Molotch and Lester, 1974; Smith and Asher, 1977). Moreover, when the bureaucratic process that produces the newscasts (including the commercialism, scheduling, use of news sources, and entertaining angles) are glossed over on the screen and are allowed to disappear before the viewer's eyes, then an important dimension of reality has been distorted—the news producing process itself. The limitations of both technique and perspective are not apparent; disclaimers do not appear, and errors that often result are not acknowledged when subsequent events make them apparent. In short, information is being used for organizational purposes; "news" becomes a justification for another form of bureaucratic hype. Only a complete awareness of our complex reality goes wanting. In Batscha's (1975: 229) words:

> To create an interest in the news is a worthy and legitimate activity that fulfills the democratic requisite of a responsible press. However, to base news judgements on the preexisting interests of the audience through the employment of the medium's positive facilitators, is to dislocate its primary role as a conscientious and steadfast contributor to a well-informed public. . . . My point is that there exist operating criteria within the news departments that potentially mitigate against sound, journalistic selection and composition.†

News, then, is even more complicated and· more implicated in bureaucratic propaganda than in Irwin's day. Whereas Irwin's contemporaries in 1930 could critically assess the worth of the reports by knowing about the source of the information as well as the more common notion that "the government is feeding us a line," today's news reader and watcher must realize that just as governments used to be at war and sought to propagandize citizens, now organizations compete with each other for public support. Moreover, members of the news audience must know something about what happens to an event in the process of becoming news, and the reasons for this. Only these two orientational stances can hope to place the event that is reported back in its true context and to alleviate the complex but very real distortion of contemporary news reports. This is especially important in situations that are unfamiliar to people. As Bensman and Lilienfeld (1973: 211) note:

> But this situation . . . is precisely that situation which makes possible large-scale fraud, charlatanry, and deceit by misdirection. For the conscious manipulation of information becomes possible only when access to genuine information or direct sources of experience is obscured by the complexity of events, issues, technology, size or differentiation in society.

> The development of complex society provides the opportunity and the motivation, but the misapplication of journalism supplies the means.

3

Propaganda With Numbers: The Case of Television Ratings

INTRODUCTION

Organizations use bureaucratic propaganda to establish, promote, and sustain their legitimacy. What is legitimate, of course, is not established before the fact, but is usually presented to a relevant audience as a fait accompli, after the fact. This chapter looks at how the widespread belief in and use of polls and statistics by bureaucracies has served to promote certain practices and to justify particular courses of action. We will examine in some detail how one form of this massive cultural tendency to equate truth or accuracy with quantification has led to the development and use of "ratings" in television. How these numbers are obtained, how they are used by newsworkers and television managers, and the legitimizing role they play in current television programming will be explained.

BUREAUCRATIC COUNTING

All communication occurs in a meaningful context of shared experience that enables a reader, listener, or viewer to take for granted certain aspects of the communication process and not to challenge or be puzzled by everything, such as the grammar, used by the message sender in conveying the message. As we have noted earlier, much of this shared stock of knowledge that enables the parties to a communicative act to place the specific messages they receive in a broader context is influenced by our culture. The message in turn becomes reified and no longer doubted;

it becomes a symbolic reality that can be ritually referred to as a justification but is itself beyond question and disconfirmation (cf. Berger and Luckmann, 1966). In brief, more of our world becomes unproblematic, especially activities with which we have only a superficial acquaintance rather than a great deal of knowledge (cf. Schutz, 1967: 14 ff).

Quantitative forms of bureaucratic propaganda are widely accepted because of their mystical association with science and knowledge on the one hand and the widespread superficial acquaintance by which most people derive their knowledge about them on the other hand. Relatively few people in our society fully understand the detailed dimensions and assumptions involved in accurately translating the world of experience into quantitative terms, and even many of those who do, continue to inappropriately use quantification. Understanding why this occurs is an important step toward an awareness of how firmly embedded in our culture quantitative uses (and abuses) are.

The broader cultural support of quantitative "proof" of all kinds is geared to our increasingly technological society and to the concomitant expanded and technical-rational oriented education required for many jobs today. As noted earlier, this training renders people more susceptible to "scientific" reasoning than to emotional appeals; often, anything not presented in "objective" quantitative terms is actually regarded as "opinion," "value judgment," and the like. As these dimensions of knowledge have grown, they have become taken-for-granted by people throughout our society, especially the more educated segments. This in turn has led social scientists to reach for research funding and to legitimatize themselves as "scientists" by surrounding their ideas in a cloak of numbers. By the same token, any business, government agency, or group that aspires to be believed and given a place in the bureaucratically oriented marketplace of ideas and projects must also appear "numerically legitimate."

We stress the appearance of legitimacy in terms of quantitative assessments because the justification of a particular course of action is the end goal; the warrant to continue along the same lines, pursuing the same policy is what most bureaucracies strive for. Indeed, in a government report, Stockfish (1971: 473–474) cautions evaluators to be aware of the process of information construction:

> . . . the subject of government information systems, including the production and use of statistics, cannot be intelligently dealt with, let alone understood, if treated abstractly and hence devoid of an awareness of the complex interactions between producers and users of government statistics. These parties are also political 'actors.'

An example is the Defense Department's annual request for more money to buy the "absolutely necessary" personnel, equipment, and so forth.

The necessity is always couched in terms of what the enemy is doing, and how many tanks, aircraft, and other items they have compared to ours. Part of the problem, of course, is "what counts." A study by the Congressional Budget Office found, for example, that analysts are sharply divided over what NATO's strength is, including troops and equipment.

> One of the problems faced in trying to weigh the balance between the two sides is whether to count only forces already facing each other or to include those which could be mobilized during any period of political tension before the actual outbreak of war (The Arizona Republic, Jan. 8, 1978).

A similar point was made by Stockfish (1971: 47):

> Military organizations have been known to exaggerate the capability of possible opponents and to understate friendly capability. One way to do this is to count only the equipment (e.g., tanks or aircraft) in friendly *combat* organizations and to compare that number with the other side's total equipment procurement, which also includes items in repair depots, those used for training, and stocks procured for combat consumption allowances.

That the defense readiness of a nation is largely a product of the practical concern at the time (such as getting more men and material) rather than an assessment of all facets of defense capability is further suggested by the government's decision not to use information it has generated about the substantive meaning of statistics, such as the excerpt from Stockfish noted above (cf. Wilensky, 1967). Moreover, the efficacy of any analysis that equates "one-on-one" comparisons of, say, tanks is misleading. Some experts demonstrate this by noting that on the basis of "bean counts" France and Britain should have easily defeated Germany in 1940! Nevertheless, such comparisons are used and are given great credence, largely because they are practical: how else can we "know" if we are as prepared for war as the other side is?

The logic of "quantophrenia"—that quantification equals science—is well suited to organizational needs since only the insiders know the true picture. All outsiders simply deduce that these figures, obtained in a way they do not understand, are somehow valid; after all, the insiders must know what they are talking about. Such pluralistic ignorance about the simple and complex ways in which all information—and especially quantitative data—can be perverted makes all potential victims quite vulnerable. The situation has become more serious as more issues and problems come to be first "proven" and then "solved" through this kind of information.

The nationwide interest in educational test scores is a good example of how the logic of numbers can be systematically twisted to achieve some practical purposes. Tests were originally intended to assist educators in their work; students weak in certain areas could be spotted, and hopefully aided. However, the teacher was in charge of the content. All this has changed during the last several decades as the standardized tests have grown in prominence. Data have been accumulated to establish national norms of performance by which children in various school districts could be compared. More recently, how well children in one district did compared to another came to have political implications, as critics would charge that the children were learning relatively less than children elsewhere, and that certain people were to blame. Undoubtedly, such claims are partially true, but this can be known independently of the standardized tests. However, when low test scores came to be understood as an "official" and even "scientific" indication that one's school or district was below the norms established by other schools and other districts, then the nature of test scores fundamentally changed. Educators came to realize that their jobs could be threatened and, as politicians at all levels sensed that "quality education" was a safe issue, they stressed the test scores and demanded that everyone have a quality education. Two things changed due to this pressure. One was the establishment of programmed courses of instruction that were oriented to the standardized tests. Another was the reduced autonomy of the teacher in the classroom. Now, although neither of these trends is necessarily bad in itself, it is important to note that the net result was essentially to teach tests and to work with children on how to take tests and achieve good scores. School boards across the country are now demanding standardized tests for their own high schools in order to overcome the "deplorable state of affairs when many of our high school graduates cannot read." What they think will happen is that these students will really learn to read better; what will undoubtedly happen is that the reading proficiency tests will be effectively taught to the students so that they will be able to "objectively" demonstrate their reading ability. This will be necessary if school districts are to be evaluated on how many "illiterate" students improve. The information will have changed, but the reality will remain clouded due to bureaucratic logic.

The most intriguing aspect of the entire movement to "objectify" educational competence is that it is all based on some very questionable findings derived from surveys and polls about the inability of students and adults to pass a "functional literacy" test (Los Angeles *Times*, Feb. 28, 1978). A study by Donald L. Fisher from the University of Michigan agrees that some students are functionally illiterate, but most of these people did not progress with their class and usually did not graduate from high school. In his examination of the forms and questions that provided the data that led pollster Louis Harris to identify "18 million adults as having less than adequate reading skills," Fisher found serious problems with the meaning of the term "functional literacy" and noted that many of the errors were due to the test-takers' fatigue. Moreover, analysis shows the meaning of "functional illiteracy" to be vague, if not meaningless. Fisher notes that all the surveys classified between 5 and 14 percent of professionals and managers as functionally illiterate, even though the very nature of their position indicates that, if they are in fact illiterate, it has not sufficiently held them back in their careers. Thus, the term functional illiterate is misapplied. For our purposes, this suggests that perhaps many of the campaigns further to standardize education and to teach students tests may be both unnecessary and misdirected. Of course, such questions as these are irrelevant to the practical use of information to justify actions.

PUBLIC OPINION POLLS
AND THE MASS MEDIA

The bureaucratic purpose creates and then quantitatively focuses on its goal. Public opinion polls are an excellent example of creating a phenomenon that can have real consequences: a skilled poll user can be elected President of the United States! Pollsters have long been aware that sophisticated polling techniques can give some impression about public views on clear and well-defined issues, such as which person they will vote for in the upcoming election. But as numerous critics have pointed out, issues are seldom well-defined and the pluralistic interests in our society only infrequently seem deeply concerned about the same matters. In short, it is not at all clear that a public actually exists the way opinion polls imply (cf. Blumer, 1948). But pollsters are in the business of polling the public, and usually they are paid by someone to obtain such information for a very practical reason, such as running for office or justifying a plan of action. Thus, publics must be created. This is where the media becomes so important.

The news media are sensitive to poll results because of the interest in reporting on newsworthy trends, especially if they are exciting and dramatic.

> Television is a very bad medium for the reporting of polls because it demands emphasis on the dramatic and the visually interesting at the expense of things which are subtle and ambiguous. For a poll to get on the air, it must be timely and newsworthy. It need not be correct (Wheeler, 1976: 202).*

* From Michael Wheeler, LIES, DAMN LIES, AND STATISTICS. Liveright Publishing Corp., New York, 1976. Reprinted by permission.

Pollsters are now routinely employed by the major networks and news magazines to ascertain public views on a number of issues that are already newsworthy, such as the president's popularity. The statistics that are reported are then used as evidence or proof of a "downward trend in popularity." Since this is what the public hears, politicians are sensitive to these messages and have become skilled in promoting their own public impressions, including publishing polls that claim they are well-known, trusted, and believed to be a good candidate. If such results are then presented via the news media, the candidate's popularity (read 'name recognition') increases, and future polls, even if conducted by someone else, are likely to show a rise in recognizability. These factors are important, as Wheeler (1976) has shown, because campaign contributors look to these official figures for trends in popularity. Polltaker Mervin Field (Wheeler, 1976: 178) observed:

> There's a lot of stupidity among those who make major contributions to candidates. You wonder how they were able to make their money in the first place.*

Despite the substantive meaninglessness of early polls, their influence on campaign money can promote a self-fulfilling prophecy; but counter-information provided by opponents and even other pollsters must be combated with one's own "scientific" polls. Wheeler (1976: 192) provides an apt example:

> In 1972, one of Pat Caddell's principal functions for McGovern was to deal with the press, to try to counteract the bad news coming from other pollsters. Caddell prefers to think of his role as that of educating the press. . . .†

On the whole, we know little about the effects of polls on political life, but there are indications that some elections have been greatly influenced by them. When polls precede elections, and particularly in primaries, the news media tend to treat poll results as evidence of a "race" being waged and dramatically report on any gains or losses. This had a profound effect on Senator Muskie's campaign for the Presidency in 1972 when he did not get at least 50 percent of the vote in the New Hampshire primary, a plausible target based on early poll results. The 47 percent he did get (which was more than anyone else) helped brand him as a loser and as not a strong candidate (cf. Wheeler, 1976: 191 ff). He withdrew from the race a short time later.

These comments make it clear that the political and media-related

---

* From Michael Wheeler, LIES, DAMN LIES, AND STATISTICS. Liveright Publishing Corp., New York, 1976. Reprinted by permission.
† Ibid.

dimensions of polling are self-promotive; a constituency is made more than it is found. This can be done by attempting to discover what the "public" feels is important and then by tabulating the results to give a political candidate something to talk about and to appear to be in touch with the constituency. During the 1972 Presidential election, McGovern's pollster, Pat Caddell, teamed with Frank Mankiewicz, the campaign manager, to hype their campaign for the press. This would be done by selectively feeding the press "scientific" information about how well McGovern had done in certain precincts. Mankiewicz recalled what he would then do at a post-election press conference:

> I'd say something like, 'Okay, here is Precinct thirty-four, a working class district in Kenosha, 54 per cent Slavic, McGovern ran strong.' The press ate it up. We never would have persuaded them that we were getting the blue collar vote if we hadn't made these presentations (Wheeler, 1976: 192).*

In short, from the perspective of polls and the role they play in the media-dominated campaigns, "issues" are simply "least common denominator" appeals. That such efforts do not always get someone elected merely indicates that people may be becoming more sensitive to blasé rhetoric, or that one candidate is more convincing, but it in no way denies the significance of this logic for our political process. The crucial point is that the focus and orientation to some phenomenon as a product, such as a "public," greatly influences how the phenomenon is treated and constructed as a matter of practical concern.

TELEVISION RATINGS

Just as politicians have become more skilled in convincing media agents and then the citizens in this country that they represent certain publics (as indicated by scientific polls), the media workers themselves are quick to argue that they are in touch with their respective "audiences." They do this with contracted poll information about programming preferences. The tastes of their audience will be determined by the marketing interests that inform their enterprise:

Economic interest in the size and (demographic) shape of the audience (read, *market*) required an accounting procedure acceptable to the buyer and seller. For stations to sell time—and presumably a chunk of the market —they needed an audience gauge to translate viewers into dollars per minute. Likewise, the buyers wanted assurance that their messages were being received by the relevant "demographics," for example, women,

* Ibid.

aged 18 to 49. The answer was found in probability theory, especially the central-limit theorem and the law of large numbers. These principles underlie statistical inference whereby a random sample of viewers can be said to represent the population. Rating services contributed to the commercialization of television by providing the means to estimate numerically the nature of the market. According to the A. C. Nielsen Company (1964: 3), one of the largest rating services,

> In television, an audience rating is a statistical estimate of the number of homes viewing a program as a percent of all homes having a television set.

The relationship between the sellers (television stations), the buyers (advertisers) and rating services can be simply stated: (1) television staffs sold access to the audience; (2) advertisers bought this air time; (3) the rating services provided the "official" market. Programming decisions could now be "scientifically" assessed. If low ratings reduced the selling price, and if this were the most relevant consideration, then programs that "captured" the largest share of the audience for potential sponsors were likely to be pursued by the programming department. This link of seller, buyer, and market is the basic reason for cancelling programs, for having few in-depth documentary reports, and in general, for using television for entertainment rather than information (Bagdakian, 1971).

These estimates occur in the practical context. The purpose for which they are used—"proving that the audience is a certain size and has certain preferences—produces distortions that must be understood if one is not to be misled.

Consider the significance of technological limitations and their effect on how the audience is viewed. For example, radio and television programmers differ radically in their interpretations of the audience. Radio programming is targeted for specific tastes, such as "rock-n-roll," "country," "classical," "middle-of-the-road," or "all news" (cf. Denisoff, 1975), whereas television programming is geared to a "mass" of viewers (Elliott, 1972). Thus, radio sees its audience in very pluralistic terms, and no single radio station would hope to provide the kind of programming all people would enjoy and tune in.

However, because of the limited range in the television spectrum, only a handful of stations, and all three major networks, compete for all the people. Moreover, both radio and television managers have "rating" figures to prove that they are programming for their audience. How can this be? How can the audience be both regarded as a mass and also as pluralistic and segmented? More specifically, an individual radio listener would be regarded as far more selective, and in a sense, more difficult to please, by a radio station manager, whereas a television network executive would argue that the same person (but now a viewer) really prefers the limited range of material that is currently being broadcast. Who is correct?

An examination of the nature, logic, and use of ratings helps answer such questions and simultaneously clarifies their status as bureaucratic propaganda. The important point is to be aware of how the organizational and commercial constraints of television promote the use of "ratings" to justify programming decisions, including news content, and in the process produce a definition and image of the audience compatible with their perspective.

Even within television, all parties to the rating process do not look at it the same way. These "official statistics" (cf. Johnson, 1975) can be treated as having a career and passing through four stages:

1. Audience members who provide the data by being plugged into a Nielsen computer or by filling out viewing diaries
2. The sales staff who use this information to promote "commercial spots"
3. The station management who interprets these numbers and makes changes in the hope of raising a particular program's ratings, such as the evening news
4. The newsmen who use these "objective" indicators to verify a number of complaints and interpretations of "what's wrong with this place."

The next section treats as data the varied perspectives of all those involved in the rating process in order to unravel the multiple purposes of what is otherwise treated as "objective," "reliable," and "valid" "scientific" information. First, a brief look at how the ratings are done.

The A. C. Nielsen Co. and the American Research Bureau (ABR) measure viewing habits throughout the country, but their methods vary depending on whether they are measuring network programming or 'local" markets. In measuring network programming, approximately 1,200 "representative" homes (according to age, sex, family size, ethnicity, region) are contacted. Those agreeing to participate in the survey have audimeters installed in their homes. This device records whether the television receiver is "on," and if so, which channel is tuned in. The audimeter also monitors the tuning status of the television every thirty seconds and indicates any changes that are made. All of this information is then fed, via phone lines, to a central computer twice a day (see Wheeler, 1976: 211). Numerical accounts are then provided on: the percentage of the nearly 70 million television families viewing each broadcast (this is a program's rating); each program's "share" of the audience watching anything at a particular time; and the number and percent of viewers according to age and sex. The latter information is especially useful for the sales staff in "hitting" certain "targets." A member of Channel B's sales staff explained.

If we're selling women's girdles, we probably should not be playing in the middle of baseball. If we're selling a soap product or a toothpaste we probably should be hitting in the center of a family or a woman's program, because the most important demographic, and that is a word we use to talk about the audience composition, is women 18 to 49. Why? Because women 18 to 49 control the pursestrings of the average family. . . .

The mechanics of the sampling, extrapolation, and use of audimeters have been harshly criticized by Harry Skornia (1965: 129). After noting that only about 57 percent of those randomly selected will permit audimeters to be installed in their homes, he adds,

At any given time probably not more than about nine hundred of the Nielsen Audimeters across the country are in working order. Of those turned on, depending on the competition which in turn determines how many ways the audience is split, in a typical area, perhaps 32 sets may be tuned to one station, 24 to another, and so on. Since about 25 percent of the films are not usable because of human or mechanical failure, these 32 or 24 are reduced to 24 and 18 respectively. These sets bear the burden of reflecting the nation's taste. The House Committee which investigated ratings in March, 1963 found that one of the sets had been on over twenty-four hours. One Nielsen customer explained that she had turned the set on as a baby sitter. Another noted that the Nielsen-equipped set was in the children's bedroom, where no one else watched. In some cases, there may be only two or three Audimeters in a given city. Such is the so-called rating research carried out with Audimeters and similar attachments. By concealing the small numbers involved in the sample through the simple device of transforming them into percentages, the illusion of adequacy is created.

More recently, Wheeler has raised important questions about the logic of counting program preferences. Since there is an audimeter for each television set in Nielsen member households, it is possible that within a given home with, say, three sets that each set could be tuned to a different station. Wheeler (1976: 218) observes the consequences this would have:

Ratings thus go up, but actual audience does not. At the same time that the number of televisions is expanding, the average number of viewers per set is decreasing.*

To make matters even more ambiguous, all that a household needs to be credited for watching an entire program is to have it tuned in for six

---

* From Michael Wheeler, LIES, DAMN LIES, AND STATISTICS. Liveright Publishing Corp., New York, 1976. Reprinted by permission.

minutes. Thus, if a Nielsen viewer watches a program for six minutes, and then flips to another station for the remaining portion of an hour's program, both programs will be recorded as having been watched.

Participation in the Nielsen ratings is voluntary, and there are strong indications that many of the people who agree to join the Nielsen family watch television proportionately more than do nonmembers.

> The inflationary effect of Nielsen's peculiar manner of counting is huge. In 1966 the Politz research organization telephoned twelve thousand households to check their viewing habits. Their survey showed 41 percent of the households using television in the evenings. By contrast, Nielsen reported 55 percent. More significantly, the Politz survey found both fewer viewers per household and fewer adults watching prime-time television, 24 percent. Nielsen had adult viewership at 41 percent, well over one and a half times as much. *Life,* using an electronic device which detects the presence of a functioning television set, confirmed the Politz results (Wheeler, 1976: 219).*

The tendency to accept without question what may be inflated estimates because they benefit the television industry rather than to examine critically the nature of the data is suggested by what the networks and the Nielsen company do if the ratings show a decrease in television viewing. The practical dimensions of acceptable definitions of the size and preference of the television audience became more evident when Nielsen data showed a 6 percent decline in television viewers for the period September 8 to October 19, 1975. After cancelling several programs for low ratings and losing some advertising revenue, the networks began pressuring Nielsen to find out what was wrong, especially since other audience estimates did not reflect the downward shift. Some four months later, the Nielsen company conceded that some mistakes in interpretation and equipment malfunction had caused an illusory deflation in audience size (*TV Guide,* May 8, 1976). The important point for our purposes is that the entire process was closely scrutinized only when underinflation was suspected, although there is every reason to believe that Nielsen data overestimate the size of the audience Still another problem with treating the Nielsen data as highly reliable is how networks and even local stations will "hype" their programming with special movies and events during rating periods in order to increase their share of the audience.

A further difficulty with interpreting Nielsen results is related to the range of error or variation that the sample may have from the population it is presumed to represent. The central limit theorem and the law of large numbers provide guidelines for inferring the likelihood of a particular

---

* From Michael Wheeler, LIES, DAMN LIES, AND STATISTICS. Liveright Publishing Corp., New York, 1976. Reprinted by permission.

sample representing a larger population, but this is only true if repeated sampling occurs. Nielsen uses the same families over and over again. By not drawing repeated samples, the chance of error grows. In practical terms, this means that the sample families may not represent the broader population and their television preferences may even be untypical. Stated differently, if by chance a sample is overrepresented with football fans, then that bias will continue since the nonfans will not have a chance of being included in subsequent samples—it is too expensive to do so. Thus, since the rating is already subject to a 3 percent error, either plus or minus, and since sampling through replacement further compounds this error, it is evident that the Nielson numbers cannot be relied on for a truly accurate picture of viewing behavior (cf. Wheeler, 1976: 220 ff). Many of the same problems exist with the use of diaries as a data source for viewer preferences.

Western City was rated four times a year in 1972 by the Nielsen Co. and three times annually by ARB. Rating periods last for approximately one month. There are estimated to be 451,000 and 456,000 television households in Western City by Nielsen and ARB respectively. From this population, a residential telephone directory aids in the selection of a "representative" sample of 1,000. Of the original 1,000 between 560 and 600 households agree to fill out viewing "diaries." The sample size is then split into four sections, one section for each of the four weeks of the "rating period," for example, October 26 to November 22. Upon completion of the "rating period," the diaries are collected, the data analyzed, and an "average viewing week" is presented as "ratings" in Nielsen's *Viewers in Profile* and in the *ARB Audience Estimates*. This information booklet is sold to various clients, including advertisers, advertising agencies, and television stations. Since each sample household represents approximately 1,000 television families, a brief look at the diary procedure seems appropriate. We begin with the first stage of this numerical career.

Stage 1: Respondents and the Ratings

It is commonplace that any data are only as good as their source. This takes on more significance with television ratings since the people who provide this primary data seem less interested in doing a good job, of filling out the viewing diary as directed, than they are with "getting it done" because "it's such a pain in the ass." At any rate, the meaning of this diary account to the people who do it provides a basis for comparing other uses of these "data."

Several important assumptions underlie diaries as a data source. A major belief, of course, is that diary respondents are representative of all television viewers. Although there are no reliable data to verify this (Nielsen uses percentage of its respondents who consume goods compared to other consumers), it is likely that there is at least some over-representation of people more prone to television viewing.

> Nielsen's reliance on diaries for its sweep week information significantly inflates the ratings, perhaps as much as the networks' special programming efforts. Although the company puts diaries in a lot of households, it is lucky to get back 60 percent of them completed; sometimes the return rate is less. The people who take the trouble to log all their viewing probably care about television more than the people who do not cooperate. Again the method produces erroneous data, but the error benefits the networks and stations which sponsor the survey (Wheeler, 1976: 223).*

A related assumption is that the rating diaries are filled out while people watch the program (every fifteen minutes a notation is to be made). In other words, the viewer's response is believed to correspond more or less with what he actually watched, especially since it is assumed that very little time separated the "watching" from the "noting." Of course, subscribers to the rating services are told in "fine print" about possible problems.

> Simple basic instructions in the diary aid accurate and complete entries of stations, channels and programs viewed for more than five minutes and the individual's viewing. Subscribers are reminded that diary-keeping is necessarily entrusted to the cooperating households and may thus in part reflect estimates of hearsay. *In other words, the recorded diary data—both viewing and demographic information—are subject to response error* [Italics added] (Nielsen Station Index, 1971).[1]

ARB (1972) also cautions its clients,

> The diary contains specific instructions to record viewing and tuning. The data are affected to the extent that these instructions are understood and followed by the diary keepers.
>
> Some diary entries may have been made on the basis of hearsay, recall, or the estimates of the diary keeper.
>
> It is possible that human and computer processing errors may occur after the diaries are received at ARB headquarters. Consequently, *the degree of variance in the data may be greater than that expected from sampling variation alone* [Italics added].

There are no in-depth studies, to our knowledge, of "diary behavior," or the process by which people account for their television viewing (cf. Bechtel, *et al.*, 1972). And as noted earlier, we do not have any systematic

---

* From Michael Wheeler, LIES, DAMN LIES, AND STATISTICS. Liveright Publishing Corp., New York, 1976. Reprinted by permission.

data about the behavior of Nielsen participants, partly because they are asked to sign an agreement that promises to keep their identity as a Nielson family a secret. Several journalists have tried to study them, and failed. Apart from some comments to an NBC reporter by the members of one Nielsen family in 1977, the most insightful view of what may be a unique case (we don't know) was described by Los Angeles *Times* reporter Dick Adler on June 14, 1974. The person he interviewed, "Deep Eyes," was aware of his special status in the mammoth Los Angeles market area, and it made a difference in what he watched. He would turn on programs if he felt they were important, although he personally did not care for them and did not view them. As Deep Eyes said:

> My one-twelfth of a rating point doesn't mean much in the national ratings, but we've had a lot of luck in the local Los Angeles market.

Although other Nielsen family members have claimed that Deep Eyes is not typical of their actions, it obviously does not take very many people out of 1,200 to alter a program's rating by one point (exactly 12), which is a large enough margin for a program to be cancelled.

Although no one has ever systematically studied how rating data are collected, an audio recording of one couple (referred to as "P." and "K.") filling out an ARB diary suggests relevant research foci. These comments should be taken as illustrative of the "diary process" and not as data per se, although informal interviews with a dozen "raters" in three states support these findings. Most interesting was the viewers' enlistment of *TV Guide* to help remind them what they watched the previous week.

> *P:* What about the *TV Guide;* are you going to use that ... ?
> *K:* No, I know what I watch, I told you that.
> *P:* How do you know what I watch?
> *K:* You can fill out what you watch (*Laughs*).

TV Guide was important because the diary was being filled out at the end of the week. Another segment of the tape suggests how handy the *TV Guide* is.

> *P:* They should have their things set up from Sunday to Sunday or whatever the *TV Guide* does because that would make it a lot easier.

"Proper" use of the diary assumes that people are aware of very basic information, such as how many channels they receive.

> *K:* Okay, what channels do we get: 2, no; 3, no; 4, no. . . .
> *P:* We get 4.

K: Four, we don't get, we don't watch anything on 4.

P: We do if there is something good on that isn't on 8 or 10 I mean We can get 4 well enough to watch it but not very often. . . . We get 9 . . . we get 11 . . . we get 13 . . . okay, we get channel 15. . . .

K: We don't get that well enough to watch anything.

P: Yes we do. Sure we do.

K: We do not.

P: We do too. We do. All you have to do is hook up the regular antenna to the UHF antenna and it works. I found this out the other night. . . . We get 39 too. . . .

Another assumption is that people are aware of what they watched.

K: Did we watch *Adam-12* on Wednesday night?

P: Is *Adam-12* on Wednesday night?

K: We just got through watching it tonight (Wednesday), I hope it is. . . .

P: Okay, now wait a minute now. *Adam-12* isn't on . . .

K: On Wednesday . . .

P: No, not at 7:00 . . .

K: At 7:30.

P: We watched the *Untamed World.*

K: I assume that you watched the news yesterday?

P: Oh yeah.

K: We're very predictable, dear. That's what this really shows.

P: No, it doesn't really because I haven't watched the news every day.

K: Yes you do.

P: No I don't.

K: Yes you do too.

P: No I don't.

K: Oh no, no, we watched *You Asked For it.*

P: But that isn't on.

K: But, that's what we watched.

P: It isn't on tonight.

K: Uh huh.

P: This is December 20, right. At 7:00 it *[TV Guide]* has *Truth or Consequences* . . . we're in trouble, dear.

K: We watched *You Asked For It.*

P: That was on at 7:30. At 7:00 we eat dinner and we don't really watch anything although we do have the *Untamed World* on

> this set out here [in the kitchen]. Now are you going to move
> to this other book here and say that we watch *Untamed
> World* . . . ?
>
> **K:** I am not!
>
> **P:** Dear, come on, it's important . . . actually we have both of them
> [sets] going at the same time usually because you're in here
> doing this [cooking] and I'm out there watching the news.
>
> **K:** Well this is absurd! [Laughter]

Since this part of the "representative" sample had two televisions, they
were given two diaries to fill out, but there was a problem because one
set had been loaned to a friend half way through the week.

> **P:** No, now wait though; you had to use this set only [the big tele-
> vision] because this set we had given to Pat. . . .
>
> **K:** I see, what do you suppose he was watching? [Laughs]
>
> **P:** Do you suppose we ought to give him the pad to fill out be-
> tween Wednesday and Sunday? [Laughs]

The issue is resolved.

> **P:** What are we going to do with this one [the other diary]? Are
> you going to keep this one? Maybe we ought to write on this
> one that the set broke or something like that, do you think, and
> return it empty because . . . they have got to have it back.
>
> **K:** Tell them that was the week . . . we loaned the second TV to
> friends; that's reasonably true; true is true.
>
> **P:** But it isn't entirely true.
>
> **K:** Well the damn thing hasn't been on like 5 minutes in the last
> month.
>
> **P:** Well, okay . . .

The problems with accounting for time spent watching television are
added to when regular programming is interrupted. This occurred when a
space shot delayed programming.

> **P:** Channel 24 is the *Mystery Movie*, but they interrupted that with
> the splashdown, or the take off.
>
> **K:** Well, I don't care what they did . . . we didn't change the chan-
> nels.
>
> **P:** Actually it went on for 45 minutes or so beyond 10:00; we don't
> know when it was? What are we going to do, lie?

K: It was a half-hour.

P: Okay, then we're a half-hour off.... Wasn't that the night that we had to call down and find out what the hell happened because everything was off? That happened several times recently.... So *Cannon* was at 10:00.

Au.: You watched *Cannon* at 10:00? Did it come on at 10:00?

P: No, probably not.

K: [Laughs] This must be the week before.

P: I wonder if they check that, that would be real interesting.

K: Well if they would, it just blew their whole study.

Finally, the general feeling about doing this kind of accounting was obvious.

Au.: That goddamn thing is complicated.

P: That's why [my wife] is doing it. [He then discusses her banking experience]. . . . That took almost an hour and 15 minutes to do. . . . One of the main problems with this is that when you watch television this is the worst thing to do because it takes a certain amount of time and ability to concentrate on . . . something about it ought to be simplified . . . it interrupted my TV watching (*Laughs*).

It will become more apparent later in this chapter that this process was not regarded as problematic and was generally not understood by sales, management, and newsmen.

Once the diaries are filled out, mailed in, and analyzed, the information is converted to "rating points." In the Western City market, each "rating point," or the number of homes viewing a program as a percent of all homes having a television set, represents roughly 4,500 homes. These summaries are presented in the Nielsen and ARB booklets somewhat as follows:

MONDAY–FRIDAY: 5:30 P.M. (*Newstime*)

CHANNEL	RATING	SHARE
D	5	9
A	17	34
B	10	21
E	2	3
F	7	14

A brief interpretation may be helpful. All five stations in Western City are presented, along with their "ratings" and "share" of the audience.[2] "Share" refers to the percent of sets tuned to a particular station of all sets turned on at this time. In other words, 21 percent of those watching television at 5:30 were tuned to Channel B. "Rating" refers to the percent of all sets in the area that are tuned to a particular channel. Thus, Channel B had 10 percent of all television households, but 21 percent of those watching at 5:30. Once all the data are in, the business of television can proceed. This is where the second stage makes its own contribution to the ratings.

Stage 2: Sales and the Ratings

Just as the viewers have their interpretation of the ratings so does the sales division at Channel B. They are less interested in how the data are arrived at than in how they are to be used; sales purpose finds *relevance* and specific meaning in these numbers. One salesman explained:

> *Au.:*   Do you have any idea how big this sample is . . . ?
>
> *Sales:*   Yes, I think it's about 1,500. I'm not exactly sure but I presume that they try to get that split apart into certain kinds of educational groups and things like that . . . income groups, etc. But that's something that ARB takes care of. *It's hard enough to take one of these books apart without worrying about how they do it.* We pay them a lot of money to do it, by the way. . . . [Emphasis added.]

The overall use of the ratings can now be easily understood. A member of the sales staff explained.

> But, at any rate the basic reason that sales uses this is that we have to have some justification for setting prices, and we have to have some idea what the target audience is. For example, if a car dealer comes on the air, he probably shouldn't be playing in this morning's cartoons where we're hitting kids between 3 years old and 11 years old.

The practical use of these largely ad hoc diary accounts presented as ratings is complex but fairly specific.

> *Sales:*   . . . the stations are the brunt of [the expense of the rating services] not the advertising agencies who also get these books and use it as a club over our head. Even we are the ones who buy it. The agencies buy out of this to make the most efficient buy, to get the greatest audience for the dollar

spent. And the way that we do, the way we frequently sell on TV and radio is [by] cost per thousand. How many thousand people am I reaching in my target audience (for example, women 18–49) for the amount of dollar being expended? That's easily done by dividing the number of people in the target into the cost of the spot. Now we see here that 30 seconds cost $28 in the _____ Show and we are reaching a target audience of 12,000 women which roughly [equals] a little over $2 to reach a thousand people. . . .[3]

Au.: Can you show me roughly how that $28 is arrived at?

Sales: Yes. The station comes to an arbitrary figure of what they feel they can sell . . . either a rating point or a thousand homes at . . . somewhere in the daytime around $10, maybe in prime time at night, $12 to $14 a rating point. So, if we get a rating of three and our cost in the daytime was roughly $10, that would be 3 x 10; we've got $30; actually about $28.

According to this accounting principle, the higher the ratings, the more money comes into the station. These numbers were *relevant* to the news operation since the competition outrated Channel B for two years by a margin of nearly 2:1. The newsroom's explanation will be dealt with later in the chapter, but it will be more meaningful when compared to the sales' perspective, especially since the latter exerts tremendous pressure on the former "to do something."

Au.: How do you alter what you charge compared to another station? That is, if another station is higher [the "ratings"] . . . does that affect what you charge for advertising time?

Sales: You mean when it's diametrically opposed to us? Well, let's take our news.

Au.: Yes, take the news, Channels B and A.

Sales: Okay. Our news has been floundering in the rating area for some time. About two years.

Au.: What do you consider a good rating?

Sales: Well, it used to be 15. Channel A's rating is between 15 and 18; in other words their news audience is almost double what our news audience is. Interestingly enough, demographically, for the most desired portion of that audience, 18 to 49, women and men, we have more than they do. They have something like 16,000; we have 18,000, 18 to 49, with about half the audience. And, we charge $85 for our news—30 second [commercials], and they charge like $140.

Au.: May I ask, is there a certain bottom where, let's say, that the news could get to, that it simply no longer would pay?

Sales: I would imagine that on any program that when the viewing

> diminishes to a point where clients do not want to buy ad-
> vertising in it, and you can't even crack the nut for the cost
> of the program, that *a businessman has to take a hard look
> at that.* . . . [Emphasis added]

The "hard look" comes from the management.

Stage 3: Management and the Ratings

It was apparent that the first two stages in the ratings career were
not the same. The respondents' interests clearly differed from the sales
division. Still another perspective is the management, who must decide
what to do about low ratings.

Apart from relatively straight forward accounting practices, ratings
also define "good" and "bad" programming and, by implication, "good"
and "bad" work. It was noted above that in order to earn as much money
as possible from advertising, the ratings must reflect a larger share of the
audience than the competition. Programming that brings in the "numbers"
is "good" and programming that is less successful is "bad." The primarily
descriptive nature of the ratings (to provide an indication of *how many*
people are watching) is merged with an interpretive function. Station
management not only looks to the ratings for quantitative assessments of
how many people watch various programs, but they also use these largely
ad hoc indices as explanations of viewing behavior. According to this
perspective, low ratings mean that viewers choose to not watch a
particular program. To this extent, motives and rationale are attributed
to the audience that are not only unwarranted by the diary data but that
are also warned against by the rating services. A Nielsen brochure (1964:
12) cautions that

> it makes no sense to talk about the TV tunings of any one sample
> home as though it specifically represents other homes presumed to be
> similar.

Nevertheless, that is exactly what is done!

The management's efforts to improve the ratings "at all costs" further
indicates the great indecisiveness about "what's wrong." Attempts to
raise the "floundering news" included presenting the news a half-hour
earlier than Channel A's newscast; format changes such as more "happy
talk" between anchormen; changing sets; framing the anchormen "tighter"
in order to bring them closer to the viewers; personnel changes, including
firing the news director and changing anchormen. All these changes had
exasperatingly little effect on "how the numbers" fell during "rating
periods."

One central reason that such efforts were largely unsuccessful was their incongruity with the original data source. Recall that the interpretation and use of the ratings reflect peculiar interests. Viewers who provide these data are certainly less concerned about providing "objective" indications of their feelings, motives, and preferences than about "getting it done." However, both sales and management acted as if this were not the case; they treated this official information as having some correspondence with viewer preferences and the reasoning underlying such choices. The upshot is that each of the three parties discussed thus far brought their own interests to the data, and these interests were in turn informed by dominant *meaning contexts,* such as, "We have to have some justification for setting prices. . . ." In understanding how these parties use the ratings we have learned something about their *contexts of meaning.* Similarly, it is evident that news workers' use of this information reflects something about their perspective.

Stage 4: Newsworkers and the Ratings

News agents imparted their experience and understanding in making sense of ratings. They were vaguely aware that these "numbers" affected advertising revenue, but they were more conscious of the impact of low ratings on their budget, on pressure from the "front office," and on the news director's moodiness. These phenomena were manifestations of pressure from "above" that were directly pertinent to the daily operation of the newsroom. Burns (1969: 71) has described the anxiety that "bad numbers" can generate in another research setting.

> The shock of a reported Audience Response figure of 63 for a programme in a series which had touched 75 was enough to disrupt the first hour or two of rehearsal of subsequent production. Very little work was done. The atmosphere of dejection deepened with every new arrival. Clusters formed around the leading actors, the floor manager, and the assistant floor manager, with the producer circulating between them and the telephone. The whole assembly was, in fact, engaged in a more preoccupying task than rehearsal for the next show: the search for an explanation.

As one of Channel B's "on-set" directors explained:

> DR.: The big problem we have now in news is ratings and that's taking everything. The point is we have to bring up our ratings and how we're going to do it, we don't know yet. . . . If we had good ratings now the newsroom could call the shots in the station. And by good I mean if we beat Channel A by 3 or

> 4 points (or 5) across the board; not by the 5 or 10
> points where they beat us across the board. So ratings continue
> to be the primary concern of [the news director] and literally
> everybody in the newsroom. . . . News is our biggest money . . .
> loser . . . now.

News workers, like the sales staff and station management offered
their own interpretations of what these figures meant. Many of the otherwise routine (and perhaps inevitable) problems of a news operation, such
as personality disputes, took on special significance in the *context* of
"objective" assessments of newswork. Thus, news personnel reflected their
interests and perspectives in their accounts of "low numbers." Understanding why certain accounts and not others are offered further articulates
their perspective.

There are several explanations offered for losing the "rating" race.
The same director attributed it to the inconsistent production and organization.

> **DR.:** I'd like to talk . . . about my feelings about the whole news
> show from a technical viewpoint and the way it's presented
> on the air. . . . It seems to go in cycles. That is, the production
> of the news show and the final look of it on the air, which has
> always been my concern, seems to go in cycles . . . of two or
> three months . . . the show could not be smoother if I would
> dream it so for a couple of months and slowly things start fall-
> ing apart. B-rolls [silent film] on news stories suddenly become
> shorter than they were, and they don't cover the A-rolls [sound
> film] completely. . . . Or film commercials will—as we had one
> tonight—suddenly we'll lose the sound loop. . . . The commands
> that I give to the floor man are not understood. . . . Things
> seem to go in cycles and it affects the whole station. . . . A
> manic-depressive effect almost. It's almost as though the place
> is going through a menstrual period. . . . I can almost feel them
> coming on. . . .

The organization of presenting the news was not the only reason given
for low ratings. Another suggestion was the anchormen's presentation, and
especially the importance of "loosening up."

> **DR.:** The highest rated stations are the ones that are putting a lot
> of nonsense on their show . . a horseplay format. . . . Channel
> A had a more folksie attitude all the way through their news
> presentation. . . . We're very hard bitten . . . we present a very
> excellent presentation but like a robot. . . .

Another newsman concurred that the format was perhaps as important as
the news content—"people want to be entertained." In the end, the search

for an answer to the ratings question came full cycle when one member suggested that too many changes had been tried and that viewers preferred something more stable. She cautioned the operation to "settle down" and "give it a chance."

The majority of news workers were unaware of the "proper" interpretation of the ratings. This was largely because they did not understand the statistical terminology and assumptions underlying these measures, not to mention "legitimate" inferences. This seemed remarkable since other statistical studies were questioned. For example, a reporter questioned a study done by the local school district on the degree of violence and harassment of students. Contrary to numerous reports by students and parents, the school survey found scant evidence that anything of the sort went on and concluded that the violence had been "blown out of proportion." This reporter was never satisfied with these results and sensed that something was wrong, although he did not understand statistical inference and study design well enough to judge whether the school survey was properly done. When it was explained that the survey was improperly conducted, (for example, that the nonrandom sample size[4] was far too small) he reopened his investigation of the matter.[5] However, these kinds of questions were never raised about the research procedures of rating services, which more directly affected his livelihood.

Newsmen did not understand the research procedures that provided the "numbers" but they did take advantage of the widespread "belief" in such "scientific surveys." Virtually any complaint about the "way things are done around here" has been used to explain poor ratings. For example, one anchorman complained about the news format and argued that the ratings reflect the viewer's rejection of the status quo. On another occasion he explained that the sportscaster "really wasn't well-liked in Western City and that the ratings showed it." Other news workers agreed that the ratings proved the truth of their concerns. One reporter claimed that there was no direction in the newsroom, "no rudder," and pointed to the latest ARB results for verification. Another added that morale was at an all-time ebb because of the "shit that goes on," and held up the Nielsen rating book as support. Similarly, a former member of the news department felt that Channel A did a better reporting job than Channel B. He said the former had far more content, and that the latter was biased. He added that "their ratings show it." Presumably, from the members' perspective, the ratings were "proof" that a wide range of problems existed that in turn produced low ratings. If the ratings are high, you are doing things right. Indeed, the staff at Channel A occasionally seemed befuddled over their lead, but nevertheless remained convinced that they were doing the better job—"We're beating the competition two to one in the ratings so our news must be good."

It was plain that these figures became accepted as reliable indications of competent newswork, but there were exceptions. These arose when newsmen's common sense told them that the "numbers" could not be high because of quality newswork. The weekend anchorman's standard reply to colleagues' criticisms of his leadership was, "We've got the numbers." One cameraman was asked if his show was that good. He explained that the main reason for the "numbers" was not the anchorman ("it couldn't be") but that more people watched on the weekends in order to get the sports scores. On another occasion a reporter was amazed when he learned that a "nothing news operation" (in another city) "had the numbers." From the newsman's perspective, then, ratings generally confirm impressions about "the way things are here." Like the three prior stages of the ratings career, newsmen have their own uses and meanings.

The "numbers" are an important source of feedback for television operations. Their importance lies more in the practical purposes to which they are put—numerically evaluating how many viewers are being reached. The next task these practitioners face is to offer some explanation of why people watch—or don't watch. This is especially important if "low ratings" are to be raised. However, any change will be made according to the presumed preferences of the audience, such as more "happy talk." In other words, the logic of the ratings requires a conception of the audience.

THE AUDIENCE

The use of ratings is grounded in ad hoc and largely unverified views of the audience. Official uses are not compatible with the lack of systematic information about audiences (DeFleur, 1970: 150):

> Interest subsided some time ago in discovering how broad uniformities among people, in terms of age, sex, ethnicity, or other variables, lead to certain uniformities or response to mass communicated messages. . . . We have barely begun to assemble truly reliable, systematized, and complete knowledge on such issues.

Media agents act as if the facts are in.

The preferences of the audience are claimed to be understood as a matter of course.[6] As Batscha observes (1975: 197) of network news:

> One impression above all pervades this research on the producers, and that is that the producers' belief that the audience is attracted and maintained through the visual and mechanical characteristics of the medium is instinctive and based on faith, not research or knowledge. Not one producer could document this impression of his audience, either with studies conducted by the network or independently. . . . Why people watch one news program instead of another; why they remain interested throughout or lose interest midway; whether they

truly like the dramatic and lively; whether the news must appeal to their own lives; or whether, indeed, it must conform to that vague criterion of being "interesting," are things the producers say they "intuit." They possess no studies, nor are they aware of any data that confirm their intuitions.*

The most explicit invocation of the ratings as an indication of the nature of the audience occurred when an anchorman received a fan letter. He felt the writer was a former Channel A watcher who became a fan of Channel B. The interesting point came a bit later when he said that even though she liked the show she fell into the wrong "demographic" category —she was older than the typical audience depicted in their ratings. He commented to the other anchorman that he bet with a little more promotion they could get more viewers in this "demographic." He assumed that people watched because of age factors that their show somehow appealed to.

Many news people claimed to know what the viewer wanted. For one thing, viewers were assumed to have a short attention span. A cameraman stated his position on the matter.

> **CM.:** I think ... when I was going to school they did a study on people's retention. In a half-hour news program they could remember maybe two stories. ... So when you come up against things like that ... you have to make news entertaining ... [because] unfortunately, people's attention spans aren't too long.

A reporter concurred.

> **Rep.:** A person can only listen to a story for a minute and a half before he starts getting bored, or *so we believe.* [Emphasis added]

More accounts were wrapped up with the viewer's psyche. An anchorman explained that unless there was continuity within the show, such as having all stories relating to Vietnam presented together, the viewer "gets confused . . . [and] psychologically you just can't take it." The same thing was said about too much violence: unless "heavy" news is interspersed with "light" pieces, the viewer will "psychologically explode." A reporter's appraisal of what the audience looks for typifies no fewer than a half-dozen similar comments.

* From FOREIGN AFFAIRS NEWS AND THE BROADCAST JOURNALIST by Robert M. Batscha. Copyright © 1975 by Praeger Publishers, Inc. Reprinted by permission of Holt, Rinehart, and Winston.

> We can spark his interest if I can start off with a flashy lead that
> will at least keep him there chewing his TV dinner and sipping his
> beer, til the next bigger news story comes up, we will have succeeded.

These images of the viewer inform what is done to "keep his interest."
A reporter explained that the news should be what the viewer is interested
in. He believed that in June, 1972, the top things on people's minds
were pollution, sex, racism, and the war in Vietnam. He added that any
"sample survey" will show that those are the things people are interested
in Merely presenting what is interesting is not enough. The technique of
presentation is also important. One reporter felt that voice inflection in
addition to "good" appearance could make a difference. By "punching,"
or emphasizing certain words, the viewer would be convinced that you
were really interested in the story. He added that if he, the reporter, were
not interested in the material, then the viewer probably will not be.

This view seems to have generally been the opinion, but news workers
were not in perfect agreement about the viewer. Disputes occurred about
the best way to present the evening news. One evening a heated disagreement centered on the best format to "capture the numbers." One person
felt that more "show biz" was in order; another cautioned against "having
a circus." A third challenged these interpretations by arguing that he
did not think the audience was really taken in by all that "crap." The
others rejoined by pointing to the ratings but this "proof" was partially
deflated when someone said that he understood one of the stations in
question had not been doing very well.

Second-guessing what the viewers wanted merged into criticism.
News agents were aware that the people on the other side of the camera
could not fully understand their problems, but they still got impatient
when "obvious" points were not understood. These unshared perspectives
were manifested when callers wanted to talk to a network anchorman
located 3,000 miles away, or wanted to speak to Channel B's anchorman
while he was still on the air! One frustrated newsman said that viewers
really did not understand that they tried to present the news in an understandable way, and that they do not have time to memorize the script.
He added that if viewers cannot understand what they are trying to
present, and if they continue to criticize them for not doing something
else, then "they're so stupid that they shouldn't be watching." The confusion reached its nadir when viewers treated a news story as "political
opinion" and demanded equal time. The lack of shared perspective was
set forth when the reporter taking the call responded, "Did we take a
position on that?" In these instances, the newsmen's sense of the audience
depended on "feedback."

The ratings had the aura of scientific feedback, but other forms were
eagerly sought, especially since the competition was winning the "num-

bers" race. There were other ways of obtaining feedback: letters, telephone calls, and comments from friends.

Letters and telephone calls provided personal evidence about specific newswork. In fact, the relatively small number of calls and letters were given unwarranted importance, because, like the small sample size of the rating services, a few were taken to indicate the feelings of many people (cf. Tuchman, 1969: 5). This "iceberg" assumption is seldom questioned, but it is regarded as another way to feel the "public pulse." Comments ranged from the anchorman's dress (color of ties and not wearing glasses) to charges of bias. Some comments were praiseworthy, such as congratulating the staff about a story on the dangers of an unfenced pond.

Callers and letter writers were often interested in the same things. News people would often take time to talk with callers and explain things. For example, one caller accused Channel B of always presenting the Democratic views. The reporter took several minutes to explain that over a period of time they had to balance the coverage in order to comply with federal regulations. In other instances, callers were treated courteously but dismissed as "nuts." One caller gave a reporter a reference in *Intellectual Digest*, which provided a different slant on a story. The message was written down but subsequently discarded. This was done in many cases in which newsmen did not want to be bothered with the details of a particular call or were simply in a hurry.

Letter writers usually were taken more seriously than callers. Letters were "recordable"—they could be filed, passed around the newsroom, and presented to colleagues and management as "proof" of good work and popularity. Consequently, newsmen would encourage some callers to write letters in order to make their comments more "official." This was not always done, but if the caller's comment was regarded as reasonable and useful (read, agreeable) from the newsman's perspective, the caller would often be encouraged to write to the station. In one instance a caller complained about the news director's handling of the Friday evening *Discussion Show* and wanted him taken off the air. According to the newsman who took the call, the viewer wanted to know if a "petition" with several hundred names would be taken seriously by the station management. The caller was assured that any "petition" would be hand-delivered by this newsman to the proper people. The extra effort would have been gladly extended since this newsman passionately disliked the news director. In short, information more compatible with the receiver's interest was more likely to be disseminated, although selective handling of feedback worked both ways.

Management could also control what newsmen heard from viewers. I asked two fellow graduate students to write letters congratulating Channel B for having both a black and a white anchorman for several days on the morning newscast. According to these people, the messages were never received, although they suspected that negative feedback was having little difficulty getting through. The advantage of letter writing thus had concomitant disadvantages: anything tangible could be filed in one's personal records, or other people could intercept the messages and file them in the waste basket.

Although the concern with feedback favored letters over calls because the former could be more easily filed, recorded calls were also given great consideration. Since most feedback came from calls, an accounting scheme was established to record these messages. Most calls taken at the front desk were recorded, but those that made their way through to the newsroom were not. At any rate, the station kept a close watch on the subject and number of calls on a daily "call sheet." The frequency varied greatly, but the average was around forty per day. Most calls requested information such as, "Do you carry the Mike Douglas show," sports scores, and the like. Some referred to the news operation—"I want to thank Channel B for the weekend news announcer instead of the regular mushed-mouth man. He's such a delight." The range of topics seemed too great to warrant serious consideration, but this was not the case; the station management paid close attention to this account of viewer interests. Suggestions for change would be made on the basis of a few calls. In fact several members complained vigorously that the "news operation [was] being run by the call sheet." [7] One man noted that a handful of calls was treated like the word of God and this was unwarranted since "most [calls] were kooks anyway." This view seemed corroborated from a newsman's perspective when exceptionally well-done stories elicited no viewer response. A cameraman complained that people did not seem interested in good reporting on "top quality stories"—"I never even heard comments" about an exclusive on a plane hijacking. And, nothing was said "even by his neighbor" about a story involving the bribing of prison officials that permitted several local financial tycoons to spend time away from prison. This apparent inconsistency on the part of viewers frustrates news personnel even more when their suggestions go unheeded only to have a half-dozen calls institute serious discussion about change. For these reasons, newsmen often reacted angrily to callers. When a lady complained that a story on a POW's sister who had switched her support from Nixon to McGovern was unfair, the anchorman said, "I think I'll use that tonight." In this way he sought to strike back at the uninformed viewer who did not understand the nature of newswork. But the problem of feedback does not end with letters and telephone calls.

Another important source of feedback for news workers was their families and friends, but not all feedback was equally weighted. [8] The station manager's "cronies" were more important vis-à-vis newsroom policies than a reporter's although the staff was sensitive to any comments made by acquaintances and often translated these into images of the viewer. Two or three opinions about a particular story at a dinner engagement were enough to elevate spirits and convinced newsmen that their work was good.

The problem of audience feedback is inextricably tied to its uses apart from evaluating good newswork. The primary concern of getting the "largest share" of the audience and providing the entertainment that brings in the "numbers"—and the advertising revenues—induces a peculiar emphasis on bits and pieces of evidence.

THE RATINGS AS PROPAGANDA

Television ratings provide a scientific basis for charging advertisers for having access to a specified number of viewers for a specified period of time. Like the other examples of objective information described in this book, television ratings fall far short of the goal of presenting a valid picture of audience preferences and especially of assessing the quality of a particular program. Nevertheless, in the face of organizational claims that ratings do this in an adequate way, the public is confronted with an *incorrigible proposition*: they have little choice but to accept these claims since they have no other assessments of either audience preferences or program quality.

Television programming is determined by the ratings. To this extent, what people see in the way of entertainment and public information programs is influenced by the reified ratings. What began as a practical way for organizations to provide *some* basis for charging air time to advertisers in order to reap revenue from television (and radio before this) has been transformed into a barometer of public preferences. Television programmers argue that their selections merely reflect what the people want, as measured by the ratings. Other people argue that people watch what is on the air, and since a national rating of 8 or 9 (translated as 8 or 9 million households—perhaps 22 million people) is not enough to obtain the maximum revenue, many programs are dropped, while the content in others changes. To this extent, ratings play a big part in influencing the kind of programs we receive, and by implication, the kind of images of society we receive. This is also true of newscasts.

News programs are evaluated primarily on the numbers of people who watch them: the more, the better. This logic has promoted current efforts to "capture the largest share of the audience" with entertaining newscasts anchored by physically appealing anchor persons spouting short and grossly incomplete reports about crime, issues, politicians, and problems. From this perspective it comes as no surprise that ABC has transferred the man who directed its "sports specials" to producing its news. The logic of ratings entails the practical assumption that viewers select programs for specifiable and object-like reasons, even when the most fragmented research shows that this is not true. However, ratings, like other organizationally relevant accounts discussed in this book, are imbedded in a practical view of truth, one that usually makes sense from an "internal" logic of the organization and those who actually work on it. But as this chapter shows, even the workers on news do not agree on the nature and significance of ratings. Nevertheless, ratings are used for practical reasons; they work to achieve the results that count and that maintain the organization and the public fiction that objective assessments are easy to accomplish. This is why they have been taken for granted by the television industry, as well as by many television viewers, and this is why ratings are one of the most extreme examples of bureaucratic propaganda. Most importantly, these figures help legitimate television news as a conduit for other bureaucratic propaganda.

NOTES

1. This study (Bechtel, *et al.*, 1972) compared questionnaire reporting of viewing behavior with video recordings. Essentially, there was very little agreement—"This means that for over half the time they reported viewing, the subjects were not watching television" (p. 286). Furthermore, subjects who had *volunteered* for the study were compared with those who were *selected*. The former's viewing time per day was closer to what Nielsen surveys have found, approximately six hours per day. The researchers note (p. 298), "While the numbers are too small to be definitive, the possibility that Nielsen ratings might correspond with a volunteer rather than a random population needs further investigation."

2. Other information is also presented, including separate ratings and shares for each day of the week, number of total persons, total adults, and several age ranges of men, women, teens, and children.

3. This salesman strongly believed in television's efficiency and expressed frustration with those people who did not use it to advertise.

> It's the least expensive thing. You can't approach it. I think for what we deliver for a couple of bucks is about $10 or $12 in the newspaper. And only 60 percent of the people in the county ever see a newspaper . . . and yet 96 percent of the people in Western City see Channel B every week. . . . So you would think that perhaps the most intelligent buy a department store could make would be a combination of the two. And do most of the department stores do that? Absolutely not! They spend a half million to a million dollars a year . . . in the newspaper and don't put one nickel . . . on the TV . . . because the advertising directors are usually older people who are . . . print-oriented . . . and they have their own little dynasties. . . .

4. Every Nth name was drawn from an alphabetical listing of the student body.
5. He also became interested for "personal reasons"; see chapter 7.
6. The most recent studies of attention indicate that people succumb to many distractions. Bechtel, et al. (1972) found that people watched news a little more than half the time it was on.
7. The news director seemed constantly to have a "call sheet" in front of him. He would circle items, attach notes, and circulate them throughout the newsroom. I discovered how he felt about this "record" when I was "caught" attempting to photocopy one. I was told that it was for "in house" use only and was nearly thrown out of the station.
8. McQuail (1969: 92) also notes that some opinions are given more credence.

> Audience research, as it is typically carried out by the survey method, may also fail to indicate what for the communicator are salient features of an audience. He will tend to be most interested in the response of significant individuals—those he knows he wants to contact, or whose opinion he respects. . . . Not surprisingly, broadcasters appear at times to attach more importance to the views of colleagues, or those of friends, neighbors, or chance acquaintances than to audience research statistics.

4

The Welfare Time
Track as Propaganda

Previous chapters have shown the impact of trends toward relying on "rational" criteria of activities in changing the nature of those acts. As we have argued, bureaucratic propaganda results when people of common sense try to present their work within the categories and perspective of "official evaluation." As these categories become widespread, they become objectified and reified to the point at which many people regard them as "real" properties. One example is time.

This chapter shows how welfare workers' time was conceived by various parties to the welfare process in general, and welfare evaluation in particular. The thrust of our argument is that the institutionalization of time and its various components is one way to demonstrate that activities are rule governed, orderly, and predictable—in short, rational. Relatedly, accounting for one's time within a rational framework of bureaucratic procedures and rules permits workers to foster the impression demanded by their "superiors" that not only are they efficient, but also that efficiency, as measured by "time" categories, implicitly supports the notion that time is somehow a real and meaningful reflection of one's work. Thus, emphasizing how one's time is spent and becoming skilled in budgeting one's time—especially for official purposes—become the quintessential indicators that one is a good worker. More generally, they show that time is a kind of "scarce resource," which, if allotted properly, provides a key structural ingredient to doing any job.

These more abstract considerations of the relationship between time, worker evaluation, and the rationalization of the Western world are particularly crucial in understanding connections between public attitudes about welfare on the one hand, and public welfare work on the other hand.

WELFARE TIME IS PUBLIC TIME

Public dollars pay for welfare workers to provide and administer welfare services to people, who, although part of the public, are not permitted legitimately to question the nature and extent of welfare workers' activities. This means, for example, that recipients of welfare services are not accorded the right to demand more of the worker's time than the latter can allot. The recipients are dependent on the workers, and thus must conform to the worker's schedule and status. As Barry Schwartz (1975: 22) notes,

> The privileged also wait less because they are least likely to tolerate its cost; they are more inclined to renege from, as well as balk at, entering congested waiting channels. On the other hand, the less advantaged may wait longer not only because of their lack of re- sources but also because their willingness to wait exceeds the readi- ness of those in higher places.

Thus, in regulating the worker's time, the recipient's time is also affected.

Because welfare time is public time (that is, the time of those who pay for but do not receive the services) guardians of the public virtue and treasure have demanded more and more accounts of welfare workers' time. The aim is to not only avoid waste, but also not to provide more time for certain services than is regarded as necessary. Still another reason is to not spend the public time and money providing services not sanctioned by the public guardians. This is the general context for more recent attacks on welfare recipients, welfare budgets, and welfare bureaucrats.

These statements are one way to make sense out of a complex issue, and especially the constant but powerful subterranean class conflicts in this society. But this does not adequately depict the reality of welfare clients and workers. First, welfare workers are attuned to the plight of many of their clients and realize in many instances that the official rules do not provide enough support. Second, the workers also know that they provide other services not often recognized by politicians and distant supervisors, who are more concerned with convincing legislators and other influentials that the public good is being served by "their people." The upshot is this: Public officials, supervisors, workers, and recipients are involved in a complex relationship that is not in any sense a "system." Each of the parties engage in degrees of overt and covert conflict over "goals," "means," and "rights." As the issues have grown and become more publicized and further distorted via the mass media, greater emphasis has been put on following rules and official accounting of expenditures, includ- ing how welfare workers spend their time. Focusing on how welfare workers in one setting understood these demands and officially presented their work days via sanctioned time categories tells us a lot about welfare work. It provides yet another example of how such records qualify as bureaucratic propaganda.

THE PURPOSE AND CONTEXT

The remainder of this chapter will present detailed ethnographic materials gained from a year-long field research investigation that included five district offices of two metropolitan Departments of Public Welfare.

Being a social worker in a public welfare agency involves many different tasks, but agency members commonly distinguish their diverse everyday experiences into two broad areas. The first is "working with people," by which is intended a broad reference to the face-to-face (and other) daily interactions taking place between social workers and public welfare clients. The second is "paper work"; and this phrase refers to the many and diverse forms of documentation that are completed and used by agency members on a routine basis.

The social workers studied during these research investigations were involved in providing "Child Welfare Services," meaning that their assigned tasks related to intervention into a wide (and ambiguously defined) range of family troubles. Even though public welfare activities such as these have been traditionally conceived as a "legal" institution guided by various sets of formally codified rules (laws, statutes, regulations), such formally codified rules related to these troubling features of family life (such as child battering, child neglect, sex molestation) were either unknown or considered too ambiguous (or even irrelevant) by the Child Welfare Services (CWS) social workers at the Metro Office. Therefore the research investigation conceives "social work" as a gloss for the complex understanding-work whereby social workers use their commonsense knowledge of typical social events to define and thereby constitute the "problems" of welfare clients and to prepare the existent interactional sequences for subsequent courses of action intending the solutions to these problems.

One important resource used by the social worker in this process is the dossier (or case record) of the welfare client. The dossier is a collection of narrative and other forms of documentary evidence concerning the client's societal existence. This case record provides one resource for "looking again" at "the facts" of the client's life as conceived by the appropriate cognitive criteria of social work. The client's case record is one important form of "paper work" done by the CWS social workers on a routine basis. The case record as a form of propaganda will be discussed in chapter 5.

In addition to the case record of the welfare client, the CWS social workers also completed and used a wide variety of other documentary forms. These included various reports, forms, and statistical summaries and tabulations. Many of these other forms of documentation were designed by and for higher administrative personnel interested in having some measure of the "efficiency" of the various public welfare programs. In order to complete successfully such statistical summaries and tabulations, the social workers were asked to "reduce" their knowledgeable understandings of their daily activities in the linguistic terms provided by a given reporting format. Because the social workers were held rationally accountable to so many different administrative structures and in so many different terms, only by using their understanding of the situated official reporting context allowed for the possibility of "making sense" of a given report and further imputed the intentions of the reporting format. This means that the situational reporting context is partially independent of the organized features of the other official work contexts. The social workers recognized this as one of their organizational facts of life. The social construction of official records and statistics by agency members, then, consisted of a continuous improvisation of practical procedures for achieving a solution to some problem immediately at hand. The various terms actually used by the social workers to refer to their procedures for managing these record-making contingencies included: accounting, ball-parking, claiming, clustering, cross-checking, cutting corners, crystal-balling, digging, doctoring, dredging up, dry-labbing, estimating, faking, feeding (the computer), fudging, highlighting, juggling, justifying, over-claiming, padding, pinpointing, projecting, revising, reviewing, rounding (for rounding off), scratching, stretching, taking up slack, tampering, totaling, and so on. The meanings of some of these terms were biographically unique ("accounting" and "dry-labbing," for example) whereas others were widely shared and commonly used (such as "faking," "fudging," "feeding the computer," "estimating," and "over-claiming"). These latter represented practical resolutions to commonly encountered problems of official reporting. In many instances some of these terms could be (and often were) used interchangeably by the social workers, whereas others were specific for a given reporting format. To understand the social meaning of any one of these terms, then, it is necessary to understand the situation (or context) within which the term is used. For the social workers at the Metro Office, the immediate situation at hand was the most important factor influencing their decisions.

The practicalities of the official reporting context were many and often of an emergent nature. These practicalities included such features as the time available for completing a given report, its temporal coordination with other activities, the space provided on a given form for particular entries, the importance (or "relevance") then being placed on the report by others in the setting, and so on. In addition to such "practicalities," however, there were some occasions when the relevance of the social worker's official reporting activities was established by their futuristically rational determinations of the use of such reports in advancing what they (variously) defined as the desirable goals of the organization generally, or Child Welfare Services specifically. The remainder of this paper describes a series of events of this nature.

THE ANNUAL TIME STUDY

In addition to the record-making, which the social workers at the Metro Office did on a routine basis as one of their many everyday activities, and their constructions of various weekly, biweekly, monthly, and quarterly statistical reports, there were other occasions when they were called on to produce reports of a less routine nature. One such occasion involved The Annual Time Study, which is a report distributed every thirteen months by the State Department of Social Welfare. Preceding the two pages of additional department instructions for completing this report (attached as a department memorandum) were the following statements (all in capital letters) which presumably sought to establish the relevance and importance of this report for the social workers:

EACH EMPLOYEE OF THIS DEPARTMENT IS REQUIRED, BY STATE AND FEDERAL REGULATIONS, TO <u>COMPLETE</u> FORM XXX–93 FOR THE MONTH OF NOVEMBER, 1970.

IT IS IMPORTANT TO ALLOCATE TIME WORKED TO PROGRAMS AS ACCURATELY AS POSSIBLE BECAUSE THE FORM XXX–93 IS THE BASIS FOR COST-SHARING (FEDERAL-STATE-COUNTY) OF THE TOTAL ADMINISTRATIVE COSTS OF THE DEPARTMENT.

The Annual Time Study was usually distributed during the last week of the month immediately preceding the one for which the report was (presumably) intended to measure. This official report sought to measure (as accurately as possible) the exact amounts of time that each social worker devoted to each of his or her welfare cases *according to the classifications listed on the report.* The allocations of financial resources (which one of the various cost-sharing formulas) were thought to be highly related to these classifications by the members within the setting (and other administrative officials as well). Although it might be plausibly argued that any particular measure of "time spent" by the members is only tangentially related to a sociological understanding of official agencies and their record-keeping activities, the actual caseload breakdowns (or classifications) used in such reports are taken for granted in many scholarly analyses of such phenomena, including analyses highly partisan toward social welfare institutions as well as those highly critical of them.

Figuring It Out

This particular Time Study was intended for the month of November, 1970. At the Metro Office, the two Child Welfare Services supervisors received the report and the accompanying instructions during the last week of October and distributed these documents to their respective units. The supervisor of Unit One distributed these forms to her workers individually, commenting only that the workers should fill out the report conscientiously because the entries would determine how much money the County could claim from the State and Federal government. As with many other such reports, several of the social workers received this one with such mutterings as ". . . another damn report to fill out." Even though the worker's personal experiences with this report varied greatly (as the following sections will detail), they commonly saw The Annual Time Study as another encroachment on their time, as another contingency to manage along with all of the others.

Upon receiving The Annual Time Study and the instructions, three (of the five) social workers in Unit One sat down together to try to "figure it out," as they put it. They immediately began reading the two pages of instructions contained within the Department memo and then the two additional pages of instructions included on the reverse side of the Time Study report itself. After reading the instructions, these three workers began joking that, even after reading the instructions, they didn't know any more now than they did before they began. These remarks were followed by their respective speculations about what the various categories listed on the report might be taken to mean. One social worker commented on how incredibly funny for someone in the state administration to think that there actually was something that could be termed "pure social services" (see Table III).

Most of the social workers appeared to regard most of the entries on the form as "self-explanatory," meaning that many of the boxes at the top of the form (those not included in Table III) did not warrant or receive any joint discussion. The discussion among the three workers of Unit One centered on one feature of the report that was not clarified by the instructions and that remained problematic for them: the meanings of line C of Part I ("Children") and line G of of Part I ("Child Welfare"). The instructions defined "Child Welfare" (line G) as those duties pertaining to child welfare that were not being handled by the Child Welfare Services social workers, an apparent anomaly from their perspective. Several workers from Unit Two (who had not yet received the Time Study report from their supervisor) joined this group, and the discussion centered on the possible distinction between an entry on line C and an entry on

TABLE III.—*The Annual Time Study* *

	PART 1—PURE SOCIAL SERVICES								
Programs	1	2	3	4	5	...	29	30	31
A–Aged									
B–Blind									
C–Children									
D–Disabled									
E–Medical Aid									
F–Adoptions									
G–Child Welfare									
I–General Relief									
K–Joint Programs									

* Table III only includes Part 1 of The Annual Time Study as this is the only section of the report relevant for the Child Welfare Services social workers' reports of their time spent. Part II of the report included entries for welfare activities other than service activities, and a third section included boxes for time spent on special projects, time off (such as vacation or illness), or nonallocable time.

line G. One worker suggested the line titled "Children" probably referred to the cases that were "aided" or "linked," meaning that the families receiving the services of these Child Welfare Services workers also were the recipients of one of the categorical aids (such as AFDC, ATD, AB, OAS, or the Medical Aid program) dispensed by the county Department of Public Welfare (hence, under the shared subsidy of the State and Federal government); whereas the line titled "Child Welfare" probably referred to cases that were "nonaided, nonlinked," meaning that the county completely subsidized the administrative costs of the services. Another worker suggested the opposite, and a third said that both interpretations appeared equally as plausible. Then another worker suggested that both of these formulations were absurd: since the form contained no spaces for entries on how they *really* spent their time (much of which is taken up by paper work, filling out various forms and requests, driving time to and from home visits, phone calls, training sessions, and so on), then it would be absurd to suggest that either formulation would render any accurate account of their time.

What appeared to be an insoluable impasse was (for the moment, at least) resolved by the advice offered by a experienced veteran of Unit One. He established the relevance of his advice by referring to how this report had been accomplished the previous year and suggested that line C was for the aided/linked cases and line G was for the nonaided/nonlinked cases. Another social worker then asked about the cases involving families that were receiving "GR" (or General Relief the only welfare program of financial assistance solely subsidized by county funds and not subject to the various shared cost formulas involving state and federal financial participation). The "veteran" present commented on his awareness that such cases did not easily fit into the aided/nonaided and linked/nonlinked categories, and said "Oh, what the hell, throw them on line G," perhaps a reflection of his exasperation that the oversimplified entries on the form were not true to the complexities of their everyday work at the Metro Office. As they left, several workers commented on the "irrelevance" and "unimportance" of this particular report and said that they would be "wasting their time" by filling it out.

"Fudging Heavy"

On the same afternoon as this informal meeting, the social workers of Unit Two who were still in the office were called to a unit meeting by their supervisor to discuss the completion of The Annual Time Study. Attending this meeting were most of the social workers in Unit Two. Similar to the aforementioned discussion, the conversation during this meeting focused on the possible meanings of lines C and G on the form. For the members of Unit Two, however, the nature of such a distinction (however conceived) was much different than it had been for the social workers in Unit One. Since all three of the *intake* workers of these two units were in Unit Two, and since most of their everyday work involved a wide variety of "screening out" and "one-shot service" activities (such as answering out-of-town inquiries, or OTI's, responding to requests for information and referrals to other agencies, or I & R's, and investigating "neighbor complaints" wherein it is determined that the problem is with the neighbor), which never reach the stage of becoming transformed into an "official case," then, regardless of what criteria they decided on for reporting their various work activities, The Annual Time Study would not accurately reflect how the intake workers actually spend most of their time. All of those present appeared to agree that this was indeed the problem at hand.

At this point, the supervisor of Unit Two and two of the three intake workers discussed the *possible uses* of the report. The statements at the top of the two pages of instructions noted that the report was in some manner related to the cost-sharing formulas used by federal, state, and county officials to determine the funding for the various welfare programs, but the exact nature of such a relationship was not spelled out in detail. Also, one question of these discussions related the status of the funding for the present fiscal year to any changes that the entries on the form might imply. After some discussion, the following general conclusion was reached about the report: the greater the magnitude of the numbers entered on the "Child Welfare" line of the report (that is, the more time that the workers indicated they spent on those cases in which the administrative costs were completely subsidized by county funds and in which the families involved in these cases were *not* receiving any financial assistance from the cost-shared categorical aids), then the statistical compilations of these reports could be used subsequently for one of two purposes by the workers. First, if the resulting compilations of the Time Study reports indicated that the Child Welfare Services social workers were spending more and more of their time on the nonaided/nonlinked welfare cases (line G), then these results could subsequently be used to justify a request (or "demand") to the county administration for a reduction of their "yardstick" number (the number of cases that each social worker is supposed to carry at any one time, which is determined solely on the basis of the cost-sharing formulas and which excludes any of their efforts in behalf of the nonaided/nonlinked welfare cases). The desirability of such a practical goal was not disputed by any of those present, since the social workers often comment about not having enough time to accomplish all of the tasks that they would like to accomplish for their clients. Second, if the resulting compilations of the report indicated that the workers were spending more and more of their time for their nonaided/nonlinked cases, meaning that such efforts were being accomplished *in addition to* the work done on cases within the yardstick number, then it might be possible to make a subsequent case regarding how overworked the CWS workers had been, and hence, to request increased allocations for additional social workers for the two units. Those present also deemed this a desirable purpose for which to work.

With these emergent understandings of the potential meanings of the two categories and the *potential uses* of the report, the supervisor and workers formulated a practical strategy for completing the report. Since the classifications did not easily fit much of the work done by the intake workers, all of their "screening out" and "one-shot service" work would be placed under the "Child Welfare" category (line G) for the purposes of this report, thereby increasing the likelihood of a subsequent justification for reduced caseloads and/or increased allocations for more social workers. Even this decision, however, did not eliminate much of the ambiguity of the report categories, but the supervisor suggested that the workers might be able to use such ambiguity to their own advantage. He informed his workers that, should any doubt remain about the appropriate category for their work, then they should "fudge heavy" on their entries on the "Child Welfare" line of the report.

On hearing about the supervisor's "fudging heavy" strategy, one worker hastened to caution his colleagues. Recalling what had occurred thirteen months ago when the members completed the report, this worker enjoined his fellows to "show some moderation" in their fudging. He explained that since several workers had shared similar interests the previous year, he had "padded" his report to favor those entries for the nonaided/-nonlinked cases. But the administrative officials in the County Administration building "kicked back" the report for a "recomputation" of the entries. He offered an explanation of this by stating that even though most of the social workers shared an interest in reduced caseloads and the assignment of new workers to the units, the administrative officials were interested in providing the numerology that would serve as a justification for as much state and/or federal money as they could get. The administrators, then, (at least according to this worker) were interested in seeing that the entries on line C (titled "Children") were much greater than those on line G (because the latter would imply an increased expenditure on the part of the county without any matching funds from state and/or federal agencies). The unit meeting concluded with this worker commenting that the success of their joint efforts would require some "finesse."

The First Time Around: Getting It Done

Some of the social workers in the two CWS units expressed some interest in completing the Time Study report; they formulated their interests in terms that saw the report as a *possibility* for furthering their political goals, or what they saw as the futuristically rational purposes toward which the organization should advance. However, this was not true for all of the workers in these two units. Most workers in the setting expressed little interest with this report and frequently commented that it was useless for any of their purposes, irrelevant for their everyday tasks, and an encroachment on their (always limited) time. One worker remarked that the report ". . . was just another example of bureaucratic red tape." Another worker noted that ". . . it's just one of the many statistical forms we complete to keep the administrators off our backs, to keep 'em happy over there." Similar feelings were voiced by workers who intended manipulating the entries on the report for what they saw as the broader goals of the organization as well; The Annual Time Study was commonly seen as a relatively insignificant event by the members, but this did not preclude the possibility that the report might have some future uses.

Although a literal reading of the instructions accompanying the Time Study might suggest the appropriateness of daily entries on the report, none of the workers commented that the supervisors would "apply pressure" on a day-to-day basis; the report just was not considered to be important enough for that type of investment on the part of the supervisors. The sanctionable feature of completing the Time Study Report was its completion *as such;* several members foresaw the possibility of "pressure" at the end of the month, when it was thought the supervisors would be subjected to some pressure from those "above" them in the organizational hierarchy. One social worker said that the "conscientious" completion of the report was of no importance in and of itself; the importance of completing the report was the possibility of remembering, at some unspecified future time, that a given worker had been recalcitrant in completing the report (or in turning it in) by the deadline specified in the instructions. Such facts were periodically used for "building a case" against a given worker, which was the documentary preparation for "giving someone the ax," a practical strategy for personnel transfers within the organization.

One worker who was aware of the sanctionable features of completing the report managed this contingency by filling in all of the daily entries for the month of November on the same day on which the report was distributed (October 27th). This worker termed this *ad hoc procedure* "faking it." The relevance of this procedure on this occasion was established reflexively, involving a reference to the rules that intended such a response in the first place, combined with a reflexive understanding of typical occurrences from the past with an extrapolation to the future. He reasoned that what would undoubtedly happen was this: a few of the other workers might record entries on a weekly or biweekly basis; most of them, however, would put it off until the end of the month when they would be reminded of the deadline, at which time they would retrospectively record their entries for the entire month. Since this worker thought that most of the other workers would be filling out the entire report during the last couple of days of the reporting period, he commented that he was "hedging" against this "last minute rush" by completing the report before the month began in order to have it ready to turn in at the end of the month. As he completed the entries on the report, he was asked how he would determine the numbers he recorded. He reasoned that since he presently had twenty-four cases in his caseload (referring to the "actual [or physical] case folders" rather than the number of "cases" as counted for the purposes of determining a worker's "yardstick," whereby one actual case folder may involve as many as six or seven "cases"), and since two of these cases involved families that were nonaided/nonlinked with any other welfare program, then his estimation was that he would spend anywhere from one-tenth to one-twelfth of his time during the coming month on these cases. With this notion of "reasonable accuracy" in mind, he recorded the appropriate entries on lines C and G of the Time Study report to construct a plausible image of a social worker who would have spent one-tenth to one-twelfth of his time on these nonaided/nonlinked cases. He further said that such a plausible image did not mean that he would record entries to reflect an expenditure of time of exactly forty-five minutes per day for each of the thirty days of November. Rather, he would record entries to reflect, for example, the fact he had spent two hours on one day, and none on another. He said it was common knowledge among the workers within the office that they were never that regular in their casework scheduling. Thus, the plausibility of his entries would be assured by recording irregular amounts of time in each box.

During the month of November, the social workers within the two CWS units employed a wide variety of practical procedures in completing The Annual Time Study. Several workers, just as the worker above had speculated, did wait until the end of the month before recording their daily entries for the entire month. Even in these cases, however, different procedures were used to complete the report. Reasoning in a fashion similar to the above worker, another worker constructed a plausible image reflecting a situation in which a worker had spent approximately one-eighth of her time on the nonaided/nonlinked cases. She reasoned that since three of her twenty-four cases involved such cases, she probably spent about one-eighth of her time with them. On the other hand, however, another worker who had waited until the end of the month to complete her report reasoned that even though only two of her twenty-nine cases involved nonaided/nonlinked families, each of these two families involved many children and she spent a disproportionate amount of her time with them. Since she spent more time with these families, she established the entries to indicate that she had spent about one-sixth of her time on these cases (line G, or "Child Welfare"). Like the worker mentioned previously, this worker did not record entries showing an expenditure of the same amount of time each day, but rather she constructed her numbers in "an irregular fashion" to present the overall plausibility of the account. In these cases, then, it is apparent that the workers similarly made use of a generalized *rule of plausibility* rather than a rule of consistency, which was routinely used in constructing other records at the Metro Office.

Perhaps as many as half of the social workers within the two CWS units, however, recorded all or some of their entries for the report on a weekly or biweekly basis. They typically used the morning or afternoon when they were assigned phone duty for "catching up on paper work," a common strategy for managing their dual routines of paper work and people work. In one case, when the worker's phone duty fell on Monday, this time was used to record the entries for the previous week; in another case, when the worker's phone duty assignment occurred on Thursday, this time was used to record the entries for that particular week. And at least on one occasion, when one worker's "day in the office" occurred on Wednesday, the entries for the Time Study were recorded for the three days of that week that had already passed as well as for the two days that remained (since the worker had already scheduled her time for the next two days and therefore could reasonably determine how much time would be spent on the aided/linked cases).

In addition to some light bantering and joking related to how one might go about recording coffee breaks, trips to the lavatory, the time spent on the Time Study itself, and, of course, several consuming pre-occupations with "shooting beavers" mentioned by several of the sportsmen within the office,[1] there were a variety of other situations of a "more serious" nature when fundamental ambiguities arose regarding the appropriate classification of some activity. One such situation involved the question of the appropriate classification for time spent in training sessions, an activity in which nearly all of the members devoted a considerable amount of time, often to their abiding consternation. One worker in Unit One said she had decided to record her time spent in training sessions on line C of the report, because this would justify the receipt of more state or federal monies. Another worker from Unit Two, not one of the three intake workers, said that he had decided to record the time he spent in training on line G of the report, reasoning that this would "take up some of the slack" in his unit since the report did not adequately reflect the work of the intake workers within his unit.

During the month of November, there was little discussion among the workers regarding the Time Study report. Most of the workers within the setting saw the report as being relatively unimportant, and few attached any significance to it at all. This is not to say, however, that any of the members were insufficiently or inadequately motivated to do their best in completing the task, or, at the least, as time permitted them to do so. Several workers imputed enough importance to the report to take the time (and trouble) to cross-check their daily entries with other records (which reflected some index of where they had actually spent their time).

One worker, for example, constructed the plausibility of his entries for the report by cross-checking them with his mileage sheet (a record that the workers are required to keep on a home-call to home-call basis if they desire reimbursement for their traveling expenses). This worker reflexively established the *intention* of the Time Study report as "reasonable accuracy," and noted that his mileage sheet allowed him to "come up with a ballpark figure" that would suffice for realizing this intention. While this worker was recording his entries on the report, he was asked why he had entered a "6" within one of the boxes on line C for a given day rather than 6.278 which seemingly might reflect with greater accuracy the number of hours he had actually expended on his aided/linked cases for that particular day. He called attention to the size of the boxes on the form (which were approximately one-eighth of an inch square), and said the very size of the boxes necessitated the entry of only one digit per box. He termed this procedure "rounding off," and followed this with a sharp quip that appeared to cast some doubt on the intellectual status of sociologists. Another worker, similarly motivated to take the time and effort to establish a "more objective" index than her memory might afford, spent some time consulting all of the "317's" she had done during the month (the newly instituted "computerized" forms that replaced the dictated narratives within the case records of the welfare clients).

Thus, to say the workers typically defined the relevance of their entries for the Time Study report by making references to the various practical circumstances within the setting (such as time available, the temporal coordination of this task with others, considerations of the reports of others, the spatial limits of the form, and so on), or that the workers used various *ad hoc procedures* to complete successfully the task in a manner deemed sufficient for the purposes at hand, is not to suggest the members were less than adequately motivated to complete this task: many of the situations described above involved various *emergent features of social interaction* for which no set of formal instructions or "supervisory rigor" could have been designed (or planned) to anticipate. This will be even more apparent in the following descriptions of the several occasions on which the Time Study was "kicked back" for a "re-computation" of the entries. Given a generalized, pragmatic motive for "getting the job done" or "getting on with it," emergent situations such as these quite literally *require* the use of the member's capacities for practical reasoning, for determining the relevance of the appropriate social rule for the situation at hand, for "putting closure" on such emergent features to get the job done, and not to give a fully valid account of what is actually done.

The First Kick-Back: Putting the Tin Hat on It

The deadline for completing the Time Study reports was the first day of December. At this time, the supervisors of the two CWS units collected the reports and forwarded them to the appropriate administrative station at the County Administration Building. Three days later, the reports were "kicked-back" (or returned) to the Metro Office. The Department memo accompanying the returned reports asked the supervisor of Unit Two (the unit including the three intake workers who had classified most of their work on the "Child Welfare" line to increase the likelihood of additional expenditures/resources for CWS) to have the social workers "re-check" their entries for this category, which meant, within the context, that the magnitude of the entries for this category should be (in some unspecified manner) "reduced."

Upon receiving the reports and memo, the supervisor of Unit Two did not return the forms to the workers for a "re-check"; instead, he formulated a strategy that he termed "juggling the numbers a little" for resolving this emergent problem. In accomplishing this strategy, this supervisor went through the six reports from his unit and altered the numerical ratios (between the entries on lines C and G) in a minor fashion that he considered sufficient for the purposes of responding to the (obviously ambiguous) Department memo. In describing his actions, the supervisor reflexively grounded the relevance of this strategy by making a reference to his concern for not wanting to inconvenience further the workers with this relatively unimportant matter. Seven weeks later, at the time of the third re-computation of the Time Study Report, he again recalled these earlier efforts and reflected that, at the time, he thought his efforts had "put the tin hat on it." [2] Upon further reflection on the unanticipated consequences that emerged during the subsequent weeks, however, he noted the possibility that his earlier judgment was premature.

The Second Kick-Back: Redefining the Categories

Seven days after the Time Study reports had been submitted to the Fiscal Services Office at the Central Administration Building the second time, they were kicked-back again, this time accompanied by more elaborate and detailed instructions. The reports were not returned directly to the supervisors. They had been returned to the Assistant Chief at the Metro Office, who called the supervisors to a conference to discuss the problem. The Assistant Chief informed the two CWS supervisors that as the Time Study reports stood at that moment, they would entail a completely unrealistic budgetary request for the coming fiscal year (due to the large entries within the "Child Welfare" category). The Assistant Chief then informed the supervisors that it would be necessary to return the reports to the individual social workers for a recomputation of their entries in terms of the new instructions that she had just received.[3]

The detailed instructions accompanying the returned reports were elaborated on what the members refer to as a "gram" (slang for a Departmental memorandum) routed to the Assistant Chief at the Metro Office by the Fiscal Services office. This memorandum was marked "for limited distribution," which meant the Assistant Chief was to communicate the instructions to the supervisors *verbally*, not allowing the supervisors (or workers) to read or possess a copy of the memorandum. Such a device reflects the insider understandings of the (actual or potential) *evaluative uses* to which such documentary evidence might be put, especially its possible use for "building a case" for some sort of adjudicatory process at some (unspecified) future time when the social meanings of the events may become transformed or redefined by other people for different purposes, such as in the case of what the popular press termed "The My Lai Massacre." This is an especially delicate matter when the situation at hand involves actions that could plausibly be interpreted by outsiders (or those removed from the immediate situation in time and space, and hence, not availed to any understandings of the emergent features of such situations) as "clandestine," "surreptitious," "immoral," or the like. Reliable sources at the Metro Office have said that one may demonstrate one's organizational acumen by destroying such potentially dangerous documents before "they return to haunt you" in some unanticipated manner.[4] Such situationally specific tactics as this are typically subsumed under the more general rubric of "protecting yourself" or "covering yourself," two of the more commonly used terms from the organizational lexicon reflecting the omnipresence of the politics of everyday life.

The two CWS supervisors returned from this meeting with the Assistant Chief with detailed notes on the new instructions pertaining to the recomputation of the Time Study reports and immediately called a meeting for the social workers in their respective units. As before, the new instructions focused on the problematic meanings of the "Children" vs. "Child Welfare" categories on the report. During one of these unit meetings the supervisor explained that the purpose of the new instructions (as well as of the recomputation) was to delimit further the rules to be used for constructing the appropriateness of the entries on the "Child Welfare" line of the report, presumably intending a more realistic budgetary request related to Child Welfare Services. For the purposes of the recomputation of the Time Study report, the new instructions called for the inclusion of the following situations on the "Children" line of the report (this category refers to cases that are recipients of one of the categorical aids subject to the Federal-State-County cost-sharing formulas and cases that are "linked" to such matching financial participation via the State's Medical Aid Program): (1) all cases in which the only needs are medical (termed "Medically Needy Only"); (2) all cases involving families who have been the recipients of some form of financial assistance from the welfare department within the last three years, and all families "linked" to such aid (these were termed "former cases" within the instructions); and (3) all cases involving family disorganization or any other indications of an unsuitable or unstable environment that, in the judgment of the social worker, would or could possibly lead to the subsequent linkage of the family with one of the categorical aid programs (these were termed "potential cases" in the instructions). In addition to these cases, there was a further specification of the meaning of "potential cases." Regardless of any of the social workers' judgments regarding the suitability or stability of the family environment, all families were to be classified as "potential cases" for the purposes of this report if their income did not exceed by 50 percent that figure for a family of comparable size on AFDC.

On hearing this last instruction all of those present at the unit meeting burst into laughter, and one worker commented that the new instructions had successfully managed to include everyone he had encountered as a social worker within the last ten years. Several of those present commented:

IR: Wait a minute, this is getting as ridiculous as that piece of shit we fill out every three months [referring to one particular portion of the State Statistical Report: JMJ]. If it's a former case, then you don't have any records lying around to find out how much time you spent on it, and if it's a potential case, well then you don't have it yet. When you. . . .

OT: No, this isn't the same. The former and potentials refer to those you've got now. The way you deter-. . . .

IR: Jesus, does it really make any difference?! I mean how many of your, tell me now, how many families have you seen in the field which couldn't be called potential cases. You've just got to be kiddin' me if you really. . . .

OT: Yeah, you've got a point. [begins laughing]

SW: What about the OTI's and the I & R's? You mean after all of this rigmarole we still don't know what to do with the OTI's, the I & R's, and the general file cases?

AE: Oh, for Christ's sake! Are you still worrying about that? Can't you see that [the Assistant County Director of the Department of Public Welfare] wants us to put everything on the first line?

Even from these brief remarks it is readily apparent that the members present understood the newly formulated instructions differently—one worker understood the relevance of the new instructions in terms of the *intention* he imputed to them and another noted certain ambiguities that the new instructions did not appear to clarify. Shortly following these remarks, one intake worker again raised a question pertaining to the appropriate classification for Out-of-Town Inquiries (or OTI's), Information & Referral requests (I & R's), and cases that were "general filed," that is, when the daily work done by the intake workers did not result in an official "case" for record-keeping purposes. The supervisor said that since the new instructions did not even mention such cases, he would presume that the workers should classify these as before—under "Child Welfare." The meeting then broke up, and the workers returned to their other duties while expressing their consternation, exasperation, anger, futility, and displeasure.

After this gathering, the social work supervisor for this unit commented:

GU: I just hate things like this. I originally, I told my workers to count all of the [nonaided/nonlinked] cases under child welfare, and if they were going to fudge, they should fudge heavy. That's how we get more workers. But now I have to tell them to do just the opposite, to fudge in the other direction. . . .

These are the kind of things I call completely useless actions. This is really what people are pointing to when they talk about all of the waste and inefficiency of bureaucracies.

It's like, you know, it's like digging a hole in the morning and filling it up in the afternoon. When you ask your workers to do something like this it can only hurt their morale and diminish their respect for their jobs and the authority of their supervisors. Even their respect for the agency as a whole. . . . And we keep on using these terms which don't mean anything, which are really covering up the inefficiency and waste of the system, like 'delivery of services' and all those. . . .

Au.: It's really hard to see how so much hassle can be caused by such a seemingly simple report. Why do ya' think the administrators are getting so. . . .

GU: That's what it's all over. One set of numbers versus another set of numbers. That's what's keeping the bureaucratic cogs rolling.

Shortly thereafter one of the intake social workers commented:

TA: It's like they're saying this: we want to find out something from you, and here's what we want to find out. . . .

Later that afternoon, the supervisor for this unit approached this author and said:

PZ: I suppose you heard about classifying everyone as aided or linked if they've been aided anytime in the last five years?

Au.: What?

PZ: We had this meeting around eleven. We got this new memo form. . . .

Au.: Oh? The Time Study?

PZ: [nods head] We're now supposed to reclassify all our [non-aided/nonlinked] cases as aided or linked if there is any deprivation or unmet need. Doesn't make any difference whether or not they're on welfare. If they've been aided or linked to an aided case within the last five years, if you think they might be within the next five years, or if, in your judgment, there's any chance of danger in the home. Oh I don't know. It looks like they want nearly all our hours recorded as aided in order to justify their budgets for their federal funding. . . . The forms didn't justify what they had already decided they wanted for funding purposes, so they're asking us now to cheat on the numbers for them. . . .

Au.: Well how much difference is this from what you told them in the beginning, I mean. . . .

PZ: I didn't tell them anything! The instructions seemed pretty clear to me, 'though I realize some complications from [the other supervisor's] unit. I just passed them out.

In accomplishing the recomputation of the Time Study none of the social workers (at least insofar as was observable) made any attempt to "re-capture" any data of their time spent during the month of November by consulting some other form of documentation, to reinterpret the meanings vis-à-vis the new instructions. Several people in the setting reasoned that *however* one might interpret the *intentions* of the new instructions, it appeared obvious at this point that one intention had been eliminated—namely, that the Time Study intended an establishment of some simple "index" of "how they had really spent their time." As one worker accomplished the recomputation of the Time Study, he commented:

> *Au.:* You're back at the time study again I see.
>
> *OL:* Another day, another form. You should've learned that by now.
>
> *Au.:* How're you determining the numbers there, I mean, what....
>
> *OL:* Well, I looked into my crystal ball this morning and ... [looks up with a grin].
>
> *Au.:* No, really.
>
> *OL:* Hell, how should I know. Fiscal apparently wants the ratios lower, so I'm lowering the ratios. Mine was about half-and-half before, so I'm just changing them to about seven-to-one, more or less.

Another one of the intake workers managed this uncertainty by waiting until several workers had done their recomputations. He retrieved their completed forms from his supervisor's desk and commented that he "just juggled the numbers to come out somewhere between [the numerical ratios from the reports of two other workers]."

In commenting on these observations here it is not the author's intention to imply inadequate or insufficient motivations on the part of the social workers, or any recalcitrance in their accomplishment of the recomputation. The differences in their various manners of accomplishing the recomputation versus their initial efforts, rather, must be understood in terms of the differential *social meanings* imputed to the *intention* of the Time Study at a subsequent time, an intention that the members established reflexively by referring to what had occurred previously.

The Third Kick-Back:
"Kissing the Gunner's Daughter"

Following the successful completion of the re-computations, the Time Study reports were once again forwarded to the Fiscal Services office, arriving there around the middle of December. Within the next several weeks few comments were made about what had occurred, and presumably the various details of these events began receding from the memories of many of those at the Metro Office.

Six weeks later, another official report, which appeared to be very similar to the original Time Study report, was distributed to the social workers in the two CWS units. Each form was accompanied by two pages of instructions and carried the signature of a "very highly positioned" administrator. The supervisors distributed the new forms and instructions to the workers in the respective unit meetings called for that specific purpose.

The new instructions began with a reference to the recent completion of the Annual Time Study. The first paragraph noted the figures representing the budgetary allocation for Child Welfare Services for the present fiscal year and commented that the overall compilations of the recent Time Study would lead to a budgetary request exceeding that figure by more than 300 percent for the coming fiscal year. The first paragraph concluded with a statement to the effect that given what is commonly recognized as the existent status of Public Welfare within Western State, such a request would be very unrealistic.

The remainder of these two pages included detailed instructions for completing the attached form. These instructions noted that the attached form was *not* to be interpreted as another time study, but rather as a request for some further information regarding cases that had been classified on the "Child Welfare" line of the previous Time Study. Rather than including entries for the "time spent" on such cases, however, this new form only asked the workers to record such cases by case name, case number, whether judged to be a "former case" or a "potential case," or within the nonaided/nonlinked category. The instructions defining how such categories were to be determined for the purpose of this report were substantially the same as those transmitted by word-of-mouth at the unit meetings six weeks earlier, although these new instructions did clarify one previously ambiguous matter (and instructed the workers to classify this particular type of case as a "potential case" on this new form). This new report contained no provisions for any entries regarding how much time each social worker had spent on casework within the respective classifications.[5]

Within the unit meeting of the social workers, these new instructions were initially greeted with various expressions of anger, exasperation, chagrin, "routine bitching," and the like. When the comments subsided, the first issue raised concerned the *intention* of this new report. Was it the same as the Time Study? Or was it, as ostensively stated, *not* the same as the Time Study? The accompanying instructions begin with several statements about the time study, and then, in the next paragraph, other statements disavow any interest with it. Why would anyone want to know about their nonaided/nonlinked cases in the distinctive terms of the Time

Study? This issue was discussed by the workers for some time, without apparent resolution.

Then several workers raised essentially the same questions about the form that had been raised at the meeting six weeks earlier regarding the appropriate classification for OTI's and I & R's, none of which were further clarified within the new instructions. The supervisor left the meeting momentarily to recruit the Assistant Chief of the Metro Office as a possible resource for clarification. The Assistant Chief joined the meeting, listened to the various problems formulated by the workers, commented on her uncertainty, and departed the meeting momentarily to solicit the aid of the Chief of the Metro Office. Since the Chief could not be found at that moment, the Assistant Chief placed a telephone call to that "very highly positioned" person whose name appeared at the bottom of the instructions and returned to the meeting with the knowledge sufficient for resolving these practical problems of the moment.

Upon returning to the meeting, the Assistant Chief began addressing each of the four or five ambiguous and vague features that had not been resolved by the new instructions. The closure that was suggested for each issue, with the exception of one that had been further subdivided as a result of the phone call, involved classifying each one in the "Children" category (or what would have been equivalent to line C of the initial Time Study). In other words, these new classifications would mean that virtually none of the CWS cases would now be classified under "Child Welfare." On hearing this, the supervisor of Unit Two noted that if the workers were to use these new classifications, then the report would not reflect the real nature of the work that the CWS social workers accomplished as a matter of everyday routine. The Assistant Chief then said to the supervisor that this new form should not be seen in the same manner as the initial Time Study. The supervisor then remarked: "We'll be digging our own graves if we fill out the form like that!"—a metaphorical reference to the possibility of budget cuts in the CWS allocations. The Assistant Chief made several comments that appeared to calm the supervisor, suggesting that the consequences of such actions would probably not be as grave as the supervisor suspected, and the meeting adjourned on this note.

Immediately following this meeting, and for several days afterwards as the social workers completed this new report, the members were much more emphatic in expressing their substantive interpretations of the events relating to the Time Study than they had been at any time previously. During the meeting itself one worker scribbled a note that said, "This is bureaucratic absurdity at its peak—I don't recall Max Weber writing about this in graduate school!" Several workers of each unit who had previously interpreted the construction of the Time Study as having little importance other than a relatively trivial matter of routine practicality, on learning of this recent twist, construed new meanings for these events involving what are seen as to be "moral" linguistic categories ("lying," "cheating," and so forth). One worker who had expressed great concern three months earlier for using the Time Study as a potential resource for advancing what he defined as his own political purposes within the realm of social welfare continued to take action on this basis in spite of the new instructions promulgated in the meeting, referencing his feelings about the Assistant Chief (and "where her head is"). Another worker who had similar feelings three months earlier remarked that the recent events symbolized a defeat, a phenomenon to be expected periodically within the realm of political action. And another worker, although not having previously defined the Time Study in such "political" terms, appeared to reflexively reinterpret it as such at the conclusion of this final meeting. One of those in the setting who had witnessed these events as they unraveled over the three months was an ex-Navy member; his observation at the conclusion of this final meeting was that the recent events appeared to indicate that the CWS social workers had "kissed the gunner's daughter" once again.[6] These interpretations were additionally reinterpreted over the course of the following weeks as well, and in principle at least, are subject to further modifications as well.

THE ANNUAL TIME STUDY AS PROPAGANDA

The Annual Time Study qualifies as bureaucratic propaganda if it is used in any way to account for, or make sense of, how the Metro Office workers actually spent their time and assessed the priorities of their official and unofficial tasks. Unless the context of these reporting activities is clarified and included as a meaningful aspect of the Time Study in particular, and their work in general, anyone relying on such reports will be deceived and will reach invalid conclusions. Nevertheless, such reports are widely used by welfare officials for their purposes, as well as critics of public welfare who do not approve of one part of the public treasure being given to an "undeserving" segment of the population. In either case, a practical purpose is served as the reports are filtered through the political context of "official approval or disapproval." All that is missing is the meaningful context of how the reports were actually done.

These detailed ethnographic materials have described how one particular official statistic report was accomplished by the social workers of the two CWS units at the Metro Office, on several different occasions. The materials show that the intended purposes of some of the social workers pertained to their *futuristically rational estimations* of the potential uses of such data for supporting policy-related decisions, specifically those concerning Child Welfare Services. Furthermore, the materials show that this particular reporting situation occasioned motivations to construct numerical representations as a *presentational* (or rhetorical) device, to present a public image of "looking good" for furthering their practical purposes concerning budgetary allocations, staffing policies, and so on.

These materials have pointed out the existence of various conflicts and different meaningful interpretations occasioned by this particular reporting situation. Furthermore, they have shown that these conflicts, disagreements, and different interpretations of the meanings of these events were *not* "mere differences of opinion," or some simple derivatives thereof, but *constituted grounds for the occasioning of differential moral assessments and valuations among the members as well.* Perhaps due to the relative simplicity of The Annual Time Study (as compared with the more complicated official reports completed by the members of the Metro Office), the materials also convincingly demonstrate that the social worker's *knowledge* of what comprised an organizationally "correct" reading and/or completion of the reporting format was *not* one of the "givens" of the situation, but had to be "figured out" vis-à-vis other understandings of the setting's organized features as they emerged or changed over time. Since the Time Study form was clearly seen by the members to possess (actual or potential) meanings not explicitly stated on the form itself, then, given one's purposes to accomplish this practical task, the "correct" entries *necessarily* had to be "figured out" by the social workers by utilizing their own practical reasoning. The reporting situation *demanded* that they put *some kind* of "closure" on the reporting for the situation immediately at hand, but *that specific* "closure" was not one of the givens of the situation. All this is readily evident if one tries to place oneself in the shoes of the social workers: Is the 'correct' reading or completion of the report one in which OTI's (for example) are recorded on line G? Or line C? There existed no absolute set of rational cognitive criteria exercising a determinant influence for these official statistical constructions for the social workers at the Metro Office; hence, to determine the "reasonableness" of a given construction, they referenced their (various) other understandings of the immediate tasks at hand, and this included their varying individual ideas, purposes, plans, goals, and feelings. Some of these were highly situational in nature, and others were of a relatively trans-situational nature.

In sum, the context of their work, including the relevance of official reports for both mundane and professional interests, helped the workers understand and actually complete the reports. They, like the other people discussed in these chapters, *felt* the implications of the report as much as they *knew* how it might be used. This report occasioned one or more opportunities for the various social workers to attempt to use this situation in their continually ongoing and self-organizing efforts to stabilize or change the nature of their everyday situations in accord with their individual motives, intentions, plans, dreams, fears, hopes, interests, politics, and feelings. That such phenomena are always subject to subsequent revision, reformation, or reinterpretation does not deny them as existential possibilities in the living dialectic of everyday life.

NOTES

1. When introducing me to this activity, one knowledgeable hunter in the office said that crucial regional differences exist regarding the linguistic usage of this phrase. As he reported, only men do the shooting in the Midwest, whereas only women do the shooting in the West. In keeping with scholarly purposes, I have tried to use the phrase here in an "objective" manner.

2. This phrase originates from the infantry. "Tin hat" is one of the soldier's terms for a metal shrapnel helmet, and the phrase "to put the tin hat on it" means to bring some line of action to a conclusive termination. The supervisor using this phrase was a high-ranking officer in the U.S. Army reserves.

3. I first learned about what had occurred at this meeting on the same day by one of those present; within the next few weeks I received essentially similar accounts from the other two members present at the meeting.

4. I do not intend this comment to imply that the memo referred to in this instance was destroyed. I actually do not know whether it was or not. Dalton's (1959: 111) researches of business management-labor union relations have led him to conclude that such phenomena are commonplace occurrences for such activities. Other descriptions of these phenomena may be found elsewhere (Johnson, 1972, 1975)

5. Several of the most knowledgeable members on such matters understood the new instructions in the following manner: since the previously completed Time Study reports were seen as inappropriate by others in Fiscal Services, but since these others could not "properly" return them again, this additional report would be used as a resource by those in Fiscal Services to "rejuggle" the original numbers themselves. It was never learned with any certainty if this actually occurred.

6. When asked to clarify this unfamiliar phrase, this social worker said that it meant "getting screwed over." Further investigation by the observer revealed that the phrase originated in the folklore of the Royal Navy, and (if literally defined) refers to the time when sailors were strapped face-down to the breech of a cannon in preparation for a flogging aboard ship. The usage in the present context is intended metaphorically, of course.

5

Welfare Records
as Propaganda

The last decade has witnessed a massive increase in the use of social services, especially those termed "welfare." This is particularly true of assistance for Aid to Families with Dependent Children (AFDC). This number has increased from 975,000 families in 1964 to approximately 4.8 million in 1976. Accompanying this growth in social service dependents has been a sizeable increase in welfare workers and kindred employees. The increases in people served and the numbers of people who serve them have necessitated higher public expenditures to cover the rising costs. This situation, along with a widespread public disapproval of welfare, has transformed institutionalized "generosity" and "assistance" into a viable social issue, one certain to gain a sympathetic hearing from most people who are opposed to either the idea of welfare or its rising costs.

Since the sixteenth century some provisions have been made for unemployed workers and other persons unable to care for themselves. In extreme cases this involved debtors' prisons; in other instances people were granted licenses to beg. Although such public condoning—and in some cases, direct support—of the poor have never been extremely popular, they were tolerated out of moral commitments, as well as being regarded as less objectionable than the alternatives. Indeed, Piven and Cloward (1971) argue that past and current efforts to help provide for the poor should be seen as an attempt to regulate the poor, to buy them off and discourage them from rebellious acts. Although this interpretation is not consistent with the actual shifts in welfare policy due to practical, arbitrary, and ad hoc reasoning, the relevant point for a current understanding is that public acceptance of the welfare burden has been influenced by the perception that the costs were worth the benefits.

This has now changed. As the number of people on the "dole" has grown, more and more critics have challenged the legitimacy of the

134 Welfare Records as Propaganda

"system," arguing that so many recipients do not deserve so much of the public treasure; the critics see the costs outweighing the advantages. But the costs do not involve only the direct subsidies to the recipients. The largest share of public money goes for the employees who distribute goods and services, to the organization that maintains the relationship between those eligible for assistance, the social service employees, the goods and services, and more recently, to public officials and the public as a whole. Hardly a local, state, or national political campaign avoids descriptions of the "welfare mess" and they often treat it as part of the "growing" and "insensitive" bureaucracy. Promises are offered to voters, and threats are made to opponents—especially the welfare recipients—that the status quo will change and that the public will be rid of freeloaders. In brief, welfare has become a major social concern.

One thing both friend and foe of welfare rely on is statistics. Statistics are used to attack and show up "cheaters" as well as to cite the growing number of cases added at an ever expanding cost to the public treasure. But statistics are also used by the officials and workers who provide welfare services. They are used to describe what occurs, how eligibility is arrived at, and how efficiently the public's dollars are being used to meet organizational needs as well as to provide services to the needy. Moreover, the past decade has witnessed a growth in the number of forms and statistical estimates that infuse daily activities. How well these estimates actually describe the day-to-day activities they are claimed to depict is the focus of this chapter.

Public services are not valued for their own sake but are informed by a utilitarian philosophy: what good does it do, and at what cost. In short—Is a program worth the expense? This general philosophy found its way into contemporary monetary policies through cost accounting and other rational means of depicting credits and debits. Public money could not merely be given because someone felt that another person needed it. First, criteria were established to distinguish between those who really needed it and also deserved it and those who did not. The aim was to take much of the decision out of the hands of the individual caseworker, who would be trained and instructed to defer to rules.

The formula is quite simple: Following rules assures compliance with codes and statutes, as well as assuring that the recipient is dealt with fairly. Another part of this formulation is: Treating welfare clients according to rule permits workers to document transactions, which can be tabulated and statistically summarized in order to provide an objective record of the type of goods and services provided and of how this was done.

This chapter focuses on how a new record keeping procedure—"the 317"—was understood and used by welfare workers. Delineating the career of each instance of this record and noting how the "objective" aspects of it are irremediably bound up with the context and practical pursuits of the workers illustrate how welfare records qualify as bureaucratic propaganda.

THE PURPOSE AND CONTEXT

The descriptive materials in this chapter were drawn from a year-long field study in 1970 that included a total of five district offices of two large metropolitan Departments of Public Welfare. The research project was organized to allow for the integration of the observer into the everyday working routines of the agency personnel. Tape recordings of the actual interactions in the setting, tape-recorded interviews, field notes, official records and documents, and the observer's experiences and reflections provide the data.

About three months before beginning field observations at the Southern Metro Office, agency personnel began a series of policy and procedural changes that would eventually replace the dictated case record with a one-page summary designed for computerized processing and control.

This new computerized format, "the 317," was designed to maximize features of existent records and reports. It included spaces for recording both the number and nature of contacts between social workers and welfare clients, and it would supposedly give those interested in such matters a rough approximation of employee work load and efficacy. The format also included more than twenty boxes for coding information about a client's life, present circumstances, and needs; the resulting data could be used for comparative research or analysis. The 317 also included a small space at the bottom of each page, approximately five to six lines, designated for the narrative account of a home visit or event. It is ironic that the 317s were developed at approximately the same time as The President's Commission on Federal Statistics (1971: 71–72) recommended replacement of traditional statistical indices with "longitudinal statistics" to be developed from individual units of life history. The dictated narrative of a welfare case record, perhaps the most detailed account of one's life ever collected on a mass basis, was to be replaced by a more truncated recording format in Metro Office at precisely the time The President's Commission was calling for more detailed, longitudinal records to make official statistics more accurate.

A MAJOR PROCEDURAL CHANGE: THE 317

In March (1970) the administrators, supervisors, and social workers at Metro Office began making plans and preparations for procedural changes related to replacement of the dictated case record with the abbreviated recording format called the 317. Meetings were held for discussing the mechanics of change as well as the formal policy objectives involved.

Within these meetings, supervisors and social workers raised questions and expressed a variety of anxieties.[1] The workers agreed that dictation took a great deal of time and effort and was sometimes of dubious value. In this respect, computerized forms would save time and labor. The new recording procedures would therefore free social workers to devote more time to casework activities. On the other hand, many workers said dictation was often a valuable aid in their efforts to understand the nature of a given family situation. Also, the narrative accounts provided supervisors with information that could be used to help the workers with casework decisions. Some workers thought existing dictation helped them prepare for an initial home visit. Therefore, the social workers viewed replacement of dictation with mixed feelings. Although replacement of the narrative would not pose any immediate disadvantage for the social workers, in the long run replacement would mean that with the receipt of each new case, a worker would be going into a case "cold."

A recognized advantage of the 317 was elimination of repetition within existent practices. Previously, dictation was done in addition to weekly, biweekly, monthly, and quarterly statistical reports. Overlapping was frequent and accurate measurement difficult.[2] Replacement of contradictory and confusing reporting forms with one unified reporting format was presented as a long-range advantage of the computerized 317s. The social workers were apprehensive about having less information in the case record, but most agreed that potential elimination of repetitious reporting might be an eventual advantage.

One worker was deeply concerned about how the new 317s would be used, by whom, and for what purpose. Workers' experience showed dictation to have actual or potential evaluative use by supervisory personnel, and this feature exercised some influence on what went into a narrative account. Since the computerized 317s contained only a few lines at the bottom of the page for narrative, the worker's supervisor would now have less information to use when making evaluations of a worker's performance. What impact would the new procedures have on matters of evaluation? Would social workers now be evaluated solely on the basis of number of direct contacts made during the month? The lack of answers to questions of procedure left staff members feeling quite apprehensive about the inevitable changes.

These concerns, on the other hand, only constituted part of the discussion in the early meetings. Most of the time was taken up with instruction and discussion on how the new recording forms were to be completed. Since the number of possible entries on each recording form were quite

TABLE IV. New Case Record Reporting

FORM: (THE 317) *

Serial No. of Report	09		Soc. Wkr's No. MC 32
Client's Name	SMITH, Claudia Marie		
Client's Address	507 West Main Street	Phone:	583–8632
Employer's Name	Maud's Beauty Salon	Phone:	754–9911

Priority Information   TO PREVENT SCAPE-GOATING

SOCIAL CHARACTERISTICS

2 5 3 M 3 3   4 N H 7 8 8   2 2 M 9 3 N   N N 3 4 2 1 1

CASE CODE: 01   DATE CASE OPENED: 02 01   DATE SRVC: 02 13

SERVICE CODES: Primary 85   Secondary 20

SERVICE CONTACTS: Direct 2   0   Indirect 0   4

                                        H.V.   Office   H.V.   Office

NARRATIVE COMMENTS: Made Home Visit on 3–5 and 3–12; Phoncon w/Dr. Peters at CMH on 3–5, 3–8, and 3–11; Phoncon w/Mrs. E. Parsons, Mrs. Smith's sister, on 3–8. NM still in depressed state due loss of husband and job. Resistive to Rx and very manipulative; still using Debbie as scape-goat; plan to continue trying to get her to CMH for Out-Patient Rx; still on phenobarb.

* This Table does not represent an exact replica of the 317 recording format. The Table includes all of the categories that are of major significance for the reporting, but several other categories were eliminated to make enough room for labeling the various entries, many of which are coded rather than titled in printed form on the actual 317 record (meaning that most of the form entries would be unintelligible to any outsider seeing it for the first time).

extensive (see Table IV), and since most of the entries were encoded by combinations of digits and/or letters, each form could only be completed if a worker learned literally scores of new rules about the appropriate entry of case information.

During the instruction sessions on appropriate entries, shared agreements were reached that appeared sufficient for the tasks ahead. Over subsequent months, however, shared agreements were modified in the light of new understanding, perhaps only to be rendered problematic by other emergent events.

The Early Months: Getting the Bugs Out

When the social workers reflected on the introduction of the 317s, most recalled approaching the changeover with anxiety and uncertainty about how the new records should be constructed, used, and what they would mean. One worker used a commonsense analogy in likening experiences of social workers preparing for the changeover to those of neophyte foster parents preparing for the first placement of a foster child in their home. Even though workers routinely made preplacement visits to new foster parents to provide them with as much knowledge as possible about what they might expect from their up-coming experience, veteran workers commonly recognized such efforts have limited success because new foster parents typically do not know what questions to ask. With the 317s, the social workers were situated similarly. They had yet to learn what could, and subsequently did, go wrong with actual application of new rules for a uniform ordering of the 317s.

The first few months were a period of trial and error. The workers frequently consulted written regulations and instructions about coded numbers for the various boxes on the form. They constantly conferred among themselves and with their supervisors on appropriate entries. Despite their efforts, errors and misunderstandings occurred regularly. For example, in the first month, one social worker conscientiously used the rules in what she and others interpreted as a competent reading of the formal schema, only to discover the computer read-out for the month listed her "service contacts" as "0" (zero). The worker had submitted her 317 on the last day of the month according to instruction. However, any 317s submitted after noon on that last day were not fed to the computer and were held over for computations in the next month. The experience of this worker and several others led to a collective redefinition of the self-evident phrase "last day of the month" to "by noon of the last day of the month." Such modifications of formal procedures were frequent and recognized as being in accord with what the procedures intended in the first place.

There were other instances when formal procedures were initially seen as unambiguous until workers put them into use and discovered that modifications would have to be made if the rules were to work. For example, one rule required submission of a 317 after each home visit. At first this appeared unproblematic, but the social workers soon discovered that it took seven or eight days before a new 317 was returned to them. In some casework situations, workers made more than one home call per week, and it was not possible to submit a new 317 for each contact. Formal procedures did not adequately reflect such contextual features of the worker's practical situation, so rules were modified. In this specific case, workers held recordings on the 317 for a period of time and then lumped together "service contacts" for that period.[3] Again, such minor modifications were seen by the members as in accord with the intent of the procedures.

In summary, for the first few months, workers used the formal procedures as they understood them. They learned how various entries in the boxes of the recording format fit together, learned which information was essential if the form was to be processed and which information was optional. They made minor modifications in formal procedures in order to make rules workable vis-à-vis other formal rules, procedures, and practical constraints existent in the setting. Members occasionally observed that they were getting the bugs out of the system. As months passed, however, it became obvious that the bugs were never exterminated in any absolute sense.

An Unresolved Conflict

During the first meetings and training sessions, the three CWS intake social workers raised questions about the capacity of the 317 to illustrate the distinctive nature of their work. The 317 was designed to record information only for activity in "official cases"—cases for which a numerical designation was assigned and an official file opened. Therefore, much of what CWS intake workers did as a matter of everyday routine could not be recorded if the formal procedures of the 317 were used. For example, CWS intake screened out many cases. They also had frequent short-term cases involving one-shot service, and these were recorded on a general file form but not on a 317. Other activity in unofficial cases included providing information and referral service, accepting of out-of-town inquiries for service, and instructing non-CWS workers about foster home placement procedures. Though the intake workers raised specific questions about how the 317 was going to reflect this type of casework activity accurately, these questions and concerns were not sufficiently answered at this time.

During the first month that the 317s were used, one intake worker called an informal meeting with his two colleagues.[4] He presented the following argument with respect to the new recording form. The 317s could not reflect much of what CWS intake did as a matter of everyday routine, and it appeared probable that the monthly summaries of the 317s would be used in some evaluative manner, the most important being a foundation for subsequent policy determinations of a worker's "yardstick." Therefore, it would be advisable for intake workers to begin recording their nonofficial case activities on the 317s of those cases that were officially opened to them. Even though they might make one home call, to the Smith family, for example, they should begin recording six or seven calls. "Padding" entries on the cases officially opened to them was the only way they could hope to achieve an accurate reflection of the work they actually accomplished. The other two workers disagreed with this argument. They argued that the computer read-outs were not intended to show a gross measure of everything that occurred within Child Welfare Services. They were only intended as a measure of service activities in continuing service cases. They also argued that none of the workers using the monthly summaries would use them for purposes of comparison between CWS intake workers and continuing services workers, and any people who would have some use of these numbers would understand that intake accomplished many activities not reflected on the 317s. The three workers agreed that the possible uses of the 317 summaries were uncertain, but disagreed on what they might do about it. The conflict remained unresolved, and all three workers continued to record entries only for those cases that were designated as official cases, at the possible danger they would look bad should someone decide to use the monthly or quarterly summaries as a comparison of their work with that of CWS continuing services.

Normalizing the Numbers: Staying Off the Fink Sheet

Approximately a week after the first month of 317 reporting, the workers began to learn how their efforts were to be compiled. The computer compilations were received in the form of computer print-out pages officially titled "Service Management Report," (SMR), which soon was unofficially termed by the workers "the fink sheet." [5]

Although workers and supervisors of both units more or less assumed the meanings of 317 categories to be self-evident, their initial review of the computer print-outs produced anomalous results. Three workers in Unit One had desks adjacent to one another and had frequently conferred on appropriate entries. Yet, their entries in the category, "number of services given," turned out to be 0, 174, and 34 respectively. Ironically, this category had been considered very important because of its potential comparative and evaluative usefulness to administrative personnel. Immediately, meetings and requests for instruction were initiated in a group effort to remedy the troubling results appearing on the SMR.

In usage, the discrepancies in reporting procedures were many and complex, and the remedial efforts begun in May, 1970 continued throughout the ten months of field observations. These attempts to remedy the situation have remained fundamentally problematic ever since. Since it would be impossible to describe many efforts in detail, we will depict primarily what occurred in the example above.

The error committed by the worker who achieved zero under "number of services given" was described earlier in the chapter. The 317s were indeed due on the last day of the month, but as a practical consideration for the processors at the computer center, only those reports received before noon were in fact processed. The members of Unit One quickly adapted to the processors' "working interpretation" and avoided the problem thereafter. Even so, new staff sometimes made the same mistake if they were not alerted in time and allowed to interpret 317 procedures literally.

Resolving the wide difference between 34 and 174 under "number of services given" was more difficult. It was known to all the worker who listed 174 services for the month was indeed a hard and conscientious worker. But it initially appeared implausible that any one worker within the setting could render *five times* as many services as one other colleague. Discussions centered on respective definitions and meanings each had used in the classification of an event as a "direct service contact" or an "indirect service contact" under "number of services given." Discussions also revealed different interpretations of these two categories. The worker with 174 counted all face-to-face contacts in the field that pertained to a case. In addition to a direct home visit to the client, he counted visits to the homes of neighbors, friends, relatives, and other offices or agencies. He also counted out-of-office conferences with other professionals. The worker with 34 counted only home visits to the client, although he, too, had other face-to-face contacts in the field. All involved agreed that both workers had justification for their respective interpretations of the categories.[6]

Throughout discussions and conferences, the existence of discrepancies remained problematic. For example, the discrepancy between 174 and 34 services could remain if it were not regarded as troublesome by higher authority. Remedial action would be unnecessary if "number of services given" were not a classification of relevance or importance. Also, individual worker differences were taken into consideration. One worker was known as a "talker," and he spent a great deal of time managing his caseload via the telephone. His colleague had particular distaste for the telephone and avoided it as much as possible. The "talker" would of course produce a greater number of service contacts. The geographical distribution of caseloads would also affect service contacts. One worker's caseload was clustered in one area of town, thus allowing him to make more home visits within a shorter period of time. Agreement on a normal state of affairs for 317 reporting did not come quickly; and even when something resembling a consensus was reached, unique situations would arise and new interpretations become necessary.

Over the months, the members gradually began to normalize the numbers on the SMR monthly summaries. Sometimes they coordinated their actions and reached shared agreements. It would be a misconception, however, to say each worker actually decided to normalize the numbers in a specific, concrete manner. The process occurred by bits and pieces. A particular worker's decision in a given context was continually informed by the worker's understandings and knowledge of previous situations and by his or her relevant definitions by both self and others. The facts of situations were subject to continual, ongoing interpretation and reinterpretation. Actions were dialectically linked to interpretations. Stated differently, actions and decisions were in part retrospective determinations and justifications of what a worker understood to be the social meaning(s) of previous courses of action and the relevance of that action to present and future situations.

Approximately seven to nine months after 317 reporting started, many of the social workers began expressing the opinion that "around 140–150" was a normal number for "services given" in a particular month. Within this range, a home visit under "direct service contact" was defined in the manner used by the worker who listed 174 on the first SMR. An "indirect service contact" was eventually interpreted to include nearly all phone calls as well as a wide variety of other actions both within and outside the office.

It is of crucial importance in understanding the members' decisions to recognize that the *normalized numbers* (140–150) did not represent a particular course of action that workers decided to adopt from among various alternatives. Rather, the workers' very conception and verbalization of this normalized number represented an interpretation of the findings gradually clarified through continual discussions of their actions throughout the on-going improvisations of previous months.[7] Once this common understanding was expressed verbally, or "externalized," to use the terminology of Berger and Luckmann (1966), and shared publicly, or "objectivated," it did serve to exercise a certain constraining influence on subsequent CWS social work actions. By no means, however, did this objectivation exercise a determinant influence in some emergent and unique situations.

Talking to the Computer

In preceding parts of the book, reflexivity in human communications received particular attention. This property of human interaction has been analyzed in great detail by phenomenologists or ethnomethodologists in sociology.[8] Generally, reflexivity refers to the necessary linkage between a linguistic account and its contextual, or indexical, features.[9] All communcations are necessarily grounded within other indexical, or taken-for-granted, understandings, which are made only partially explicit within the context of communication, if at all. At the most basic level, taken-for-granted meanings of linguistic communications include the cognitive rules of communications themselves. At a substantive level, taken-for-granted meanings include other background meanings that one must necessarily understand in order to make sense of a particular linguistic statement or utterance.

Such reflexivity became especially evident when social workers "talked to the computer." It is true, in a sense, that the computer constructed certain communications with respect to the 317, but they were distinguished by the absence of reflexive properties. Although the logic of everyday talking is conditional, the logic of computer processing is formal; and this difference led to a peculiar set of troubles for CWS workers.

In everyday life, members of society have certain understandings about the reflexivity of their own communications and expect others also to have such understandings. For example, we often realize, on reflection, that the "wrong" word was used to describe a certain event or phenomenon. However, the correctness of the word choice is never called into question. It becomes trivial because we often know what the other person means due to our understanding of the context of the statement. For this substantive rationality of everyday life, the computer substitutes a formal rationality, or formal logic. The 317 reporting procedures left no room for compromise between the parties concerned, so CWS social workers developed a distinctive way of talking to resolve the dilemma: computer talk. Consider the following example.

It was routine in CWS intake for the worker to make home visits and other service contacts to a family who was not at that moment classified as an official case. If considered eligible to receive monetary assistance via one of the categorical aid programs, the family was assisted by the worker to make the appropriate application. If judged ineligible, the family might still need on-going social services and the intake worker would forward the case to a continuing services worker, who then officially processed it as an "OI" case, or, services only case. In either instance, it was possible for many contacts to occur before the case became official. Within the logic of computer processing and recording, however, the date of first service contact could not precede the date the case opened. It was not a logical possibility. Therefore, if the social worker recorded the true dates of service, the computer kicked back the 317, and the case would be listed on the fink sheet as needing service for the following months. Since the cause of this problem was not self-evident, it took months for workers to discover how to talk to the computer so that it would properly record services for a given case. One worker finally began to "play around with the numbers," as he put it, and discovered one had to submit an erroneous date for date-case-opened in order to have the computer record one's service activity. So, even though an outsider might interpret the faking of a date as a deviation from formal rules and procedure, the workers in this case considered it a reasonable course of action to achieve what they thought 317 reporting procedures required in the first place.

Doing Services and Claiming Services

Earlier we mentioned that one worker felt 317 reports would be used by administration as a measure of work accomplished. Since intake workers provided many services to unofficial cases, the worker felt intake should begin padding entries on official cases. Padding would have the effect of making the monthly computer read-outs more accurate as a reflection of intake work accomplishment. As the reader will recall, the other two intake workers disagreed with this assessment at the time. They argued that the 317 was explicitly designed to reflect only on-going social services in official cases and that anyone reading and/or using the reports would do so with this in mind. The 317 computerized reporting was not intended as a measurement of the range of intake work activity.

The conflict was not resolved, so the intake workers used the 317s only for recording direct and indirect service contacts on official cases. Since the typical caseload yardstick number for intake was around 10 to 12 official cases, as compared with 25 to 30 official cases for continuing services, the monthly result was predictable. The number of services given by continuing services for the month varied between 130 and 170 per worker, whereas the number of services given for intake varied between 30 and 40.

During the third month of reporting, this situation changed. However, change did not come because the one intake worker was successful in convincing his colleagues that his definition of the situation was in fact the better one. Rather, during the first few months there were hints that administrative personnel were using the monthly summaries as a measure of work accomplished and of social worker efficiency. Though exact use of the 317 was not definitely known, the available indications led intake workers quickly to revise their criteria for recording. As one intake worker commented at the time:

> . . . I remember thinking at first intake was getting off easy on that because we didn't have to report much on them. Chuck kept coming to Bud and I [sic] and telling us that we were going to look bad as compared to the other workers, but we just laughed at him at the time. I told him I thought it was crazy to think that they [administrative personnel] were going to use those silly numbers to compare one worker with another month in and month out. I told Chuck and Bud that the only number that would be important would be cases closed [one of the categories on the SMR] because of [another Welfare Department bulletin that had recently established "time limits" for the length of time that a social worker was allowed to keep a case]. But then [the two supervisors] started getting this feedback from [the Assistant Chief] and it was obvious as hell the number totals were being used to compare one unit with another, even CWS with [the

AFDC social workers]. I was finally convinced Chuck was right, and now I claim like a son-of-a-gun. . . .

Thus, intake reporting changed drastically. Basically the workers reported unofficial screening-out and one-shot service actions on 317s for official cases. This led to the linguistic distinction between doing services and claiming services, a recognition that numerically presented claims were to be used as the public front for everyday work. The numbers became a presentational device to convince others to take a particular course of action with respect to the organization. *The immediate result was number of services given by intake increased by nearly 1,000 percent.*

Overclaiming

One of the heated conflicts that occurred throughout the field research observations took place between the CWS intake workers and concerned overclaiming. Overclaiming was a way of providing statistical justification for an increase in the allotment of staff positions for Child Welfare Services. Arguments about overclaiming concerned whether this strategy was justified within the context of the situation, and, if justified, to what extent.

For several years prior to the research, social workers in Metro frequently expressed interests in advancing resources allocated to the various social welfare programs. Both an increase and shift in resources could decrease a worker's yardstick number and allow more time to devote to fewer cases. Workers made use of a number of strategies and tactics to realize such changes. Many workers supported the activities of the local and state Social Services Union, which publicly promoted such changes. In addition to this, there were two methods that had proven consistently successful within recent years—reaching-out and overclaiming.

Reaching-out was a general term referring to a limitless number of ways by which social workers recruited clients for various welfare programs.[10] Such a recruitment process could simply add more work, so reaching-out practices were typically combined with claiming practices. In this way, those with control over resource allocations were advised about a new-found, increasing demand for social services which would justify an increase or change in allotment of resources.[11] Within this context, claiming activities were very important. They were typically constructed within those existent official records used to measure welfare programs and were used to justify expansion.[12]

At Metro, a recent success of such efforts had culminated in the allotment of an additional staffing position to Child Welfare Services. According to those present at the time of the increased allotment, the additional position was achieved largely through the entrepreneurial efforts of one CWS intake worker. This was in December, 1969. This worker later explained some of his efforts:

> **S:** ... Chuck's screwin' off, everybody knows it. He's spending a lot of his time lookin' for another job, and probably everyone knows he spends a lot of time visiting his relatives during the day, too. Not a big secret to anyone either ... Can't say that I blame him a great deal either. . . .
>
> **Au.:** Doesn't that show up on his [317s]?
>
> **S:** I really don't know if, don't know. Doubt if he even bothers to fake it. He's being protected by [the District Chief], special relationship and all that shit. . . . It's hampering my efforts, too, and if he would only keep track of, goddammit I was solely and completely responsible for generating the statistics for Chuck's job, his position as of last December, that's our newest slot in [Child Welfare Services]. Now whatever's on mine [referring to the cases handled and services given in excess of this worker's yardstick commitment] just makes up for what Chuck doesn't claim. Basically I'm now claiming enough for two [workers]. . . .

During the initial months of 317 reporting, there were some efforts planned by intake workers to create the symbolic justification for another request for additional allocations to Child Welfare Services. Discussion took place almost simultaneously with the aforementioned conflict over whether or not service on unofficial cases should be counted on 317s for official cases. One recurring topic concerned whether or not intake workers should use the practice of overclaiming [13] to justify a request for an additional position.

The worker who was the strongest promoter of overclaiming, as well as the most consistent user of the practice, commented on the nature of the issues and conflicting interpretations:

> This afternoon Jim told me about a meeting which the three intake workers had held during the lunch hour. Jim said that he told Chuck and Bud once again about his plans to build a case to support his request for another CWS slot, how he was going about it, when it was going to happen, and so on. Jim said his case will not only include all of the state [various statistical reports of the CWS work], but—and perhaps even more importantly—copies of all of the memos and grams he's written during this last year to [his supervisor] and [the Assistant District Chief]. These grams detail all of the complaints and hassles with the CWS intake work, especially the uneven work loads which have resulted from the intake scheduling, all of the times he or one of the others has had to cover the intake phone [due to Chuck's

absence at the time he is scheduled to be on intake duty], and all of the problems and troubles they've had whenever some crisis or emergency situation comes up [meaning that the intake worker on duty may have to leave the office for some "crisis intervention" situation when the other two intake workers are also gone]. Jim said that when the time comes for him to make his case to [the Assistant Chief], obviously the first thing that's going to happen is that [the Assistant Chief] is going to review the work for all three of the workers, and if the other two [especially Chuck] don't have their records in order then somebody is going to get in trouble. Jim also said that Chuck and Bud apparently aren't taking him seriously; they don't seem to think that he's going to follow through with these plans.[14]

One of the other intake workers (Bud) offered his thoughts in a separate conversation:

> *Bud:* ... Jim's crazy as hell if he thinks he's going to fool anybody with whatever in the hell he's up to this time. I'm sure [laughs], I don't have the slightest idea what he wants this time, and I'm sure he doesn't know either. [The Supervisor] and [the Assistant Chief] aren't going to be—I'm sure both of them see through it by now. He just wants attention. His feelings are ruffled because he thinks he's doing all the work and nobody's givin' him any credit for it. ... If [Jim] ever does get around to making a big stink about intake, [the Supervisor and/or Assistant District Chief] will give 'em a couple of days off on comp time and that'll probably be all there is to it.
>
> *Au.:* What does all this mean for you, I mean, does this mean you have to be sure to record everything you do just in case Jim does sub— ...
>
> *Bud:* Are you kidding? Really, I mean, really, what do you think could happen to me? Nah, this is just water running off my back ... [laughing]. I'll probably get a refill for my phenobarbitals I suppose, if not for this, then probably for something else though. ... I learned the game from [my supervisor] shortly after I came to [Metro], so I'll play their statistical numbers game for fifteen minutes at the end of each month. For no more time than it'll take me to take a coffee break I can keep everybody happy and off my back. ...[15]

The third of the three intake workers, Chuck, was also the one who earlier argued with Jim and Bud about the advisability of padding the 317 reporting forms so that the monthly computer summaries, or fink sheets, would more accurately reflect the amount of work accomplished by intake. Paradoxically, Chuck later voiced his opposition to Jim's futuristically rational plans for creation of justification for a staff increase. Specifically,

he opposed overclaiming on the 317. Possibly his promotion of padding
was motivated by a certain self-defense posture. He did not want intake
to look bad. But Chuck's advocacy of padding within this context seemed
to possess no necessary relationship to his subsequent stance against overclaiming.[16] He also offered some observations on the emergent events.

> *Chuck:*   ... I think Jim's headed for trouble this time. If he doesn't
> quit screwing around he's going to get *all* of us in
> hot water eventually, and—eventually it's going to make all
> of us look bad, and not just the intake either, I don't think.
> *Everybody* can see, Jesus, see through what's going on, see
> what's really—damn, we've been *through* this before!
> What's—I mean, did you see the read-outs just out? Jim
> had a total of 360 services down for his total for July, and
> the figures for, Jes–, I think [Bud] and I together had a
> total of about 50 or so together, for *both* of us. *Everybody*
> here knows Jim sends in a [317 form] every time he
> takes a crap, and you can't be—it's only a matter of time
> until the shit hits the fan over this, too. [The Supervisor]
> and [the District Chief] know all about this, they can see
> right through what's happening. They can tell.
>
> *Au.:*   How can [Jim] get by with recording like that? Doesn't
> he think [the supervisor] ...
>
> *Chuck:*   [The District Chief]—Jim apparently doesn't think [he]
> knows all about the numbers game as he does. I don't think
> it would be possible for someone to get to be as high as a
> District Chief without knowing—especially [name of Chief]!
> He's a sharp cookie, sharper than most of them. He's un-
> doubtedly known more the in's and out's of this than [Jim],
> and I think [Jim] will have his day of, quite a surprise in
> store for him. ...
>
>   Right at the time everybody's running scared about the
> so-called welfare reforms and the possible cut-backs in the
> welfare programs, Jim keeps firing out these incredible
> memos demanding more slots for [Child Welfare Services].
> Too many intakes, the need for another intake worker, ro-
> tating intake, God knows what all! We'll probably be the
> ones to get the axe first. ... This is really the time *not* to
> make any waves of any kind. All we should worry about
> now is keeping our noses clean and staying out of any
> hassles that we don't need to be in in the first place. ...[17]

The actions and counteractions undertaken by the workers did eventually come to a head, in a manner of speaking. However, by the time
proposals for official policy changes were made and justified with typical
data, so many contingencies had emerged in the interim that it became

progressively unclear what was at issue. Many of the participants were polarized in the process and considerable bitterness was publicly expressed toward resultant changes and everyone involved. The end result did involve some changes in CWS policies and resources. Another social worker was added to Unit One to take over the other worker's BHI cases. Also there was a reassignment of duties for one of the workers in Unit Two to include part-time service as a fourth CWS intake worker. For the most part, these changes were of the nature of practical compromises situationally hammered out among the contending parties involved.

WELFARE RECORDS AS PROPAGANDA

In view of our reformulation of propaganda presented in the first chapter, welfare records qualify as decontextualized information that can be useful for a variety of purposes. These materials show that the workers' understanding of the general context of welfare administration and accountability, plus the specific situation of treating "the 317s" as adequate records of their service to clients, forged a meaningful context in which to emphasize how the records appeared and what officials and others would get out of them, rather than a serious effort to reflect validly what actually occurred. Administrators, politicians, journalists, or curious laymen would be grossly misled if they approached these records as a resource for understanding the nature of welfare work and the problematics of recipient eligibility.

The complete and necessary meaning of these reports cannot be divorced from the situations in which they are constructed and from the reasons for such work. It would be nearly impossible to make sense out of the 317 format when first confronting it. Although it is perhaps obvious, any competent reading of these records presupposes knowledge of a distinctive terminology; such a vocabulary does not describe an orderly state of affairs. Rather, these records presuppose an understanding of such an order. For those people accorded authority to read or use such records, it is assumed that they not only know the relevant practical, legal-bureaucratic tasks but also that they will adopt the official perspective in order to make sense of the documented representations within. The 317 records, then, rather than showing an ordered state of affairs, *constitute* such an order.

The events of the normalization process show that the successful use of such criteria is a morally sanctionable condition of one's organizationally recognized competence and membership. Members' comments presented in this chapter show the social workers not only assume this is so, but also expect others, as a matter of moral obligation, to use contextual features of the setting's organized ways in order to understand the substantive rationality of their conduct. Other materials presented also show, however, that the moral order constituted by record-making practices is not one of simple homogeneity, nor is it unproblematic for the members. The materials illustrate that it is possible to use different methods to complete practical tasks; and more importantly, that different methods serve as foundations for imputing different moral judgments about social competence and membership in the setting. To say that different methods were used by social workers is to make it possible to conclude that record-keeping operations were inefficient and sloppy or that administrators and supervisors were not diligent in overseeing tasks. But such a judgment necessarily distorts realities. Metaphorically speaking, this would be like faulting tennis for not being football; that is, faulting tennis for being precisely what it is. More to the point, to judge these actions by invoking external criteria of efficiency is to fail to appreciate that it is the criteria of efficiency that justified the procedural change over to computerized record-keeping operations. Furthermore, many of the resultant problems of the change over were generated by the motivated concern of workers to make records more accurate and efficient. Indeed, one's efficiency as a record keeper was an important and sanctionable criterion in the moral order of the record-keeping setting.

However, not all people who may have access to such reports, and who may use them for their own purposes, research, explanations, exposes, and so forth, share this moral and practical perspective. Or in cases in which they may do so, their reports to others may exclude this important feature of the information contained in "the 317s." In either case, the context is important; if it is not part of any use of such information, it qualifies as bureaucratic propaganda.

NOTES

1. Since these meetings antedated the beginning of the research by approximately three months, I have necessarily relied on members' reflections in order to provide background information on the procedural changes. Since some of the working practices used subsequently to construct these records were related to these early efforts, I think this quasi-natural history of these efforts is essential for understanding some of the subsequent ethnographie materials.

2. A detailed example of this appears in the previous chapter.

3. The phenomenon of holding onto a case possessed other uses as well. For example, in later months, after the workers had grown more familiar with the recording processes, some would hold their recordings until the next month if they had already made their required number of contacts for the previous month.

4. Since this meeting occurred before field observations at Metro began, this account is based on reflections of intimates at a later time. The reason I

am sure about this account is that the argument that allegedly occurred during this meeting was still existent among the three CWS intake workers by the time I arrived within the setting and continued for several months thereafter.

5. Etymologically the term "fink" was originally "pink," a contraction of Pinkerton (originally workers and/or private policemen hired by a factory, mine, or company to aid in the breaking of a strike around 1892) and was reputedly one of the most derogatory terms in the lexicon of the Wobblies. Since around 1910–1920, however, the term "fink" has been used within the underworld to refer to an informer, squealer, or stool pigeon, and it is this meaning intended by the phrase "the fink sheet," which social workers used in referring to the SMR since the SMR informed others of their discrepant actions.

6. Because of the relative simplicity of this particular example, it is plausible to interpret these events in terms of one of several traditional frameworks, namely either as an instance of (1) the oft-noted and analyzed gap between the formal rules and the informal rules existent within a particular setting (as noted by sociologists Bensman & Gerver, Blau, Cohen, Dalton, Page, Roy, Scheff, Turner, and many others); or of (2) the commonsensical understanding that any initial learning or socialization process, such as those taking place among children within any cultural setting, and presumably any adults learning anything the first time around, is essentially and necessarily openended or emergent (see Berger & Luckmann, 1966); or of (3) what some sociologists have termed "the recalcitrance of the tools of action" (see Selznick, 1948), a fancy reformulation of what Plato and subsequent commonsense observers have seen as the necessary gap between the ideals and the realities.

7. The essential reflexivity of commonsense accounts of everyday actions is, according to Professor Harold Garfinkel (1967), the singular feature allowing for topics studied by ethnomethodologists within sociology. More detailed analyses of reflexive properties of decision making in everyday life may be found in Garfinkel (1967, 1970) and Pollner (1970).

8. Harold Garfinkel (1967) defines the distinctive nature of those scholarly analyses termed "ethnomethodology" in terms of an exclusive reliance and emphasis on reflexivity.

9. The scholarship of Garfinkel, Cicourel, Sacks, McHugh, and Churchill is especially relevant in this respect.

10. The prevailing commonsense view of welfare programs, as with official agencies in general, is that such programs represent a functional response to a set of conditions that precede them in social space and time. This view has been recently expressed in the award-winning analysis by Frances Fox Piven and Richard A. Cloward, *Regulating the Poor* (1971). To those sharing this conception of social welfare, my brief description here of reaching-out practices may appear to be news, perhaps of the nature of a revelation of an organizational secret. Personally, I do not think that many social workers would see this as newsworthy. The phrase *reaching out* has been around social welfare for a long time. Many professional publications

describe, promote, and analyze the phenomenon, and it is one of the routine features of graduate education within social work. In addition, the publications of various professional organizations such as The National Association of Social Work, Child Welfare League of America, and The American Humane Association in particular contain a variety of pamphlets promoting reaching out as a rational strategy for increasing the service delivery in the field of Child Welfare Services.

11. Any such claims are always subject to a counterclaim of self-interest on the part of one presenting the claim, and this is especially true for the recent years for social welfare programs. Having a rather sophisticated understanding of such phenomena, one CWS intake social worker was largely responsible for creating what I thought was an ingenuous organizational device for resolving such a dilemma. Largely on this social worker's entrepreneurial initiative, a group of Foster Parents was mobilized for the ostensive purpose of advancing their own interests and for creating a common forum for discussing common problems as foster parents. Called "The Foster Parent Association," this was officially a voluntary organization whose membership was open to private citizens who were either foster parents, prospective foster parents, or interested parents within the caseload of the entrepreneurial social worker. Largely on the basis of this worker's advice and counsel regarding what was feasible and practical as a demand within the present situation, this group made frequent public presentations and demands for increased allocations of resources to foster parents within the county at monthly meetings of the County Board of Supervisors. On occasions throughout the period of my research, such actions achieved some success.

12. From what I was able to learn about these activities in previous years from my trusted intimates within the office, the claims had been traditionally justified by making use of existing official records, reports, and/or statistical compilations. During the course of my research, however, when some administrators at the State level were trying to use similar official records and reports to justify various cut-backs and decreases of allocation of resources to some social welfare programs, the counterclaims used to combat such proposals sometimes involved independent sources of data such as researches by the state of local Social Services Union and professional organizations and associations. Sometimes the relevant data from academic sources were used for these purposes.

13. Within this context, "overclaiming" refers to recording facetious entries to represent intakes handled, services rendered, and so forth, or, on some occasions, recording phenomena not typically counted (such as a phone call that is a wrong number) as a "service given."

14. I recorded the details of this meeting within my written field notes several hours after my conversation with CWS intake worker referred to above (Jim). The excerpt cited here represents a shorter summary of the major details of this conversation.

15. This portion of my conversation with this worker was tape recorded during one of our conversations within the office.

16. Saying that there existed conflicts and disagreements between social workers

on some issues and that their conflicting interpretations resulted in differential use of a particular practice is not to imply that the adoption of one stance or other rendered all subsequent record-making activities unproblematic. Whether or not padding, faking, claiming, overclaiming, and so on were judged a reasonable course of action was not dependent on one's commitment to one abstractly stated side of an issue, but rather the tasks in the situation immediately at hand.

In the case of the intake worker mentioned above (Chuck), for example, one day at eight o'clock in the morning, just as he was about to assume his four hours of phone duty, he received a call involving a crisis situation that necessitated his departure from the office for a period of about seven hours. Chuck and I made five or six different stops in connection with the immediate crisis and the placement of the client's children within a Subsidized Foster Home located approximately 35 miles from town. In completing the 317 report for these actions, Chuck later recorded the stops as 36 service contacts. Even though this occurred when overclaiming was a relevant issue within CWS intake, and even though this example might commonsensically appear as an obvious example of overclaiming, this worker's padding of 36 service contacts was not undertaken with the intention of developing subsequent justification for a proposed change in CWS resources. In this situation, rather, the worker's departure from the office during his scheduled duty time deprived him of that period of time that typically produced the greatest number of contacts that were recorded on various official forms and reports as measures of one's workload accomplishment. Furthermore, his absence during this time also meant that one of his fellow colleagues was getting contacts that he would have been able to record as his if this crisis situation had not called him from the office. In this instance, then, the worker's use of padding could be seen as a competent reading and use of formal rules and regulations in that such a usage allowed him to accomplish his assigned duties in a successful and competent manner. It also allowed him to maintain his competitive position vis-à-vis the other members in the setting.

17. These comments represent a portion of a tape-recorded conversation that I had with this worker during one of our lunch hours. The comments in the last paragraph were actually made several days after the preceding comments and were recorded within my daily field notes for that day.

6

Propaganda Dimensions
of Evangelical Crusades

We have cited examples from public organizations in illustrating the claim that bureaucratic propaganda takes a different form and is usually more subtle than that of traditional propaganda. One reason for this is that bureaucratic propaganda builds on conventional cultural wisdom—especially that of more sophisticated people—that therefore seems less manipulative and more plausible than traditional propaganda. This chapter focuses on a private religious organization's use of its own records and documentation as evidence that the problem it is addressing is "real," but also that the problem is being solved by this organization, in its own way.

The belief in using rational means to show or prove effectiveness is also seen with segments of organized religion. The Billy Graham Evangelical Association (BGEA) is one example. These workers, like all the workers noted throughout our analysis of bureaucratic propaganda, are sincere and are committed to their tasks. However, unlike many of the other people discussed in these pages, they are not dependent on tax dollars or government organizations for their continuation. Nevertheless, they employ numerical tabulations, annual reports, and budgetary data as evidence of their work.

The variety of tasks performed, their essential open-endedness, and the general problems of trying to categorize adequately relatively uncomplicated activities have already been noted. This becomes especially problematic when highly subjective topics such as "souls," "salvation," and "true redemption" are being considered. This apparent problem notwithstanding, the BGEA workers routinely complete their rational search and documentation of newly won souls.

THE PURPOSE AND CONTEXT

This research focused primarily on the activities of religious counselors at a Billy Graham Evangelical Crusade. We report and analyze how counselors worked to provide the official information specified by organizational considerations, namely, the classifications of the "inquirers" (or converts) who came forward at the end of the ceremony to accept the evangelist's invitation to receive Jesus Christ into their lives. For these holy bureaucrats, their good work consisted of treating individual souls with a blend of least-common-denominator religious doctrine, personal congeniality, and formally rational accounting procedures.

Our team of four field researchers studied evangelistic counseling at the May, 1974 Billy Graham Crusade in Phoenix, Arizona. The research observations included observations of and interviews with religious counselors as they conducted their tasks, interviews with the crusade staff, photography and videotapes of selected features of the ceremonies, discussions with people who conducted the crusade "follow up," review of pertinent documentary materials, and talks with other interested persons. The major research strategy required the four researchers to "come forward to Christ" during the altar call following the evangelist's invitation in order to learn how the counselors did their work. We observed a dozen counselors as they ministered to the researcher converts. Once the general counseling protocol was understood, various attempts were made to manipulate experimentally the scenarios by changing researcher-convert biographies and circumstances. This strategy was intended to discover and demonstrate the counselor's definitions of the situation. This second stage of the research involved two general approaches. The first consisted of the researchers working separately, whereby each would engage a counselor individually. Our debriefings and discussions after these encounters suggested that the research objectives of systematically presenting the counselors with various topics and problems would be more adequately met by working in pairs. This second approach required one of the researchers to bring his "friend" (the researcher-convert) to the altar call. The first researcher would tell the counselor that he had "already accepted Jesus Christ into his life" and that his friend also was on the verge of doing so. This strategy afforded an opportunity for the first researcher to analyze and direct the conversational flow so that the desired information could be presented to the counselor.

Information about converts, or "inquirers" as they are called by some of the crusade staff, is recorded on a "decision card" near the completion of the counseling scenario. In addition to the convert's name, address, phone number, occupation, and religious denomination, one of three boxes is checked: (1) Acceptance of Christ as Savior and Lord, (2) Assurance of Salvation, and (3) Rededication.[1] These decision cards are tabulated and used for organizational assessments of a given crusade. Summations are stressed quantitatively, such as "nearly 10,000 people accepted Christ into their lives," and qualitatively, such as "the Gospel has been proclaimed, lives have been changed, homes have been reunited, our community has been enriched," as local newspapers depicted the Phoenix Crusade. But such ex post facto assessments and public relations work in the local communities represent only one use of this information, and not the most important one. The statistical tabulations are additionally used as evidence to support the distinctive "selling point" promoted by the members of the Billy Graham Evangelical Association, namely, Graham's ability to gain previously un-committed, *new* followers for local ministries; as such, these tabulations represent one important factor accounting for Graham's relative evangelical dominance in the United States.

Fundamentalist and evangelical crusades represent one enduring feature of the pluralistic religious and ethical traditions in the United States. Although many evangelists now work throughout the country, Billy Graham is the most widely publicized and recognized. Since his first tent crusade in Los Angeles in 1949, the "Gabriel in gabardine," as he was then known, is reputed to have preached the Christian Gospel to more millions of people throughout the World than anyone else and claims to have encouraged over one and a half million people to "step forward for Christ" during the last twenty-five years. Social scientists who have devoted their attentions to understanding the apparent appeals and successes of the movement led by this onetime Fuller brush salesman have generally focused on either its mass movement-like character (Argyle, 1959), on the "collective behavior" involved (Broom and Selznick, 1963: 437ff), on the psychological "susceptibility" of the participants (Frank, 1961: 77–8), on their social backgrounds (Cantril, 1953; Niebuhr, 1959; Berger, 1961; Whitam, 1968), or on Graham's "charisma" and/or manipulative strategies (Lang and Lang, 1960).

As a striking contrast to sociologists' persistent and puzzling tendencies to view Graham's evangelical crusades as "unstructured collective behavior" are the perceptions of the more than 8,500 groups and organizations that annually solicit his services and assistance. Most of these groups, (espe-cially the requests from ad hoc alliances of local ministries seeking remedies for their sagging market situations) are understood to seek not only Graham's personal appearance but especially the aid of "the organization."

Since its inception in 1950, the Billy Graham Evangelical Association has become a vast corporate enterprise. With an annual budget in excess of $20,000,000 for 1974, BGEA sponsors a radio program syndicated over 900 stations, the production of motion pictures, a School of Evangelism that has instructed as many as 8,000 participants at one time, an instruc-tional program for writers and other evangelical propagandists, world congresses on evangelism, and the production and distribution of vast amounts of religious literature (including the magazine *Decision,* which has a monthly circulation of 5,000,000 and is printed in ten editions and in six languages). BGEA maintains two headquarters (one each in Minneapolis and Atlanta) and full-time offices in London, Paris, Frankfurt, Buenos Aires, Mexico City, Sidney, Tokyo, Hong Kong, and Winnipeg. Specifically concerning the BGEA crusades, it is common knowledge that a local request accepted by Graham and BGEA will involve a vast organizational apparatus to insure its success. This includes preplanning activities that typically begin one year or more in advance, an orchestrated publicity and public relations campaign during the months immediately before the crusade, detailed instruction and training of the religious counselors who will work the crusade, experienced leadership in handling all the organizational practicalities of running the crusade (including auditorium, housing, transportation, amplification, lighting, and seating), and perhaps most importantly, the "follow up" on the crusade. In addition to an understanding of Graham's "charisma," a common knowledge of factors such as these is often crucial to the commitment of the "advance money" by the local ministerial alliance. One of BGEA's advance men for the Phoenix Crusade succinctly commented on this:

> S: I would say probably five, six, six thousand people [are involved in the crusade]. . . . The choir, there's maybe 3,000 in the choir, and over 1,500 counselors. There's only, for the really big and important jobs, there's only about fifteen people that really set things up. You get too many people and you get too much of a mess. They delegate a lot of responsibility. . . .
>
> Au.: Do some of the counselors come every night?
>
> S: Oh yeah, just about all of them. Most of them come every night, and most of the choir comes every night. . . . Most of the people who work in colabor in these different jobs [come nightly]. They're pretty dedicated, most of them, and besides that they really enjoy it. They realize they're seeing, you know, a chance of a lifetime. Phoenix probably won't have another crusade like this for another ten years plus. They're seeing the biggest invitation in the world, you know, history, so, uh, it gives them inspiration. . . .
>
> Au.: Yeah, the counselors I talked with are very energetic. It's like it's very personal. . . .
>
> S: Well, this has been twenty-five years of this, you know. Billy's personality is only a small part of the whole thing. We feel that the key to our crusades is the invitation and the follow up, and we feel that we have the best follow up by far of anything we have ever seen. That's where we've really got it over the other [evangelical crusaders]. We've worked on it twenty-five years, you know, and we know what to do.

e more ceremonial "witnessing" previously stressed by fundamentalist elievers, in part reflects the desire of many people to translate the sacred eachings of the Gospel for applicability to modern problems and relevancies. One BGEA staff assistant remarked on this emergent emphasis on counseling:

> **S:** You can pick up a lot of things. Counseling is really getting to be, you know, there is just going to be a whole lot more counseling going on in the future than there has been before.
>
> **Au.:** That does seem to be a really important part of it all.
>
> **S:** For one thing, people are more open now about their problems and, for another thing, you know, there are so many problems with demonology, mysticism, and all that kind of stuff. . . . People are going to be searching out counselors [to help them with their problems]. We're ready for anything at our crusades, and we have gotten some pretty strange things. But I know, you've just got to be ready, ready for anything. You could be going out to your car, even tonight, and you could be confronted with somebody with a serious problem of some kind. You just have to take authority. You can't think, "Now I have to call my preacher," or something like that, because God might send somebody your way that needs help that could be delivered from the demons.

Although it is recognized that modern times are characterized by many, long-standing moral problems (such as sinfulness, pride, sensuality, and greed) as well as by some relatively new and emergent ones (such as demonology, divorce, and drugs), fundamentalist believers argue that a mastery and appropriately literal interpretation of Biblical teachings will provide one with solutions for these problems, whether for self or others. But it is both essential and necessary to be prepared for any and all eventualities, to learn and gain knowledge about how the sacred teachings actually apply to seemingly new problems and to the eternally ingenious ways of the devil. At the most abstract level, then, the present emphasis on religious counseling reflects a reaffirmation of faith in the applicability, utility, and therapeutic success of the traditional writings.

All religious counselors involved in a BGEA crusade are drawn from the local area where the crusade is held. All undergo an extensive instructional and training program, typically conducted in two or three hour sessions over a period of four to six weeks. Even though this "Christian Life and Witness Course" is presented under the guise of preparing Christians for being able to cope with any situation, when translated into the organizational context of the impending crusade, the instruction is more concrete, immediate, and practical. Counselors receive instructions

Contrary to sociologists' repeated assertions that evan
such as the Graham crusades represent instances of relativel
collective behavior, the remarks of the BGEA staff assista
above indicate the existence of formally organized actions in\
individuals. Furthermore, these rational actions consistently
"success rate" in the form of *new* converts (or previously un
church goers or believers) for which experienced BGEA vete\
some distinction over other evangelical enterprises. This "succ\
supported by the hard statistical evidence, is what BGEA vete\
as the primary factor explaining their effectiveness and relative eva\
dominance in the United States.

The field observations of this research were motivated to answ\
primary questions of how the "successes" of the Billy Graham Ph\
Crusade were socially defined in the face-to-face counseling work and \
this official information was subsequently used. Toward this end, infor\
tion on two aspects of evangelistic counseling is of central importanc\
first, the counselor's decision that an individual is a "convert" (that i\
that he or she is appropriately classified in the first of the three available
categories); and second, whether counselors would consider "disconfirming\
information" in their classifications (whether they would change a prior
evaluation of "convert" in the light of additional and contradictory information). For all of the cases collected by our team of researcher-converts
during the field observations, the end result was the same. All counselors
checked the first box (Acceptance of Christ as Savior and Lord) on the
decision card indicating a new convert, as opposed to the second (Assurance of Salvation) or third (Rededication). This was the case despite our
use of the most unmitigated, explicit, decisive, and unequivocal statements
(short of using force) to promote the other two categories. An understanding of the religious counselor's perspective, preparatory instruction, and
practical tasks in the organized evangelical context further clarifies this
phenomenon, and thus the nature of evangelical conversions.

THE COUNSELING PERSPECTIVE AND TASKS

Religious counseling is now regarded as an activity that requires
specialized instruction and training. This view reflects a partial change
in the traditional perspective of many Protestants, especially the fundamentalists who perceive themselves closely akin to Graham's evangelism.
Traditionally, untrained laymen were accorded an acknowledged license
to minister to convert and nonbelievers alike if they had had a personal
experience with God. Indeed, many fundamentalists have traditionally
shunned "book preparation" as an inauthentic call to the ministry. This
changing and increasing emphasis on religious *counseling,* as opposed to

on how to recognize the coded name tags, coded hand signals to be used during the altar call, how to fill out daily statistical break-downs, what brand of mint to chew immediately before encountering a new convert to make one's breath less offensive, and many other mundane bits of knowledge necessary to insure a smooth performance. Most importantly, however, counselors receive instructions about their interactions with and classifications of prospective converts, and also on the crucial follow-up contacts.

Counselors begin their work after the singing, testimonials, collection, and Billy Graham's sermon, which culminates in the altar call. At the moment of Graham's invitation to "come forward to Christ," counselors and choir members begin moving forward to an area usually in front of the speaker's platform or rostrum. To a naïve member of the audience or a television viewer, this movement creates an illusion of a spontaneous and mass response to the invitation. Having been assigned seating in strategic areas of the auditorium or arena and given instructions on the staggered time-sequencing for coming forward, the counselors move forward toward the rostrum in such a fashion so as to create the illusion of individuals "flowing" into the center of the arena from all quarters, in a steady outpouring of individual decision. Unless an outsider or observer of these events has been instructed to look for the name tags and ribbons worn by those moving forward, it is all too esay to infer from these appearances the "charismatic" impact of Graham and his invitation. Needless to say, these troop-movement strategies promote the respectability of making a public commitment and represent methods calculated to manipulate the consent of the passive, the uncertain, the wary, and the indecisive.

Following the ceremonial benediction, the public portion of the crusade is terminated and those standing in the area in front of the rostrum are asked to remain for an additional brief message. At this point, possibly a sizable majority of those in front of the rostrum represent the counselors, choir, and staff of the crusade.[2] During this additional message, new converts are informed that they will be immediately contacted by a person standing close to them to give Billy's "mass evangelism" a more personal and individual touch. Though the new converts are unaware of this, by this point virtually all those in the area have been "paired off" with one another on the basis of sex and approximate age. The pairing off was accomplished by a combination of self-selection, standardized assignment procedures, and the silent hand signals of "advisors," who are at this point managing the performance. Indeed, many of the new converts have been specifically "followed" by a given counselor since leaving their seats. (Counselors are instructed, for example, to bow their heads and close their eyes at the beginning of the final prayer of the sermon, but to open their eyes immediately in order to keep track of certain individuals who may begin moving forward during the prayer.) Following this final message, the process of translating mass to personal evangelism begins with the counselor's work; at first, a hand on a shoulder, a smile, and a welcome.

Religious counseling to evangelical converts involves the production of a step-by-step protocol. Confidential crusade training manuals containing the standard operating procedures variously depict eight to ten broad depictions of the steps; each step is further broken down into as many as seventeen additional subcategories. These steps are standardized so as to effect a warm and friendly welcome, a direct introduction to Christ through mutual prayer and scripture reading affording enough opportunity for expression so that the convert maintains a sense of participation in the interaction, winning the convert's confidence, making an assessment of the nature of the convert's decision and commitment, eliciting and recording the information needed for the follow up, and terminating the encounter by introducing the convert to one of the roaming advisors (usually a local minister), and hopefully in time to minister to another convert. The progressive enactment of the BGEA protocol, similar to that used by door-to-door encyclopedia salesmen, is partially contingent on passing through a series of "check-off points" at which the convert's verbal responses partially influence what occurs next. If all goes smoothly and the counselor has efficaciously used the rules about being warm, congenial, friendly, and yet not too talkative, then the encounter will last about eight to fourteen minutes. This time sequence is partially based on the BGEA understandings about how long the people have been there already (perhaps two to three hours), their transportation problems, and other factors. But counselors will, if judged necessary, spend up to sixty to ninety minutes or more with the new convert, explaining and encouraging the decision for Christ. For the most part, however, the religious counseling in the evangelical context is not designed to "convince" or "persuade" individuals, but rather to obtain the information needed for the follow up. The more personal follow up, always made within forty-eight hours by phone, visit, or letter, is seen as a more appropriate context for persuasion.

In addition to learning about the practical aspects of putting on a smoothly organized crusade, evangelical counselors also receive extensive doctrinal instruction and preparation. This might seem strange to an outsider. The religious counselors who volunteer their services for one of the BGEA crusades are self-selected from a rather specific segment of the range of all Protestant believers and are drawn from an extremely narrow range of all religious believers. They identify or at least feel comfortable with the crusade's explicitly Biblical fundamentalism. A reader who is not familiar with the daily realities of these believers might all too readily infer that they share in common a homogeneous set of moral meanings. In some respects, this is true, but in others, it is not.

The 1,500 to 1,600 counselors who volunteered to work the Phoenix

Crusade, and explicitly expressed their commitments to Christian principles on the application forms, were drawn from the congregations of many different local churches and denominations. Merely being committed is not sufficient for a BGEA crusade, however, since denominations vary widely in Biblical interpretation. Some denominational perspectives are frequently accused of preaching "false doctrine" by the true believers of others. The most vehement and categorical moral judgments are often reserved for these heretical enemies since, unlike those yet to be exposed to the truth, they have access to it and hence should "know better." In the daily lives of members of fundamentalist denominations, there are many people who literally are not on speaking terms with members of other denominations. It is relatively easy to find many analogies to this general kind of situation in the contemporary university.

It is clear that public visibility of the existent fundamentalist warfare in the local communities might have a potentially disastrous effect on potential converts, on neophytes, and on people whose newfound beliefs are without sanctionable social supports. One way to resolve momentarily these doctrinal battles, at least for the immediately practical purposes of the conversion enterprise, is to provide all volunteers with a standardized biblical interpretation, a counseling protocol, and some accommodative "ground rules" for playing the game. Volunteers are asked to suspend whatever differences may exist among them in favor of that least-common-denominator that unites them—their assurance of salvation and the Word of God. These beliefs are what allegedly subsume and unite all the minor denominational differences into one, according to one of the BGEA staff assistants, as opposed to those beliefs that promote "false doctrine."

> We went to St. Louis, and St. Louis is dead. There are so many cities that are cold, that you don't get much cooperation. Like St. Louis is a real big Catholic city . . . like I say, the ministers that are saved, and are interested in evangelism, cooperated. But when you just go to just the regular churches, you know, where they preach the Gospel a little bit, they're not that interested. . . . Of course, *the Catholic churches, we don't work with them at all—that's the only church we just don't work with. They've got too much false doctrine.* [Emphases added]

Stressing a standardized, literal interpretation of the Biblical scriptures not only serves to encourage a collective consciousness of their (immediate) common purpose, of feelings that "we're all in this together," but also serves a more important utilitarian purpose. According to the BGEA conception of the conversion process, "true" Christians will *only* be converted by the Word of God and *not* because of Billy Graham's "personality," the interpretations or proselytizing of the counselor, the convert's feelings or personal problems, and so forth. According to the BGEA staff who instruct the counselors, people only become converts and come forward to accept Christ because of God's word, and therefore only a knowledge of scriptures will "work" to gain converts. One counselor for the Phoenix Crusade stressed the significance of maintaining the proper religious stance to the conversion process:

> They do that to make sure you know what you're talking about, because any guru or somebody could come down here and counsel and give off false doctrines. Anybody, if it were not for [the stand-ardized interpretations], could come up and say, "God is everything, and if you meditate, that is how you become one with the universe," or something like that. That wouldn't bring us any true Christians.

The general idea behind the counselor training courses is to ensure that the counselors have a standardized knowledge of the scriptures, which, given the organizational conception of the conversion process, is defined as utilitarian in evangelical terms. This includes attending the classes of the instructional program, memorizing key scriptural passages, learning which Biblical passages correspond to a listing of common problems or questions that converts express, and so forth. The instruction includes scriptural references to expressions of doubt, the devil's first attack on a young Christian, and even possible "reasons" for such an attack by the devil (such as the possible "blindness" of Jewish converts). But these instructions about the literal truth of the scriptures are also seen to contain possible sources of "trouble" for a counselor. They are, therefore, combined with some accommodative "ground rules" to enhance the success of the immediate organizational purpose. When counseling Jewish converts, for example, the point is made not to frighten them with the prospect of hell punishment at this time and to side-step all discussions of the Trinity and Virgin Birth. The immediate objective is to encourage the decision and to record the needed information for the follow up. In fact, given the limited time available, counselors are generally advised to avoid doctrinal argument and proselytizing altogether. It is in using methods such as these, then, that the absolutist morality of the fundamentalist beliefs becomes inter-twined with the accommodative morality of everyday life and practical affairs. Both are present in the same situation in the form of a *practical absolutism*. Jack Douglas (1971: 171–243) argues that commonsense societal members use a meaningful distinction between these two moralities to maintain the reality of each. But these observations suggest that, at least for the evangelical counselors, the accommodative morality of daily life is seen in terms of its utility for realizing the other.

To point out the purposes and emphases on the least-common-denominator Biblical interpretations and on the advised ground rules to effect them as effectively and smoothly as possible, however, should not be interpreted to mean that these rules are unproblematic for evangelical counselors. Indeed, our field observations as researcher-converts included several instances that would be defined, from the official crusade stance, as "deviance." During one conversion exchange, for example, an ex-Catholic counselor promoted his distinctively personal interpretation of the morality of consuming alcoholic beverages, a morality that directly contradicted the Graham position on such matters. The observations included two instances in which the counselors promoted their own local churches to the researcher-convert and one fairly unequivocal condemnation of a researcher-convert's expressed beliefs. Specific doctrinal or personal interpretations, promoting one's church, proselytizing, and condemning others' beliefs are all in fact widely recognized by BGEA staff assistants as endemic and recurring problems for an organizational enterprise like a crusade.

Counselors work on new converts by having them repeat certain words and scriptures. Part of this work is done with the aid of a standardized pamphlet titled "Steps to Peace with God." It is progressively organized in steps to elicit a series of responses from the convert. These procedures are intended to foster a reverence for holy words in general and especially to emphasize the meaning of their actual utterance. In addition to a theological rationale for this, these procedures are informed by a common-sense organizational theory of persons and of the conversion process.

The Power of Words

By definition, evangelism would be impossible without the unquestioned acceptance of a sacred text as the source of truth. The significance of the word in Western thought reaches beyond the Hebrews. According to the Bible (John 1:1), "In the beginning was the Word, and the Word was with God, and the Word was God." This emphasis on the absoluteness of sacred words is common to much traditional religious thought; it is not unique to fundamentalist Protestantism. This emphasis also has exercised considerable influence on our Western philosophical and scientific traditions, but in these instances it might be more fair to say that the absolutism pertains to words in general rather than to specific ones.

According to Christian theology, "the Word" was originally sacred and absolute but became contaminated by the forever sinful ways of Man. In John (1:14), for example, we learn "The Word was made flesh, and dwelt among us. . . ." Christian theology holds that Christ was the Word incarnate and to utter the proper words was to call on God and speak the truth. Indeed, scriptures depict "the Word" as both a personal being and an independent stream of life-giving energy available to all persons. Billy Graham's version of religion strictly adheres to this interpretation of "the Word." In describing how one enters the kingdom of heaven, for

example, the evangelist remarks that "it is not done with a ritual . . .
it's done in the name of the Lord Jesus Christ." Graham further describes
the place of scriptures in the Christian life in one sermon:

> In other words, learn the scriptures, learn the word of God. That's
> why—when people come forward to Christ—we give them a Bible
> study [course] and we get them involved in the scriptures, memorizing
> the scriptures. This is how we resist the devil. . . . [And] the way
> to get prepared is to learn this book [the Bible] so that when they
> [one's friends] do call upon you to witness, you know the scriptures
> and you can quote the word of God, and be a witness, and resist the
> devil. . . .

Learning the sacred words is not only viewed as an end in itself,
however, but it is also presented as a therapeutic technique that promises
success in solving social problems. Extolling one of the previous therapeutic
successes, Graham observes: "Christ resisted the devil by quoting scripture,
that's all he did. He said, 'It is written,' and when he finished quoting
the scripture the devil would leave him and the angels would come and
minister to him." The significance of the Word, and especially of the
personal commitment entailed by sincerely saying the proper words, is
also underscored by the repeated emphasis that one's salvation cannot be
gained by baptism, good deeds, communion, church membership, or
national ancestry, but only "through the Word of God."

The counseling protocol is constructed to encourage a reverence for
holy words in general, but it is specifically designed to elicit a series of
specific spoken words by the new convert. This is for the most part standardized by the pamphlet used for these purposes. In the interaction
between counselor and convert, the counselor is searching for some variation of a specific verbal utterance "I believe." This is viewed as independent
empirical evidence sufficient to warrant an inference that one has "converted." The following exchange involving a researcher (Res), the researcher's "friend" (the researcher-convert, Res-Con), and a counselor
(Couns) illustrates this:

> **Res:**   You see, I think the [researcher-convert] has accepted
> Christ, but you don't yourself know, isn't that right?
>
> **Res-Con:**   At times I think I have, but at times I'm not sure.
>
> **Res:**   I believe you have.
>
> **Couns:**   Let me give you these verses.
>
> **Res:**   [to counselor] Do you think he has?
>
> **Couns:**   Sure. If he thinks Christ died for his sins and if he accepts
> Him into his heart as Lord and Savior of his life. Just
> say, "Lord, I believe, I want to follow you." You have to
> say that. I have some doubts, too, but that's what faith is

> all about. That's what faith is. But you have to begin by
> saying it.

To result in a conversion that is sufficient for all practical, organizational purposes, the counseling process requires the convert to express
faith in the scriptures. But in actual situations, this typically includes the
counselor's exposition of one or more "rational reasons" for this faith. Our
research observations included several instances in which counselors stressed
the therapeutic value of scriptural utterances. According to one who
counseled a researcher-convert:

> I found that when Satan bothers me a lot, if I've got something that's
> really tempting me, well, instead of yielding to that temptation I'll
> recite a scripture verse. You'd be surprised how fast the temptation
> goes away!

The counselor's comments promote the therapeutic value of scriptural
utterance for one's personal problems. But other counselors promoted their
therapeutic utility for solving the problems of other people. During another
exchange between counselor and researcher-convert, this additional utility
is illustrated:

> So it is very important to get into the scriptures and have an answer
> for every man's question. You'll find that a lot of people you'll be
> talking to will have a lot of questions, and you have the answers for
> all of them right here in God's word. . . . This is the way you get
> your answers, by looking them up right here in the Bible, and then
> just letting the holy spirit teach you so that you can teach others. . . .

During the field observations and interviews with the BGEA evangelical counselors, all variously expressed one or more "rational reasons" for
making a decision to have faith in the holy scriptures. If one has faith,
according to this view, verbal utterance of the scriptures possesses the
power to solve social problems for self or others. But verbal utterance
of the proper words also is seen to possess another power, one of a
more immediate relevance to the organizational tasks of the conversion
enterprise.

The religious counseling at a BGEA crusade is based on a commonsense social theory of the self. This theory, which is not new, tends to
be completely taken for granted in the actual counseling interactions and
made only slightly more explicit in confidential training manuals. It is
a theory of the social self found in virtually all Western religious traditions
and also taken for granted in the writings of many philosophers and social
scientists. The fundamental idea of this theory is that an individual
possesses *substantial self* that is constituted by a "central core" of moral

qualities. These core qualities are belived to transcend any and all situations and practical involvements of an individual, and hence to determine what "kind" or "type" of person one is. The core qualities determine, for example, whether one is a "basically moral" or a "basically immoral" person. On this foundation, this theory proposes that an individual's thoughts, feelings, and valuations emanate from this central core in a relatively direct fashion and find their expression in one's verbal talk. Stated differently, the theory little appreciates the relevance of paralinguistic meanings, situationally bounded actions, the expressive meanings and uses of human communications, and other such phenomena. For the present discussion, the important point about this theory is that one's verbal utterances are conceived as morally sanctionable, whether by self or others. Verbal utterances are thought to reflect or mirror the qualities that constitute the substantial self. This has been and continues to be a very popular theory among theological, and philosophical and social scientific wordsmiths.

These remarks depict in general terms the official organizational theory of the self that underlies the BGEA counseling. When translated to the practical tasks of the conversion context, however, it undergoes a distinctive modification. The conversion context involves rather severe time limitations. It is obvious that the time available for the counselor-convert interaction following the altar call is insufficient to change the totality of an individual's values, beliefs, cognitions, feelings, perceptions, and attitudes. Given these practical constraints of limited time, the BGEA protocol, especially the part that requires the counselor to take the new convert through the progressively ordered steps of the pamphlet ("Steps to Peace with God"), is designed to elicit a series of verbal utterances by the convert. Since the theory about an individual's substantial self asserts the existence of a relatively direct, necessary relationship between one's verbal utterances and the morally sanctionable core qualities, encouraging or eliciting these spoken words is to insure a conversion that is successful for all practical purposes. In addition to the powers imputed to words, then, words are believed to possess power in this respect as well.[3] This point is illustrated by one of the counselors who ministered to one of the researcher-converts:

> *Couns:* Just simply say "I believe" and "I have faith." Don't worry about anything else. Don't worry about the other things. If you say that, you'll believe, and that's all it takes. God will work it out. It says in the Bible that all things will work out for those who love God.

The emphasis on the convert's verbal utterances is found in all of our transcripts of the interactions between the counselors and researcher-converts. During one conversation, when the researcher-convert expressed his realization that making the decision for faith was "not a matter of rational choice, like picking out a pair of socks or something," the counselor responded excitedly:

> *Couns:* He's come to you now. You're beginning to get it. Just say "I believe." If you want to grow in Him, and the way to grow in Him is by reading the Bible, the scriptures, get yourself a Bible. You'll only grow by learning His words. . . .

As noted previously, the pamphlet used by the counselor to instruct the convert is progressively ordered by steps. Before the counselor turns the page for the next step, he queries the convert about his understanding at that point. If the convert understands, he turns the page for the next one; if not, further clarification will be forthcoming before going on. At the concluding portion of the final step, the convert learns by way of a citation from Romans (10:9) that if one has acknowledged with his lips the fact that Jesus is Lord (which was required to progress beyond step three), then one's salvation has been assured.[4] If for any reason the convert responds in an obviously negative way at some point in this process (that is, as opposed to an expression of uncertainty), then the convert's responses to the earlier steps are used to point out the "inconsistency" of the latter response. The negative response would be defined as "inconsistent" because of the underlying theory of an individual's substantial self discussed earlier. The form of this process, incidentally, bears a striking similarity to the methods used by door-to-door encyclopedia salespersons to manipulate the consent of families; these methods were developed after years of market research and millions of dollars.[5]

The evangelical conversion process is both personal and organizational, and thereby combines a mixture of personal feelings and rationally organized procedures. Converts may cry, but the counselor who beckons him toward eternal life does so calmly and with a rational plan-of-action. Counselors are instructed to deny the relevance or importance of personal feelings in favor of the judeo-Christian rational-word tradition. The sacred scriptures emphasized literal acceptance of "the Word" through faith, but counseling employs rational procedures for ascertaining whether the person has the faith and whether the accepted truths are adequately understood. The convert's newfound faith is thereby informed by theological and organizational perspectives, resulting in a curious blend of faith and formal rationality. One counselor who ministered to a researcher-convert explicitly denied the relevance of feelings to the conversion process:

> *Couns:* Some people don't feel anything. You might not feel anything.
>
> *Res-Con:* How will I know?
>
> *Res:* [to counselor] Can you tell [the res-con] how he'll know when he's accepted Christ?

> **Couns:** Well, let me say that, first of all, we have to have the facts, right? The facts have to be laid out to us. Then we have to have faith, just believe these facts by faith. This is what God has said. We have to come to Him like a simple child. Just believe what he has told us in His word. Then the feeling will come later. It is in that order. . . .
>
> **Res:** But the feelings don't really have to be there?
>
> **Couns:** No. You don't want to count on feelings. It's like this. God said it, I believe it, that settles it. It's as simple as that, okay?

Expressions of feelings and emotions are not only officially unnecessary for religious commitment, but BGEA staff also explicitly instruct counselors not to classify an individual as a convert (the first box on the decision card) if there is an excessive display of emotion. Despite this, however, many counselors interviewed during the field observations recognized a show of emotion as a decisive indicator of acceptance. The relevant criterion for the organizational classifications is, officially, at least, the nature of the verbal utterances. Spoken words, not feelings, are presumably what symbolizes the convert's commitments.

When counselor and convert reach the conclusion of the steps outlined in the pamphlet, the convert is handed a prayer to read. This prayer invites Jesus "to come into my heart and life." In all of the field experiments in which the researcher-convert reached this point, the prayer appeared to be the crucial empirical evidence used by the counselor in recording the subsequent classification of convert. On one occasion, at the point of this prayer the counselor exclaimed with mild excitement, "You've accepted Him, You've accepted Him, You've committed your life to Him!" On another occasion the counselor assured the researcher-convert, "He's got a hold of you now and He'll never let go!" At the end of the prayer on a third occasion, the counselor asked the convert, "Where is He right now?" The researcher-convert's hesitation led the counselor to point to former's chest with his finger and say, "He's right here, right here!" During a fourth interaction, the counselor asked the researcher-convert if he had been saved. The latter's answer, "I suppose so," elicited the exclamation, "Right, you've been saved, now you've been saved!" All of these interactions occurred during the first several nights of the eight-day crusade.

The field observations also included occasions when the interaction did not progress to the point of the prayer. In one instance, the researcher-convert (a minister's son) tried to be classified as "rededicated," and on several occasions the researcher-convert emphatically expressed considerable confusion, indecision, uncertainty, or outright denial. Our transcript for one conversion on the final night of the crusade illustrates this. The first researcher initially introduced the researcher-convert as a former

Christian who wanted to "come back to the fold, to get back into it." The counselor asked if the convert had "received Christ as your Lord and Savior." The researcher-convert responded by saying that he had once belonged to a church, but had "strayed." This was met with further interrogation:

> *Couns:* Did you have a time in your life when you said "Lord, forgive me of my sins and come into my life and live with me"? Do you have a time in your life where you really did this and really believe that Christ came into my heart and into my life?
>
> *Res-Con:* Have I had this time?
>
> *Couns:* Have you had this day in your life when you said this and knew it took place?
>
> *Res:* [to friend] Did that ever happen to you?
>
> *Res-Con:* Well, several months ago I was having problems with this girl I was going with, and it caused me to drink very much. I think I wanted to then.
>
> *Couns:* Did you have this time, though, when you called and said, "Jesus, forgive me of my sins, come into my life and live here"?
>
> *Res:* I don't think you have ever said it quite like that, have you?
>
> *Res-Con:* Not that way.
>
> *Res:* [to counselor] I think you know what he meant though.
>
> *Couns:* Yeah. It doesn't have to be in those exact words, but we have to have a time when we specifically say "Lord Jesus, forgive me for what I've done," and ask him to come into my life and live with me. . . .

This excerpt further illustrates the emphasis placed on the formally rational criteria pertaining to the convert's verbal utterances to determine the appropriate organizational classification. Even in this situation in which this criteria did not appear to be even plausibly met, however, the researcher-convert was categorized as having "accepted Christ as Lord and Savior," the first box on the decision card. This was also the result for the other field experiments, including one instance in which two field workers tried strenuously to have the first classification changed to "re-dedication" by providing conclusive evidence to that effect. The field observations, experiences, and reflections suggest that several factors are important for understanding this emphasis on counting converted souls: (1) doing counseling work for a BGEA crusade is a relatively unique and much-anticipated experience for the participants, (2) the hopeful expectations are generated either by the role itself or preceding events of the

172 Propaganda Dimensions of Evangelical Crusades

evening, (3) the criteria of "good work" exists among counselors, and (4) the organizational emphasis is on soul-tallies.

Before further discussion, one point deserves mention. The fact or possibility that several BGEA counselors might have "misclassified" a group of researcher-converts, and hence produced crusade numerology that was not "completely accurate" is unimportant in itself. The major point to be made by the field observations and natural experiments reported here is that BGEA counselors were oriented to people who came forward in the practical, organizational terms emphasized in their instructions and preparations. They were asked to obtain organizationally mandated information as quickly as possible while nevertheless touching all bases of the counseling protocol. This involved using formalized criteria and a tripartite classification schema to categorize the diffuse motivations leading people to come forward at the altar call.[6] Rather than introducing a kind of influence on the crusade numbers that one could reasonably assume to be randomized—which would appear to be the case with any "misclassification" of a researcher-convert—these emphases introduce a systematic influence on the crusade statistics. This point deserves further discussion.

Practicalities and Problematics of Counting Souls

For many local church members, being selected as a religious counselor for an upcoming Graham crusade is seen as an exciting, momentous, once-in-a-lifetime opportunity. It is, perhaps, similar to playing in the World Series, the Stanley Cup, or Wimbledon. Not all those who apply are eventually chosen by the screening board, which uses the standardized BGEA guidelines for such decisions. As best we could tell, attached to a person's participation in the BGEA crusade was a certain sense of excitement and anticipation, although this was apparently subject to some denominational differences.[7] Some people saw their selection as counselors as a momentary "calling" to lead wayward souls to the Cross. In addition to this generalized excitement and anticipation, the events of a particular evening stimulated or heightened the feelings of hopeful anticipation. In a local fundamentalist context such as this, it appears reasonable to think that many counselors came forward to the altar call expecting to play a meaningful part in the process of gaining new converts for Christ. One counselor interviewed during the research observations stated this expectation:

> **Res:** Do you get many folks that you put in one of these [other two categories], a fellow who had been Rededicated?
>
> **Couns:** Yeah, there's a lot of them. A lot of them come down for

assurance. Some of them have accepted Christ, but they feel like they have to have more of a feeling about it.

Res: I mean, how do you know that's where they belong, how do you know where to check them?

Couns: Well, usually you don't know. You have to play it by ear. But a lot of times you know, you just know they have come down to accept Christ as Savior.

Res: Probably most of the people, though, are people who are accepting Christ and not the latter two?

Couns: Oh sure, yeah, I'd say so. . . .

On the basis of our extensive discussion about the critical relevance of converts' verbal utterances, it is evident that this reference by the counselor to "playing it by ear" is not meant to be a casual, metaphorical, or felicitous expression. In this context, playing-it-by-ear is an expression appropriate for emphasizing the crucial criteria for these classifications of the convert's decisions for Christ. In addition to this, however, these remarks illustrate the counselor's probabilistic expectations about people who will be coming forward. It is some indication that, for a counselor at a BGEA crusade, one's "good work" will be judged on the basis of encouraging decisions for accepting Christ as Lord and Savior and mapping out the way to the Cross.

Counselors by and large see converts in practical terms. They are oriented to the relevant dimensions of evangelical counseling, which include a friendly and personal introduction to God and the scriptures, the prayer of a commitment, a brief examination to make sure the convert understands what has taken place, and finally, collecting pertinent information for the follow up and counting this soul among the reborn. The last consideration is especially important because the previous procedures are informed by this essential organizational goal. If the converted souls are not "counted," they are organizationally "lost," although the counseling may be personally meaningful in itself. The dominance of this perspective is seen in what the counselor takes for granted about the convert.

The counselor's definition of the situation is inextricably tied to the formally rational procedures for classifying and counting souls in a context of severe time limitations. Even if a counselor wanted to work against these practical constraints, the roaming advisers were ever-present to enforce them and often chided counselors for taking too much time. This crusade context encourages a working presupposition that converts who come forward to accept Christ define their actions as the counselors do, fully understand what this entails, and rationally follow and relate to the step-by-step scripture and prayer sequences discussed above. Put differently, counselors take for granted that individuals they encounter are interested in coming to Christ in the same way they understand it—that is in the various ways they understand it. This view of the convert contributes to the counselor's definition of the ministry at the altar, the assumption that they are praying and witnessing together and, in short, sharing meanings and purposes. Even though some counselors we studied admitted to some doubts, the evangelistic context became a sensible way for them to recruit a few of the lost flock. It is this counseling perspective that enabled the holy bureaucrats to equate answering a few programmed questions and uttering a prayer with a deeply personal religious commitment. Moreover, the organizationally mandated indicators could be rationally distinguished; as one counselor explained, "It's either accepting Christ, concern for their salvation, or rededication."

The combination of theological, organizational, and contextual relevancies transforms evangelical counseling into a practical and formally rational (or bureaucratic) task. The counselors we studied and talked with appeared sincere about their personal ministries to new converts and did not cynically try to comply only with organizational dictates. In this sense, it would be unfair to say they were motivated by the crusade to produce official statistics. However, the tasks they were trained to carry out were more or less compatible with their personal beliefs but were intended to produce the desired statistical and follow-up information. This was effected by treating the ministry, prayer, and scripture reading/quizzing as guides for conversion and indicators of religious commitment. In this way, counselors made organizational sense out of a convert's uncertain walk to the altar. Even though the motivations of many counselors appeared sincere, however, this should not be taken to mean that their actions were entirely devoid of immediate self-interests. This is illustrated in the comments of one BGEA staff assistant analyzing the factors accounting for the differential denominational participation at—and sense of zeal in—the crusade:

> Of course it's worth [the local churches'] while. It's just the churches that preach the Gospel that want to cooperate. The others think it's nice, but they don't want to get involved in it because it will be more work than they want to contribute. Sure, they'll get more members, though, especially those that preach the Gospel [the more fundamentalist-oriented Protestant churches]. No doubt about that. You know, there's going to be 10,000 people that have been saved here. There's already about 8,000 [for the first seven nights] and there's going to be 2,000 tonight [the final night] because there's about 44,000 people in the stadium tonight. . . .

COUNTING SOULS AS PROPAGANDA

Without support of local churches, the Phoenix Crusade and all others would be impossible. Without the numbers from past crusades promoted as an effective track record, and the generalized belief that they are successful in gaining new converts, on the other hand, local congregations and their leadership would be less willing or eager to commit the time, effort, manpower, or advance money. The official numerology—intertwined with the publicity promoted and given the crusades through the local mass media—are important features of Graham's relative evangelical dominance at this time in the United States. Both are dialectically interrelated in the efforts to fulfill what BGEA partisans prophecize as the as yet unrealized vision.

Even though having the hard statistical evidence of their evangelical successes is crucial to BGEA's futuristically rational efforts to self-fulfill their envisioned hopes of further success, another factor is equally important as a selling point of BGEA crusades. This is BGEA's distinct claim to win *previously uncommitted* (or new) souls for Christ and local ministries. Precisely how many of the evangelical conversions represent previously uncommitted individuals (versus regular church-goers in the local communities who come forward to Christ because of the relative uniqueness of the experiences for them or people who were church-goers but have been back-sliding) remains a disputed question. BGEA and their allied research groups consistently claim that approximately 40 percent of their evangelical conversions are previously uncommitted individuals. Other people consistently claim that this figure is much lower but admit that the question remains open due to BGEA's refusal to allow outsiders to see their records.[8] One insider turned sociologist (Whitam, 1968: 123) did obtain access to the BGEA decision cards during his research. He revealed that only 6 percent of those who came forward to Christ did not express a specific denominational preference. Organizationally detached observers largely agree that evangelical crusades generally, and Graham's version specifically, for the most part "convert" their own membership.[9]

Critics who desire to do battle with BGEA over the meanings of the official numerology maintain that the people who come forward to Christ at best represent a short-term gain for local church membership and not commitments of a lengthy duration.[10] Graham and BGEA counter such claims by saying that when viewed in the broader context, the efficacy of their efforts cannot be truthfully evaluated by any such one- or two-year comparisons, that many lifetime commitments for Christ just require a longer gestation. As this research indicates, both claims miss the crucial factors about the organizational and practical context within which official numerology is constructed and used.

There is another implication of these findings. Weber and others warned us about the impact of the movement to order and depict life in rational terms. When bureaucratic forms predominate over the specific content, the latter becomes transformed by the former and the distinction becomes blurred. For the BGEA workers it is not enough merely to "make a difference" in someone's life, to raise important questions for them, or even provide a meaningful way to change one's life. Proof of this impact must be available. The upshot is that more and more rational efforts are affecting popular notions of the holy and eternal meaning of man's existence. An offshoot of this conscious effort to make the sacred intelligible and respectable through profane categories is bureaucratic propaganda.

NOTES

1. Previously there were five classifications on the decision card, but BGEA has reduced it to three in recent years. According to Douglas's historical analysis (1971: 42–132) of official information, the statistical tabulations of official agencies of social control have undergone a similar process of progressive reduction as their mandates become more specifically defined and as the records are increasingly used to assess their public accountability.

2. According to the research conducted by Lang and Lang (1960) and their forty-three mass observers during the 1957 Billy Graham Crusade in New York City, their impression was that about 60 percent of the participants in the 19,000-seat Madison Square Garden were in one way or another tied in with the organization. Given our knowledge of the procedures that counselors are instructed to use in coming forward, as detailed in the confidential training manuals and bulletins for a crusade, our impression is that perhaps slightly more than half of those who end up in front of the rostrum are in some way affiliated with the crusade. But there have been exceptions to figure, largely varying according to the size of the auditorium or arena. When BGEA used Yankee Stadium, for example, it was commonly recognized that so many would come forward that counselors might have to minister to converts in groups.

3. Oral and written examinations used in educational institutions are other examples in which this underlying theory is assumed and taken for granted. One might see some striking similarities between the process gone through by evangelical converts and, for example, Ph.D. candidates in sociology, the difference being the substantive content of the process (scriptural words vs. those of Marx, Weber, Durkheim, et al.).

4. The actual verse from Romans (10:9) is, "For if with your lips you acknowledge the fact that Jesus is Lord, and in your hearts you believe that God raised Him from the dead, you will be saved."

5. One of the authors has had previous experience in encyclopedia sales as done door to door. This protocol is designed in a series of temporally specific segments, each of short duration. The salesman must elicit an affirmative response from his clients before moving on to the next segment ("If it were free, wouldn't you love to have this beautiful set of books in your home for your children?"). If one receives a series of affirmative responses during the course of the 45 to 50 minute presentation, it is

supposedly very difficult for the people to come forth with a final "No" at the time of the "clincher."

6. When at the area in front of the rostrum following the termination of the public ceremony, it appears obvious that there are diverse motivations involved in coming forward. Children frolic about, laughing and playing, groups of non-English-speaking people are herded here and there, ushers and advisers scurry back and forth while managing their workers, organized groups from nearby communities are sometimes counseled en masse so that they can catch their buses, organizational insiders chat about the evening's success, and some individuals can be seen weeping and crying as they accept Christ into their lives. Some of these actions foster an impression of a carnival atmosphere and others of a jovial group outing.

7. To some extent this observation is based on our interviews with counselors and staff assistants; it is also partially speculative. The security precautions at a crusade are very extensive, and none of the researchers had a pass to enter areas in which the counselors went for their debriefings and meetings. For this reason, then, it was very difficult to learn about the counselor's feelings on a given evening of the crusade.

8. Specific comments on this point are made in the research reported by Lang and Lang (1960).

9. Specifically concerning the Billy Graham Crusades, this point is made by Lang and Lang (1960), Frank (1961), McLoughlin (1960), and Whitam (1968). For other crusades, or evangelism generally, see Dike (1909) and McLoughlin (1955, 1959).

10. Lang and Lang (1960: footnote 8) briefly discuss an unnamed British research project conducted one year after a crusade in London. According to this research, less than 15 percent of the evangelical "converts" who were previously uncommitted church-goers were church members one year after the crusade.

7

Military Preparedness as Propaganda

Providing rational justifications for organizational tasks is a prerequisite for more and more dimensions of social life. As noted in chapter 1, applying rules to any activity will necessarily change that activity to appear to fit the rules. This is also true of war activities. Even though warfare has always been partly governed by sentiments of procedure, tactics, and even "fair play," it has only been during the last century that standing armies, navies, air forces, and other components of international "war machines" have bureaucratized everyday life—both in and out of combat— with rules, procedures, and various modes of "being prepared." The public relations efforts of generals, admirals, and other people have emphasized the necessity of an ever-increasing and more awesome military might, whereas those persons actually charged with doing the fighting spend their time getting ready to fight. This preparation includes training, drilling, testing weapons systems, materiel, and logistics. How they later account for their combat readiness and actually demonstrate that there is such a thing as a prepared and available army, navy, or air force is contingent on the rational and bureaucratic rules and procedures they are presumed to follow and that their superiors can "objectively" evaluate. Thus, their "war between wars" is a "paper war" waged for officials, congressional committees, the news media, and for countries who serve as potential targets of attack. These organizational accounts are honored despite periodic reports that America's military forces are in a shocking state of combat readiness . . . we can rely on only a small fraction of our forces to be fully prepared at any given time" (U.P.I., March 31, 1977). It appears that a spectacular "irregularity" must occur before the image of prepared- ness and invincibility is acknowledged by military spokespersons to be an exaggeration. One such event occurred on April 14, 1977 when a Russian turbojet flew within sixty miles of American shores. One spokesperson acknowledged, "We do not have a detailed air defense system, and I assume that certain planes can penetrate it as they did in this case." Nevertheless, most accounts are accepted because the organization that generates them is also the major source of discreditable information (cf. Smith and Asher, 1977).

Periodic checks of a unit's military preparedness fulfills the organizational mandate to be viewed symbolically as an organized entity. But there is more to it. These accounts and reports also permit officers and their charges to compete with other units in their sphere of relevance, such as division, category, or class. Further, performance records provide a rational basis for assessing competence and for being used as "evidence" for or against promotions and citations.

This chapter shows how persons involved in one military setting actually viewed the organizational mandate to follow fixed procedures in documenting their combat readiness. It illustrates how the same "weapon," a U.S. Navy destroyer, performed in combat conditions and promoted its own organizational record of competence and effectiveness despite the circumstances of "being at war."

THE PURPOSE AND CONTEXT

This chapter reports on one aspect of an investigation of how petty officers and commissioned officers in the United States Navy conduct their practical affairs. The following pages describe the ways these men use rational organizational design to manage their circumstances and personal goals by determining the operational meaning of rules and procedures in everyday situations. Chapter 8 describes another dimension of the same process.

The materials of this study were drawn from research conducted (1969–71) primarily aboard one U.S. Navy Destroyer, hereafter referred to as the USS *Walden*. Additional interviews and research included personnel stationed on other ships in the same division as the USS *Walden*, as well as other persons still on active duty and some who had been separated from active duty.[1] The USS *Walden* was home-ported at a large United States naval facility in California between its scheduled cruises to the West Pacific, which lasted six to seven months. Like most of the World War II destroyers of the same class, the USS *Walden* typically carried a complement of 2 senior-grade commissioned officers, approximately 15 to 18 junior-grade commissioned officers, 18 chief petty officers, and 240 to 260 other enlisted personnel.

The USS *Walden* was one element of a division of four destroyers of the same class, and the division was one element of a squadron, composed of four divisions. The ship was under the operational command of the admiral in charge of the fleet in which the ship operated; the fleet varied depending on whether the ship was operating near its home port or deployed to the West Pacific. Like many of the older destroyers, the USS *Walden* had been "modernized" in the early 1960s and refitted with newer equipment and capabilities. Its "primary mission" was that of Anti-Submarine Warfare (ASW). However, since many of the navy ships were called on to provide "shore bombardment" during the conflict in Vietnam, the priority of this capability had been replaced with that of the gunnery operations. When the ship operated at sea near its home port, the time was spent completing a series of exercises, inspections, reviews, drills, and other forms of training to prepare the crew for the ensuing deployment to the West Pacific. Periods set aside for the maintenance and repair of the ship's equipment, as well as for various types of in-port training and inspection, accounted for time when the ship was not at sea. The important Administrative Inspection (referred to as "an Admin") was one of the crucial criteria for determining a ship's "battle readiness" and "battle efficiency." Ships in the same division and squadron competed with each other for "awards," which carried prestige for the ship's commanding officer and crew. The inspections were generally conducted when the ship was in its home port.

The formally defined objectives of the navy have been refined many times since Article I, Section 8 of the United States Constitution charged Congress with the responsibility: "To provide and maintain a navy; to make rules for the government and regulation of land and naval forces." The primary set of rules governing the activities of the navy are the *United States Navy Regulations,* although there are many additional regulations. Sufficient for our present purpose here, however, is to note that the USS *Walden* is accountable to two different chains of command. One is the "operational command," or what is called in the sociology literature the "line function," a hierarchical arrangement of fleets, squadrons, and divisions controlling the operational movements and assignments of the USS *Walden.* The other chain of command is the "type command," or what is called the "staff function," a lateral arrangement of various support functions designed to maintain the readiness of the ship's equipment and personnel training. A type commander, generally a rear admiral, promulgates various standing instructions designed to enhance a ship's battle readiness. Successfully meeting the requirements of the standing instructions, as well as successfully engaging one's "operational commitments," evaluated through the operational command, determines which ship or ships will receive various "Battle Efficiency Awards." The winning of this award is one determination of "success" for a given ship, especially for its commanding officer.

To pursue the objectives of the type commander and the operational commander, the USS *Walden* was formally organized into three departments. These were the Operations, Engineering, and Weapons Departments, each possessing sets of rules and procedures to carry out its function. Each department was headed by a junior officer, generally a lieutenant, who was directly responsible to the executive officer and commanding officer for the performance of these tasks. Each department, in turn, was organized into divisions according to the specialized functions of the department. Each division was headed by a division officer, usually an ensign or lieutenant junior grade, who was directly responsible to the department head for the completion of the specialized tasks.

Since this chapter is restricted to the consideration of the general phenomenon of "gundecking" as it applies to the Sonar Performance Report, one aspect of the maintenance of the Anti-Submarine Warfare (ASW) capability, it is concerned only with those work situations in one division of the Weapons Department.

The Everyday World of Work in the "Tin-Can Navy"

Famous historians, popular novelists, and naval folklore recite the alleged unique characteristics of the "Tin-Can Navy" (referring to destroyers and their lack of armor to protect the hull). Destroyers are the smallest ship classified as a "combatant." Thus, it is often asserted that destroyers possess a certain esprit de corps not found on larger ships. This is allegedly because the performance of the various daily tasks makes each person "indispensable," and also because certain occasions (called "special evolutions"), such as replenishments-at-sea, gunnery missions, and hi-line transfers at sea, require the services of nearly all of the ship's company regardless of their specialized rating or technical speciality. This is not to say that "goldbricking" [2] or "the philosophy of do the least" [3] (the Navy term being "skylarking") are not present. But these alternatives are just more difficult to realize, especially on such a small ship.

A fundamental feature of the processes leading to organizational competence is learning the specialized lexicon or vocabulary. This socialization involves learning the vocabulary and the situated use of the vocabulary by members in actual occasions of the everyday routine. The various branches of the military form a "natural language community," with these languages distinguishing not only the general membership categories within the community (or organization) but also subdivisions of membership. [4]

When at sea, during normal steaming operations, the USS *Walden* typically used a three-section watch bill. This meant that at any one time approximately one-third of the ship's complement designated as watch-standers (which excluded such persons as cooks, storekeepers, and yeomen) devoted their time to "standing watch." Watches were typically accomplished in four-, five-, or six-hour shifts, depending on the type of watch. This necessitated that the remainder of the ship's complement carry on the everyday working tasks without the aid of those who were "on watch." All personnel were required to "put in a full working day" between 0800 and 1615 hours, regardless of whether or not one had the midwatch the previous morning (that is, the watch from midnight to 0400).

The sequential coordination of the "normal working day" was set forth in the ship's "standing instructions." Daily modifications to this schema were promulgated in the Plan-of-the-Day (called the "Pod"), which was written by the executive officer and distributed in mimeographed form each evening for the following day. The routine working tasks could be modified by special evolutions called for in the Pod. The typical working day generally included at least one such evolution, if only for a brief "call to General Quarters" (to familiarize personnel with their assigned battle stations).

The tasks required to maintain and/or repair the ship's complex equipment and machinery were outlined in the Planned Maintenance System (PMS). This was initially operationalized as a quality control measure to insure that various preventative maintenance tasks were standardized and routinized. But in recent years, PMS had been expanded to include such mundane matters as chipping paint and swabbing passageways. The tasks were designated, for example, as a "Daily Three," which meant that this was the third maintenance procedure to be completed on a daily basis by a person of a given technical speciality. Other tasks were called a "Weekly One," a "Quarterly Two," a "Semi-Annual Two," and so on. Upon completion of a given task, the worker was required to fill out a form to his superior. The task was then marked off on the "working calendar," which delineated the scheduling of the PMS tasks to be accomplished by a given technical specialty. These forms would be mailed from the ship to the appropriate facility at regular intervals. Several months later, the ship would receive a computer readout of all of its accomplished tasks in order to have an adequate chronology of its maintenance work. Copies of this readout also went to the relevant type and operational commanders, and comparisons of "total man hours" of PMS work for a ship and its "sister ships" in the division and squadron were often used as an indication of a ship's "battle readiness" or "battle efficiency." There were some routine tasks on the *Walden*, as well as many repair tasks, which were not covered under PMS; but for the purposes of recording the man-hours there were a number of general or residual categories under which these tasks could be classified for computer coding.

After a brief discussion of the general phenomenon of "gundecking" in the navy, the remainder of this chapter concentrates on the specialized tasks of the ASW Division on the USS *Walden* as they relate to the Sonar Performance Report.

GUNDECKING

There is some disagreement about the origin of the term "gundecking" in the navy, but substantial evidence suggests that its meaning is widely shared as common inside knowledge.[5] Further evidence suggests that its meaning, if not its use, is increasingly shared by more and more people. Webster's *Dictionary* defines the term:

> **gundeck**—to fake or falsify esp. by writing up (as a series of official reports) as if meeting requirements but actually without having carried out the required procedures (e.g., gundecking the daily reports on the night before an inspection).

Although navy personnel are familiar with the "literal meaning" of the concept, there are important qualifications. From a recorded interview with a junior officer(s):

> **Au.:** What does it mean to you? How do you define it?
>
> **S:** Well, gundecking, is, ah, the job that you know, but that you don't actually go ahead and perform the job, you just go ahead and write the results down without performing the job. Remember, is that what I said before?
>
> **Au.:** Yeah, I think so. Okay, what would be an example from something involved in your job?
>
> **S:** Let's say I was supposed to go out and check certain areas or talk to certain people, but I already know what the results are going to be, so rather than do that I just go ahead and mark down the results, and then hand in the results. I haven't done the job but I've given you the results
>
> **Au.:** Okay, one thing I wondered about is—are there other times when gundecking is something other than a complete falsification of a report?
>
> **S:** Oh yeah, probably most of the time gundecking doesn't involve a *complete* falsification—I mean, you generally have a pretty good idea that everything's okay before you gundeck.
>
> **Au.:** What would be an example?
>
> **S:** Well, let's take my Hull Reports, for example. In the last three years I've probably gundecked half of the entries—you know, things like the lockers and magazines that I knew were all

right anyway. I didn't have to go down into the magazines every week to know that they were okay—you know, what in the hell can change in a magazine in the space of a week? Especially when you're in-port and nobody every goes down there, except the striker who checks the temperature gauges. If there was any change he'd probably recognize it before I would anyway. On the other hand, it kind of depends on whether or not there's any flack going on about Hull Reports. You know, if you've been in-port for a while and the Old Man's on the rag about something, and the JO's [Junior Officers] are catching a lot of flack about their jobs, then you have to be a little more careful. But, hell, when you're overseas and doing a lot of operating, then I'm sure that all of the JO's gundeck most of the entries on their Hull Reports, because they know there won't be any check because everybody is so busy . . . including the Old Man and the Exec. You know that there isn't any chance of getting caught, you've got nothing to lose by doing it. Some things you wouldn't gundeck are things of major significance.

Au.: Well, what's the crucial variable there, I mean, in other words, why would you gundeck some things and not others?

S: Well, it just depends on its significance, you know, it's how you evaluate how important something is. I think that say, ah, a prefiring check before a gun shoot is more important than a Hull Report, and more, you know, more specifically, some checks are more important than others. It depends on the situation.

Another junior officer on the *Walden* comments:

Au.: First of all, how would you define gundecking?

S: Umm [short pause] . . . that would be, ah, falsifying a document for the purposes of having the paperwork there, ah, [pause] . . . necessary completion of the paperwork without the corresponding real, the actual work being done.

Au.: Is it always a complete falsification?

S: No, most of the time you don't go on blind faith. It depends on the situation. It depends. It's not a complete falsification, but it *can be*. It depends.

Au.: What does it depend on?

S: It depends on, for me, it depends on my judgment, my decision as to the real value of the report, or the document.

Au.: What do you mean by the 'real value'?

S: What I decide the value to be. It really depends on the situation. It's hard to generalize about even one report, because there can be different considerations depending on the situation. Depends on how vital I consider it to be to my job, or whether I think it's just a useless piece of paperwork, and ah, busy-work type stuff.... It's such an individual thing, I don't know. I've never really thought much about it, I just do it.

Au.: Well, do you think you're the only one who does it?

S: [Laughing] No, I know I'm not the only one, but ... [pause] I might be the only one who does it the way I do it. Put somebody else in my position and he'd probably gundeck quite a bit, but he might not gundeck exactly the same things I do. In other words, his judgment about what would be necessary and what would be trivial might not be the same as mine.

An electronics technician:

Au.: Well, do you ever gundeck anything each and every single time?

S: No, I don't really think so. It depends on a number of things, probably one of the most important things has to do with whether or not I think there's any chance of being checked up on. For ET's, the only real sweat is the Chief, 'cause your Division Officer usually doesn't know enough to check on your work.

Evidence is persuasive, then, that gundecking "depends on the situation," and that "the situation" is an important determinant of the "reasonableness" of it, that is, of whether or not the situation seems to "call for" gundecking an official report.

Before analyzing some important features of the situation that warrant the gundecking of the Sonar Performance Report as a reasonable organizational activity, here are several estimations of the extent to which knowledge of gundecking is shared.

I'd say that before PMS began only the officers and most of the leading Petty Officers knew about it, that, well, anyone who had to do a lot of paperwork as part of his job, or who had to handle a lot of chits on an everyday basis. Since PMS I think probably everyone in the navy knows what gundecking is, even the lowest Seaman Deuce; that is, anybody who's been out of boot camp for more than a week.

Hell, I don't know. I assume that *everybody* knows what it is. I don't see how you could be in the navy for more than a couple of days without knowing what gundecking is.

These comments and others suggest that gundecking is widely shared among navy personnel and that it "depends on the situation." The following section details some practical reasons that lead to the "reasonableness" of gundecking official reports.

PRACTICAL REASONS FOR GUNDECKING

Battle Efficiency and the "ASW E"

One major criteria of "success" for a ship was its competition for Battle Efficiency Awards, although, assuredly, the meaning of this varied greatly among the personnel on the *Walden*. The most prestigious award was the "Battle E"; it was awarded to only one ship in the squadron (four divisions of destroyers) during a given competitive period. A ship deserving the "Battle E" was thought to be successful not only in terms of the criteria constituting success for the lesser awards but was also considered exceptional in meeting "operational commitments." This meant the ship had earned a reputation for proficiency in battle-related activities above and beyond the routine measures of success set forth in administrative instructions. During times of peace, this "battle-related success" was determined through a complex set of at-sea experiences involving all battle capabilities. In times of war, such as during the Vietnam years, this generally involved a successful engagement of some unusual or out-of-the-ordinary mission while in or near Vietnam.[6] To a large extent the opportunity to engage in such an unusual activity was beyond the volition of the ship's commanding officer or operational commander. A prevailing folk theory was that being a commanding officer of a destroyer was a necessary condition for a "straight line officer" to be promoted to flag rank. Thus, being the commanding officer of a ship awarded the "Battle E" was thought to be a sufficient condition for realizing that goal.[7]

In addition to the "Battle E," several other Battle Efficiency Awards were given, not to a ship as such but rather to the various departments of a ship. These were the "Operations E," the "Engineering E," the "Gunnery E," and the "ASW E," all determined by standardized criteria. The winners of these awards were determined through a competitive process. For these awards, however, unlike the "Battle E" awarded to only one ship in sixteen, it was theoretically possible for all four ships in a division to be awarded, for example, the "Gunnery E." The awards were based on cumulative scores on inspections. The administrative inspection was the most important. Generally, the four destroyers in a division would "take turns" in giving the administrative inspection to each other.

Successful competition for battle efficiency awards on a ship such as the *Walden* necessitated the construction of an immensely complex collection of records, the routine collection, production, and use of which constituted one essential feature of the organizational setting. These records, which were collected and produced about many different aspects of the organization, provided a basis for demonstrating to the various inspectors of the ship's accounts the fact that the everyday affairs had been conducted in accordance with the relevant rules and procedures. Not all "pieces of paper" were regarded as being of equal importance, as shall be seen; but in one way or another, all the paperwork collected and produced was seen as part of the routine everyday "work" of the persons doing it. Personnel were typically "evaluated" in part by their ability to produce such documentation. This research, however, suggests that many strategies are employed in the management of these practices, as well as a diversity of their meanings.

The ASW Division aboard the USS *Walden* operated and maintained all of the antisubmarine warfare equipment. This included the ship's two sonar systems, on which the remainder of the equipment systems depended; the "hull-mounted" sonar, located on the keel of the ship; and the "variable depth sonar," which could be lowered or "streamed" at considerable depths while at sea to provide a capability for penetrating the various thermal layers of the ocean. Maintaining these complex electronic systems entailed considerable technical expertise. The sonarmen charged with these responsibilities were among the more skilled technicians in the navy. Nearly all of the routine work tasks were outlined in the Planned Maintenance System (PMS) in terms of steps, theoretically to be completed "by the number," supposedly sufficient for insuring the continued operational efficiency of the equipment.

The sonarmen and torpedomen composing the ASW Division were supervised by the ASW Officer. This billet was typically occupied by a junior officer with fewer than two years of active duty service and possessing little or no knowledge of the complex electronic systems for which he was formally responsible. Generally speaking, the sonar technicians constructed the accounts providing demonstration that the technical aspects of their tasks had been accomplished in accord with the relevant procedures of the organization.

The temporal coordination of these various routines was always difficult and sometimes impossible to maintain in a smooth, consistent fashion. This was the case especially when the *Walden* was at sea and the normal working day included so many disruptions. These other than normal situations significantly altered the tasks of the ASW personnel, especially when the *Walden* was involved in long periods of battle operations in Vietnam, when some of the sonarmen and torpedomen were called on as substitutes for gunnery personnel. From the point of view of the ASW officer, the primary working tasks involved the people necessary for constructing the accountability of those tasks; "doing his job" assumed an ability to demonstrate, when called on to do so, the (recorded) "facts" of this accomplishment. His knowledge that he was personally accountable to others motivated an interest in maintaining a trouble-free development of this accountability. For the sonarmen, the "by-the-numbers" procedures in the PMS program "was just so much baloney." These procedures were thought to be unrelated to the "real needs" of keeping the equipment in an operational condition. They perceived their watch-standing duties (especially when assigned watches unrelated to the ASW functions), their extratechnical duties (such as their turn to swab the decks), and much of the paperwork as an infringement on the time needed to "do their job with the gear." Having knowledge of the practical circumstances of the ASW officer's tasks, sonarmen frequently employed strategies to insure a certain "evenness" in the flow of reports of accountability, given their knowledge of the appropriate amount for the situation, which could vary depending on the degree to which ASW was being emphasized. On the other hand, the ASW officer often employed his physical absence from the working spaces of the technicians as a kind of "strategy of nonsupervision," to allow them to accomplish tasks in an unfettered manner.

An Important Task for the "ASW E"

It is not possible to detail all of the practical exigencies of the working tasks of the ASW personnel in this brief chapter. But a more detailed consideration will be given to one important requisite—the tasks involved in taking a noise level measurement of the ship's hull-mounted sonar system. This task, which is a routine maintenance task outlined in the PMS program, also is very important because it requires, in addition to the routine documentation, the sending of a "Sonar Performance Report" in a classified message format to higher authority. It is one of perhaps only ten or twelve such reports that *routinely* leave the ship in this fashion; its routine character is established reflexively by referring to the "standing instructions" of the type commander that requires it. This report is important because persons in high governmental positions must be informed about the operational status of the fleet's antisubmarine warfare capabilities and battle readiness, much of which depends on the operational efficiency of the sonar systems employed on various vehicles as the primary sensors of an enemy submarine threat. Competent organizational actors in the lower echelons of such record-producing agencies also understand, however, that these reports represent not only the organizational activities supposedly "made to happen" in accordance with standardized procedures; in addition the fact of their submission in the typical temporal sequence documents the organizational acumen of the people producing these reports. The potential evaluational uses of such documents constitute an important feature of "what any competent actor knows" about the taken-for-granted workings of the formal organization. In this case, which involves taking a sonar noise level measurement and documenting it in the Sonar Performance Report, it was known that the use of this report was important in subsequently determining both battle efficiency and the awarding of the "ASW E." Competent actors assumed they would be called on to document that they had conducted these affairs in an efficient manner.

The sonar noise level measurement is an attempt to measure the amount of noise put into the water by the ship's machinery and electronic equipment as a function of a given speed of the ship through the water. The measurement also necessarily includes some noise introjected into the water by the many persons moving on the ship engaged in their normal working routines, which often entailed using electrical or mechanical tools. The complex procedures to provide for this measurement cannot be mentioned in detail here. It is sufficient to mention that the task calls not only for a "by-the-number" process involving relatively simple readings of electronics test equipment that sonarmen are accustomed to using in their work, but also other coordinative contingencies involving a number of the ship's personnel for whom this measurement is not a matter of daily routine (such as many engineering personnel required to monitor the fuel and engineering systems during the many speed changes required for the measurement). The procedures also call for, at least in their literal meaning, a stopping of the normal work routines of most of the remainder of the ship's personnel for several hours. What is of crucial importance is that the "routineness" of the measurement must be renegotiated on a situation-to-situation basis in terms of the reasonable judgments of the variously situated personnel involved. This particular task of taking a noise level measurement represents a routine, taken-for-granted working task, requiring no out of the ordinary efforts on the part of the ASW personnel. From the perspective of the engineering personnel, however, the measurement represents what they term "a real pain in the ass," in spite of its routine occurrence in the setting. The situation required that the reasonableness of the various judgments involve an understanding of "how it all fits together." This emergent definition of the situation is sometimes made to happen by the commanding officer's tactics of compromise in an effort to construct order from the differing social definitions proffered by the ASW Officer and the Engineering Officer. As shall be seen later, these organizationally competent actors must orient their activities to the negotiable routine in terms of "what is known" about the ship's operational situation.

The procedures informing individuals about the measurement specified that the results were to be reported by a given deadline and were to leave the ship in a classified message format. A necessary condition for constructing compliance was that the ship had to be at sea, which was not always the case for a ship within the specified time period. The formal procedures further specified, therefore, that if the ship were not at sea during a given reporting period, or for some other understandable reason could not comply with the procedures, then it was proper to submit documentation to that effect in the same manner as one would report the results of the measurement if it had been accomplished. *What is important is that failure to accomplish compliance with the lexical meaning of the formal procedures was NOT sanctionable in the terms of the formal organizational schema, at least as long as the report was properly submitted detailing the "noncompliance."*

Thus, if the "literal application" of the procedures is taken to mean the "normal" or "proper" use of the formal organizational schema, with no considerations of the "extenuating circumstances," then other uses of the formal schema would have to be deemed "pathological" or "improper" alternatives. This obscures the fact that such alternatives may be competent uses of the formal schema informed by the reasonable judgments of the exigencies of the practical situation.

"Throwing in a Fudge Factor"

Measuring the ship's sonar performance entailed stopping the normal working day for nearly all personnel on the USS *Walden*, whether or not they were actually involved in the processes of the measurement itself; most of them were not. This was necessary in order to reduce to the minimum the noise on the ship. But the ASW personnel considered that the measurement could be accomplished in a sufficient-for-all-practical-purposes manner without the necessity of requesting so many of their fellow shipmates to disrupt their tasks for several hours. Also, although "the letter" of the formal procedures called for shutting off all the electrical equipment in the ship's kitchens and galleys, the ASW personnel considered this unnecessary. There were other occasions when either the operational commitments of the ship precluded the possibility of making the sonar performance measurements at speeds that required greater and greater amounts of fuel (which might be needed for other occasions), or when the requirement for the engineers to "bring all four boilers on the line" would entail a great deal of inconvenience for them, possibly causing serious delays in their everyday maintenance routines.[8] This meant that the measurements were only accomplished for the lesser speeds, with the ASW personnel "sketching in" those for the higher speeds using a common-sense extrapolation based on the measurements taken at the lower speeds. That these practical exigencies called for relatively minor modifications of "the letter" of the formal procedures reflected the practical interests of the ASW personnel in maintaining a social environment in which they did not "catch flack" from their shipmates for an "inappropriate" disruption of the normal routines. It also reflected their knowledge that this was indeed an important consideration, given "what anyone knows" about sustaining a cooperative atmosphere for social relationships in such a physically confining setting.

For the purposes of reporting the *Walden's* sonar performance measurement in the Sonar Performance Report when practical circumstances such as these prevailed, the ASW personnel would alter the measurement readings in a relatively minor fashion in terms of their common-sense extrapolation of what they thought would be a "reasonable" factor representing the noise put into the water by, for example, the fact that the equipment in the galley was not shut off during the measurement. They spoke of these activities as "throwing in a fudge factor," or "fudging," in order that the report would reflect the "real" measurements of the efficiency of the sonar system. As the *Walden's* ASW Officer stated:

> S: And even though [the noise level measurements] wasn't a particularly difficult job for us—you know, just having a couple of ST's on the bridge with head sets [sound-powered telephones] and a couple of guys in the equipment room reading the test equipment; the coordination of the damn thing was always a hassle. I always wanted to take the readings right up to [the maximum speed of the ship] and Troxell [the Engineering Officer] always seemed to interpret this as if I wanted to sabotage his whole department. From his point of view, the measurements were, well, I must admit that I understood his situation. Bringing four boilers on the line *did* entail a fantastic amount of extra work for his people. And it was work that wasn't too related to his primary jobs. And, not only *that,* you have to understand that this was only one special evolution which involved Engineering. The snipes also ran into the same problems with everyone else who needed their help to do some little measurement or exercise. Seemed like Troxell was always involved with someone in some kind of hassle about his men. That could have been partially because of the kind of guy he was though. . . . Let's face it, we all know that nobody's going to find a submarine on sonar at [the maximum speed of the ship] anyway—maybe not even if you'd run over it on the surface—so I was usually happy just to take the readings to [the maximum speed at two boilers]. . . .
>
> Au.: What about the people in the Supply Department? Same story there?
>
> S: Yeah, same thing. The pork chops could really give a [damn] about a sonar noise level measurement. Don't blame them really. I know that I don't have much interest in many of the things that go on aboard the ship. All you have to do is ask 'em to shut down the galleys for a couple of hours and they start screaming. Even worse than the snipes, I think. We actually put the Quiet Ship Bill into effect once for the measurements. About a week later we discovered that we were

having a little difficulty, you might say, in processing our [forms requesting spare parts from storage], the Sonarmen began getting all of the torn sheets, and our watch standers were booted from the head of the chow line. . . . You eventually learn all of these things, you learn what it is that other people have to do as a part of their job, and you learn to do your own job in order to avoid a war aboard the ship at the same time you're trying to fight one. . . .

A former Engineering Officer on the *Walden* comments:

S: Sure, I knew that the noise level measurements required [the maximum speed of the ship], but I also know that the people at CINCPAC, or Washington, or wherever it is that the report goes, know that the story is with the plants [the engineering equipment] on these old cans. It's not only that [the maximum speed at four boilers] would probably shake these babies apart at the seams, it's also that these plants require many more man-hours for maintenance and repair. . . . I suspect that there are damn few [class of ship similar to *Walden*] class ships which could put four boilers on the line at any given time, even though there may be only one or two [name of a report used to inform superiors of a major boiler casualty] outstanding in the entire Fleet at any one time. Everybody knows this. I'm sure the guys who read those sonar reports understand the situation with the engineering set-ups on these old cans. They'd have to. The guys who are now on tours in the Pentagon aren't that dumb. They were here doing the job I'm doing not too many years ago.

All of these Tin Cans are different. Take the, well, ah, even though the [*Walden's* class] and the [another class of Destroyers], come under the same regulations which govern DD's [Destroyers], there's a difference of twenty-five years there in construction dates, and that means one hell of a lot when you're reading reports that have to do with the engineering plants on these ships. . . . I'm sure that the guys reading the sonar reports understand these things as well as those who are collecting all of our engineering stuff. . . .

It can be seen that modifying "the letter" of the formal procedures in terms of competent members' sense of maintaining the organizational normal working day requires reasonable judgment of relevancies for determining *what it takes* to make the measurement while maintaining *business as usual*. The *intent* of the formal organizational procedures for the sonar noise level measurements, then, is thought to be followed *in terms of the members' understandings of what it takes to maintain the "normal working day" for those men situated at other positions in the organization.*

As indicated in the comments by the *Walden's* Engineering Officer, the "markings" or "traces" on organizational reports are *not* regarded as unproblematic. This indicates that part of what is involved in developing organizational competence is *learning how to read such documents;* that is, learning what such markings stand for, refer to, or mean within the context of the report. In this instance, for example, it can be seen that the same "markings" on two pieces of paper presumably representing the "same" report may mean something entirely different, given a member's inside understanding of the class or type of ship involved.

"Juggling the Numbers": Practicalities and Priorities

A division of four destroyers usually leaves the United States for the ships' six- or seven-month Westpac Deployment at the same time. Often ships of the same division will be assigned the same "operational commitment" once they arrive in Southeast Asia. When this occurs, the commodore of the division plays an important role in assigning and coordinating the assignments and operations of the ships in the division. He usually plays an important role in monitoring the effectiveness of "his" ships through the collection of various documents and reports, from both the standardized competitive exercises and inspections as well as from those which may originate from other sources. When operating near the land areas of Southeast Asia, it is impossible literally to comply with the formal procedures of the sonar noise level measurement because the water is too shallow to permit a measurement uncontaminated by sound reverberations from the ocean floor. Thus, each ship will usually be detached from its operational duties for as many hours as are necessary for the ship to reach open sea, conduct the measurements, and return to its former position.

As stated earlier, the formal procedures included provisions for submitting an "unable to comply" report as an alternative to submitting the measurements obtained in the Sonar Performance Report. This report would include a brief statement of the "reasons" for this, and submission of such an "unable to comply" report entailed no formal sanctions. The officers and ASW personnel on the USS *Walden,* however, believed that submitting a proper report showed both a professional concern for and efficient accomplishment of the many tasks necessary for maintaining the operational readiness of the ship's primary ASW capability.

Anti-Submarine Warfare (ASW)

On one occasion during its deployment, the USS *Walden* was the fourth ship of the division to be detached from its assigned mission for several hours to conduct its noise level measurements. Several of the ship's officers knew that the other three ships had successfully conducted their measurements and had reported the results to their appropriate superiors with a message transmitted over the radio-teletype circuits. On this occasion, the USS *Walden* had a mechanical casualty to one of its boilers. This state typically required a message report to various superiors. But one had not been submitted because members believed that such casualty reports were taken to evaluate the professional competence of the commanding officer. This is not an atypical occurrence. Knowing that the present commitments required the use of no more than two of the ship's four boilers, it was decided that the ship would conduct the noise level measurements at lower speeds and then "guesstimate" the measurements for higher speeds for the purpose of the report. As the *Walden* began the measurements, it was discovered that the electronic test equipment needed to take the readings was not operative, rendering even an approximation of the measurements impossible. It was perceived that revealing either of these facts could possibly cause embarrassment to the commanding officer. Of much greater concern, at least from the commanding officer's point of view, however, was that such a revelation could subsequently cause the *Walden* to be reassigned to the nearest naval facility for repairs to the equipment. Reassigment would not only eliminate the ship from its competitive position vis-à-vis the other ships of the division in meeting its battle-related commitments, which was of greatest importance, but it could also entail the construction of documentary evidence possessing a potential evaluational use by those to whom the commodore was accountable for the operational performance of "his" ships. Thus, since there was no evidence or suspicion on the part of any of the ASW personnel that the sonar system was any less efficient than it had been the month before, it was thought that this (potential) "trouble" could be avoided by "gundecking" the Sonar Performance Report. This was accomplished by "juggling the numbers a little" from the previous report, in order to avoid detection, and submitting the figures as if the ship had actually followed the required procedures. As the ASW Officer commented on this situation:

> **S:** This was unquestionably one of the tighter situations we ever had with the noise levels. There were several other times when we were at sea, about ready to begin the measurements, when we would discover that our test equipment wasn't in calibration, or would discover some other casualty, but, at least when we were steaming in Eastpac [near the United States], that wasn't all that big a deal because we would postpone them to another time. Then we would—
>
> **Au.:** Were problems with test equipment common, or uncommon or...?

S: Yes, they were fairly common actually. I'd say, well [pause], I guess that maybe half the time in the three years I was the ASW Officer I had serious reservations about the test equipment. The reason was that it took so long to get it calibrated. You couldn't really afford to send it to the lab unless you were sure that the ship would be in-port for about two months, and nobody on a DD could *ever* be sure of that! [Laughs] When my leading ST would have some doubts about the gear, he'd usually check it out with a similar piece which the ET's [Electronic Technicians] had, but there were a number of times when we couldn't really be sure that some unusually high readings we had taken were due to the sonar system or the test equipment. . . .

That time when we had been detached by the Commodore from our shore bombardment mission to take the noise levels really made me a little nervous, I'm tellin' you. That whole cruise, the one we made with the other ships in our Division, seemed to go like that, though, from one crisis to another, with each CO constantly trying to "one-up" the others. The next one we made didn't go anything like that. It was really smooth by comparison. That's because we steamed with [number of another Division of Destroyers] all the time. But that first one was really something. We'd had the "ASW E" for four consecutive years, and were shooting for the gold one [awarded to the ship on the fifth consecutive achievement of a battle efficiency award]. The pressure was really on. The Commanding Officer's major concern at the time wasn't the "ASW E," I don't think, in fact, I'm sure it wasn't. He was more interested in keeping us on the Shorebom missions, where the action was, so to speak, and not having us transferred back to [the Philippines] for repairs. . . .

From a legalist or functionalist perspective, this example gives the appearance of a clearcut case of rule violation or "noncompliance." In fact, from this brief description, it can be seen that the organizational actors sensed the "deviant" nature of gundecking. But the "deviancy" of this instance of gundecking is established only in terms of the perceptions of those involved. In fact, gundecking is judged by them as a reasonable course of action in terms of the perceived consequences that might result from another use of the organizational schema. By constructing the appearance of formal compliance (the *intent* of which the ASW personnel believed they had accomplished, that is, having maintained an operationally efficient sonar system), the "troubles" perceived to potentially follow from a *literal usage* of the organization were avoided in order to get back to the bigger business of meeting battle-related commitments. These commitments were considered by most of the organizational members as the reason that justified the sacrifices of such a long deployment.

Covering Your Ass

As mentioned previously, the USS *Walden* had two sonar systems. One was mounted on the keel of the ship and the other was located on the main deck at the rear of the ship and could be lowered into the water at various depths while the ship was underway. This system provided the ship with a sonar system capable of penetrating the thermal layers of the ocean. The Variable Depth Sonar (VDS), as it was called, was used very infrequently. As a result of several collisions between the VDS sonar being streamed and U.S. Navy submarines, its use has been severely restricted by many official procedures. Many of these policies had been promoted by men in the submarine service.

Maintaining the primary sonar system entailed continual minor repairs and replacement of various parts. These parts, most of which were electrical components, were kept in stock on the *Walden;* the most frequently used parts were stocked in greater numbers. When a given part was needed to make a minor repair to the sonar system, the typical procedures called for the sonar technician to fill out the appropriate form at the supply office and for one of the supply department personnel to take the form and retrieve the requested part from one of the ship's many storerooms. Then the supply personnel would use this same form to reorder the part from the appropriate facility, in order to maintain an adequate stock of repair parts. When the ship was deployed overseas, however, the periods between replenishments (either in port or at sea) often exceeded the frequency with which the sonar technicians needed certain parts to meet the practical demands of their repair work and to preserve their sense of accomplishing their tasks in a proficient manner. To meet the exigent circumstances of repairing the hull-mounted sonar and to sustain this sense of proficient job accomplishment among the technicians involved in this activity, there was a tacit understanding between the sonar technicians and their division officer to the effect that, if certain electrical parts were needed to maintain the peak performance of the sonar system, and if these parts were not presently in stock aboard the ship, then parts would be taken from the Variable Depth Sonar for use in the primary sonar system. This procedure was called "cannibalizing" by the technicians. Although they clearly understood the explicit "unofficiality" of these practices, they were systematically used to manage certain kinds of contingencies with the knowledge that the official restrictions regarding the use of the Variable Depth Sonar were so great that the chances were exceptionally small that they would be called upon to account for its operational efficiency. Considerable care was exercised to keep these practices "under cover," perceiving official sanctions to follow from public disclosure.

Although these covert practices were sufficient most of the time, on one occasion the *Walden* was called on to conduct a sonar noise level measurement on its variable depth sonar and to submit the results to the commodore of the division. The commodore was then riding on one of the ships steaming in company with the *Walden*. Since some of the essential electrical components of the VDS had been "cannibalized" to provide repair parts for the other sonar system (although this was not obvious from any outward appearances of the equipment), it was not possible to construct literal compliance with the organizational procedures. In this situation, the ASW personnel "went through the motions" of compliance, and the ASW Officer and the chief sonarman gundecked a sonar performance report based on the figures from the previous measurement. They submitted the report to the commanding officer who in turn forwarded the information to the commodore of the division.

As the man who was the leading sonar technician during this occasion comments:

> S: That was probably one of the funniest noise levels we ever took. Even though I told Nash [the ASW Officer] when we planned this out there wouldn't be any trouble pulling it off—because I knew [the Commanding Officer] wouldn't come down to the sonar equipment room and couldn't even read a voltmeter if he did—he was really sweatin' it out. Nash was running around like a chicken with his head cut off.... Really incredible, all those people involved in taking the measurements when we were actually covering ourselves for cannibalizing the VDS for the hull-mounted. At that late date in the cruise I wouldn't have been surprised if everyone on the three ships wasn't doing the same thing.... In fact, I later met Erwin off [another ship in the Division] at the EM Club [Enlisted Men's Club] one night after we got back, and he said they'd been doing the same thing the whole cruise. It's the only way you can keep the gear up [operative], with the supply system as [messed up] as it is.... We'd never have to do this in Eastpac, because we can aways get the parts we need, even if we have to cumshaw them [loosely, "borrow"]....

The ASW Officer comments on the situation:

> S: That's the only time we ever had to do that, thank God! I mean, we've completely gundecked the reports, before, like the other time I told you about, but [the Commanding Officer] was usually in on the situation with us. This was strictly a case where the ST's had been cannibalizing the gear in the VDS for several months, knowing full well that the restrictions on using the goddamn contraption were so fantastic that we hardly ever got a chance to stream it. I knew about the situation. I knew about it and didn't know about it, know what I mean? [Laughs]

> I could've mentioned it to [the Commanding Officer] long ago, but that would have put him on the spot. . . .
>
> **Au.:** What do you mean?
>
> **S:** Well, officially at least, he would have then been forced to submit a [report noting an equipment casualty], and you always try to avoid that unless it's completely impossible. . . . So we had to cover ourselves, just like everyone has to do in this outfit. "Cover your ass with paper," isn't that the old adage? Went smooth as silk too, I might add. . . .

Once again, if one were to think of social action as rule-governed (or normative) activity, implied throughout various structural and functional perspectives in studying deviance or organizational behavior, this example might suggest an instance of rule violation, or noncompliance. And again, some merit to that interpretation is even suggested by the covert nature with which the ASW personnel managed these "under the table" practices. To dismiss this example as being atypical, however, as only to be found on rare occasions in formal organizations and as having no greater theoretical importance other than being "an interesting exception to the rule" obscures the critical issue of how organizationally competent actors methodically employ such "unofficial practices" to deal with certain practical exigencies, which, from their point of view, cannot be reconciled through the literal use of the "official" organization schema and its rules *at least if they are to preserve their sense of satisfactory job accomplishment.*

In this example, the ASW personnel perceived the primary consideration to be the maintenance of the primary sonar system. This objective, incidentally, was also regarded with greater importance by others as well as in the organizational rules. To avoid the potential "troubles" perceived as concomitants of the inability to accomplish this task, the covert or unofficial practices were employed to solve the problems arising out of the exigent situations within the supply system. These exigencies were indeed difficult to deal with through the "normal" use of the organizational routines, as seen by the ASW personnel. Utilizing the "unofficial routine" of cannibalizing one piece of sonar equipment to accomplish what they see as the most important tasks was one method of providing a socially meaningful and orderly routine to which they could orient themselves. This preserved a sense of accomplishment which comes, for some people, from the knowledge of "doing what it takes" in a given situation in order to be regarded by others as a "competent bureaucratic actor," a "can-do" person.

Viewed from this perspective, the actions of the ASW personnel in "going through the motions" of literal compliance and the gundecking of the official report can be interpreted as an instance of "covering your ass," to use the members' term. "Covering your ass," in this example, involved the systematic and competent use of the organizational rules for the purpose of validating and sustaining the "unofficial practices" that dealt with the exigent practical circumstances. It was a routine that worked sufficiently for the circumstances.

THE PROBLEMATICS OF GUNDECKING

As these data and comments suggest, gundecking a Sonar Performance Report may indeed be a reasonable use of the formal rules when seen from the participants' perspective. The propriety of the practice is determined by the exigencies of the situation in which they find themselves. These situations may involve the use of a "compromise," or a partial gundecking of the report ("throwing in a fudge factor"), to sustain the normal working day for those people situated at other positions in the organization. When seen in this light, gundecking is their way of constructing the larger social order of the USS *Walden* when the lexical use of the formal procedures would presumably lead to disruption. The situations may involve the overt gundecking ("juggling the numbers"), as when members' reasoning and judgment lead them to conclude that the intent of the organizational schema will be served more effectively by doing what is necessary to remain on a scene (near Vietnam) perceived to possess a higher priority among the various organizational goals. In this light, gundecking is a kind of "mini-max" strategy to construct the larger social order of the Vietnam conflict, a strategy determined by the members' judgments of the priorities of the situation. Or, the situations may involve the covert or "unofficial" use of gundecking by the members ("covering your ass") to deal with certain practical exigencies arising out of their everyday routines, which cannot be reconciled through the literal usage of the organizational schema. In such situations, gundecking is seen to preserve the members' sense of satisfactorily accomplishing their work. At any rate, the successful accomplishment of gundecking as a practical matter is *not* one of the "givens" of the situation. It is a largely problematic endeavor.

In the situations analyzed here, gundecking was seen to require the cooperation and coordination of team-work. As such, gundecking could never be one of the givens of the situation, but is instead *fundamentally problematic*. That is, as a product of the participants' reasoning and judgment, gundecking must necessarily be negotiated and renegotiated on a situation-to-situation basis in terms of individuals' perceptions of the situation. Such situations also involve, to a large extent, considerations of the unique characteristics of the persons as members of the team or audience. As situations and persons change over time, the meaning of gundecking practices must necessarily be renegotiated by the members in terms of their knowledge and perceptions of the situation. Because successful gundecking is as much a result of the people who receive it as of those who initiate it, it makes little sense, at least for the purposes of sociological theorizing, to contend that it is ever "structurally determined."

Gundecking involves presenting the appearance of orderly situations (presumably what the report is taken to stand for) by organizational members. As experienced by the participants, however, the situations often involve contingencies that could not be adequately covered by any set of formal rules, no matter how complex and intricate. Any given instance of gundecking, therefore, is necessarily problematic to its practitioners because of their *incomplete knowledge* of the reactions of the audience (the persons to whom the report is sent); the fact that they can never be sure that those who will receive their gundecked report will understand the situational contingencies of such an activity in the same manner as the members. That is, a report that is sufficient for all practical purposes at one point in the organization may not be sufficient for the practical purposes of other purposes at another point in the organization at the same time. Given a conflict of perceptions among organizational members in such matters, this may mean that the report will be renegotiated.

Also, a report deemed sufficient at one time may, at some later date, be redefined as insufficient. A contemporary example that reached the mass media were the official reports of the My Lai Massacre. In this case, the reports that accounted for the military actions at My Lai to those people in higher positions were (presumably) sufficient at that time. Eighteen months later, following an entrepreneurial initiative taken by a person who was not a member of the military organization, the reports were redefined as insufficient for the practical purposes of the new situation. Members who had demonstrated their organizational competence in the initial issuing of these reports were subsequently redefined as "incompetent" and were threatened with prosecution. Membership in military organizations often includes an understanding that such redefinitions of the situation may occur; this is another problematic feature of gundecking practices. Members commonly perceive that such actions may happen "for political reasons."

GUNDECKING AS PROPAGANDA

Rather than merely an example of noncompliance with organizational rules and procedures, gundecking an official report may be seen as competent use of the formal schema when viewed from the members' perspective. This suggests that discrepancy between how an organization "ought" to operate and how it in fact "is" operating cannot be dismissed as merely "incompetency," "inefficiency," "not following rules," and the like. Rather, since the rules themselves are not sensitive to the realities of the contexts they are intended to rationally direct, there will necessarily be a discrepancy between official prescriptions and words on the one hand, and the actual deeds on the other hand. One reason for this lack of fit is the inability of planners and others to recognize the great problem with guiding a series of events that are influenced by situational, emotional, unpredictable, and very human concerns with specific steps of operations. As this research shows, it is simply not practical to follow the rules given other priorities, such as fighting a war, getting promoted, and so forth. It is not enough to argue that these priorities should not be involved in day-to-day conduct; nor is it enough to try to frighten people into avoiding these practical considerations. Indeed, virtually any time that a complete investigaion is undertaken of the *Walden's* activities, that of other ships, or for that matter *any activity presumed to be run according to specifiable rules*, great discrepancies will be found. Exposing gaps between the "ought" and the "is" will make great headlines, will get some people in trouble, and will promote alliances between future investigators and those investigated. It will spawn more outcries for congressional investigations, closer scrutiny, and the like, but even these committees, and investigative units are likely to be faced with similar situations.

Despite the almost universal practical use of rules and official directives and the widespread recognition that such practices are absolutely essential, the final reports will seldom reflect this context of meaning. Instead, people will act as though their procedures fit the rules, as though the "ought" and the "is" are compatible. If people are unfamiliar with the context of the activities, and with the context of completing reports that may be used to sanction an individual or group, they will be misled because the reports will be partially true but very invalid portraits of the reality of the actual situation. Nevertheless, the reports, documents, and other bits of sanctionable evidence within our rational approach to research and argumentation will be used as though they are reflections of reality. As noted in chapter 1, such reports may be used by an individual or a committee to "prove" a point, as a justification for continued funding, and even in the most bizarre cases, that the unit in question is capable of doing everything claimed by the report. In the case of the *Walden*, for example, this would mean that outsiders, people removed from the context of record making, may really think that this and other ships were equipped to carry out the kinds of operations implied by the rational accounts. This would be misleading, but most importantly, if the discrepancy was ever discovered, the interpretation may be offered that a few bad people and inept officers were responsible for such rule violations. The meaningful context would be overlooked.

The final chapter (9) will discuss in some detail the ways of improving the quality of information about the *Walden's* activities along with other organizational tasks. But a point must be emphasized now about the implications of these practices. *The process of reporting any activity has itself become a meaningful act.* That is, putting one's involvement down in black and white—as an account—is seen to have consequences apart from the truth or falsity of what is presented. The problem for the people involved in a report, then, is to look as good as possible within the context of that report. The logic of this system of data collection becomes a reality in its own right, but a reality that is dependent on situated beliefs in the power of official information.

NOTES

1. The research consists of field notes and unstructured tape-recorded interviews with various petty officers and commissioned officers on active duty (during 1970–71) in the U.S. Navy, as well as of interviews with various persons having former associations with the navy. Crucial resources for the research were the personal experiences of the researcher and a number of inside informants used to check the validity of the researcher's observations.

2. Cf. D. F. Roy, "Quota Restriction and Goldbricking in a Machine Shop," *American Journal of Sociology* 62 (1962): 427–442.

3. Cf. Arthur K. Davis, "Bureaucratic Patterns in the Navy Officer Corps," *Social Forces* 27 (1948): 143–153.

4. Cf. Harold Garfinkel and Harvey Sacks, "On Formal Structures of Practical Actions" (1970).

5. A historian from the U.S. Naval Academy informed me that the term originates from the days of the square-riggers of the eighteenth century. These ships, according to this account, could have as many as three decks lined with their cannons (or gundecks). They typically trained their crew members in the use of these weapons by employing a thirteen-step exercise that began, as the first step, with a gunner's mate simulating the ignition of the fuse. Following the simulation of this first step, the other crew members would then proceed through the remaining twelve steps as if the cannon had been fired. The term "gundecking," according to this historian, originates from the simulated first step that initiates the remainder of the exercise. There are, however, many other versions of the origins of the term. Even though the definition cited from Webster's within the chapter more closely approximates contemporary usage, the remainder of the chapter should provide ample evidence that its entire meaning is not supplied by the literal or dictionary definition.

6. For example, while engaged in a "routine" shore bombardment mission near the coast of Vietnam, one destroyer came under the attack of several small gunboats and successfully engaged them in battle. Such events were typically perceived as "out of the ordinary."

7. The term "line officer" refers to a person qualified to take command at sea (or of an airborne unit). The category includes many aviators and former aviators. The term "straight line officer" refers to people who are not, or have not been, aviators, but still may be qualified to command at sea. Line

officers are distingished from staff officers, who include such specialities as doctors, dentists, chaplains, civil engineers, lawyers, and supply officers.

8. The ships in the same class as the *Walden* possessed four boilers to generate the steam on which they depended for propulsion. Nearly all of the sea operations in which these ships were engaged required the use of only two boilers that could, if needed, provide enough power for the ship to attain 80 to 85 percent of its maximum speed. Mechanical and fuel economy decreased drastically with the use of all four boilers, and this was rarely done.

8

Battle Efficiency Reports as Propaganda

The application of rational efforts to depict efficiency, as well as to justify and present many individual efforts as though they were really part of a "system," has led many people to believe that official accounts can be assumed to reflect some action, even a very complex one. This chapter illustrates how a navy "weapon," the USS *Walden*, accomplished the task of presenting official reports about its overall effectiveness in combat. Unlike the previous chapter, which emphasized how the *Walden prepared for combat* as far as official reports were concerned, this chapter focuses on the *Walden* in combat. However, like our earlier discussion, reports about combat are of more significance for success, promotion, and general recognition and approval than are the events that occur. In short, reports are what count.

THE PURPOSE AND CONTEXT

The conflict in Vietnam was one of the United States's most sophisticated and rational attempts to destroy a foe with the aid of scientific technology and organization. Many new weapons were employed; in addition, the improved communications capacity, along with more versatile hardware, including jet helicopters, were available to combine intellect and gauge reading with the blood and terror of the battlefields.

There was also another way in which the conflict in Vietnam differed from earlier campaigns. The success of the war effort was difficult to assess because of the enemy's guerilla tactics, elusiveness, and difficulty of identifi-

205

cation. Bodies were hard to find; enemy stores seemed nonexistent; captured territory would return to enemy hands within days after American forces had secured it. Compared to earlier conventional wars, Vietnam seemed confusing. It was almost impossible to measure our effectiveness. For example, there was no scrimmage line that could bulge, as occurred in a famous European campaign in World War II. To the contrary, the enemy was sought through seek and destroy patrols. And there appeared to be no central enemy authority to provide documents that could be captured to reveal our effectiveness.

The difficulty in assessing success promoted more reliance on official reports about the number of bodies counted, expended ordnance, number of air strikes, and estimates of our domination of the seaways, especially offshore naval activity. These accounts came to be the foundation for actually deducing our effectiveness. The formula was quite simple: the more American troops in Vietnam, the more bombs dropped, the more air strikes flown, and the more shells expended became the basis for deducing the amount and character of damage to the enemy. Relatedly, the people inflicting the damage—dropping the bombs and firing the shells— were given credit for the presumed impact of these acts on "bringing Hanoi to its knees." Like all rational efforts, these acts were rewarded with prestige, careers, medals, and great attention via the mass media. This context changed the purpose from fighting an abstract war to showing what one's outfit was contributing to the war effort. The USS *Walden* was part of it all.

As noted earlier, during the years of the Vietnam conflict the ships of this class were among the only ones that still possessed a capability for gunnery missions, which the newer, guided-missile destroyers could not perform. Thus, even though the "primary mission" of the USS *Walden* was officially that of antisubmarine warfare, it was scheduled to fulfill shore bombardment missions during the Vietnam conflict, as well as several other war-related activities. The priority of *Walden's* primary capability (ASW) had been replaced with that of gunnery operations in recent years.

DETERMINING BATTLE EFFICIENCY
IN EASTPAC AND WESTPAC

Chapter 7 mentioned that *Walden* crew members perceived that the major criterion of success for their ship was its competition for the battle efficiency awards. The most prestigious award, the Battle E, was awarded to only one ship of a squadron. In times of war, such as during Vietnam, this battle-related success generally involved some unusual or out of the ordinary mission while in Vietnam. To a large extent, the opportunity to engage in such an unusual activity was beyond the volition of the ship's commanding officer or operational commander.

Successful competition for battle-efficiency awards on a ship such as the USS *Walden* necessitated the construction of an immensely complex collection of records. The routine collection, production, and use of such records constituted one essential feature of the everyday activities of this organizational setting. Not all pieces of paper were regarded as being of equal importance, as we shall see. But, in one way or another, all of the paper work collected and produced on the ship was seen as a part of the everyday working routine of the persons doing it. Personnel were typically evaluated in part by their ability to produce such documentation. The importance of a given report or other form of documentation is sometimes said to lie in the necessity for persons in high governmental positions to be informed about the operational status and battle readiness of the ships in the navy. But competent members in the lower echelons also understand that these reports also represent the organizational acumen of those producing them.

ACCOUNTS OF BATTLE EFFICIENCY
FOR NAVAL GUNFIRE SUPPORT

Before deployment for its WestPac cruise, generally six to seven months in duration, the ship's personnel use a variety of inspections, drills, and exercises to construct their readiness. These preparations include a variety of predeployment inspections intended to insure that the ship, its personnel, and its materials are in satisfactory condition. The inspections and exercises, however, are also counted as fulfilling the requirements for the battle-efficiency awards. Personnel of the USS *Walden* called this "killing two birds with one stone."

Upon arriving to the West Pacific, when the ship was said to have chopped into the command of the operational commander of the Seventh Fleet, there were a variety of training sessions and briefings to familiarize everyone with the activities of the Vietnam conflict. During these discussions, those personnel permanently stationed in the West Pacific brought to the ship a variety of "Op Orders," which detailed the rules and procedures governing the activities of military units in the West Pacific. Op Orders may include detailed instructions for what will constitute compliance with an assigned mission. These missions include "plane guard," when a destroyer is assigned to an aircraft carrier to rescue any downed pilots; "search and rescue," which covers instances when the ship is detached for searching and/or rescuing a pilot lost in the ocean due to hostile fire or accident; "electronic intelligence," which includes instructions on how to monitor various electronic transmissions within a given geographical area; "antisubmarine warfare," which includes instructions for detecting and/or following enemy submarines; and naval gunfire support.

The USS *Walden* and similar ships were among those frequently used for providing naval gunfire support to ground and air forces in Vietnam. Three kinds of missions were classified as falling under the category of naval gunfire support. The first and most frequent was an "indirect firing mission." On a typical indirect firing mission, the ship would receive instructions on the locations and coordinates of targets or target areas within Vietnam. These targets were provided by a "spotter" who could be located in a small aircraft or on the ground. The ship would engage in firing missions at the direction of the spotter. These indirect firing missions were not in support of any American or Allied Forces in Vietnam. Closely associated with an indirect firing mission, the ship could be assigned "Harassment and Interdiction," which meant that the ship was provided targets on which to fire during the night at its own discretion. These "H & I missions" also were not in the support of any American or Allied Forces, but were typically directed at areas near the coast where the Viet Cong were known to frequent. The third type of mission was known as a "direct firing mission." These assignments were rare, and the instructions for them were delivered on a situation-to-situation basis depending on the exigencies of a tactical advance by ground forces. Being assigned to a direct firing mission carried very great prestige for the "tin-can navy." This meant that one was firing in direct support of ground forces and afforded an unparalleled opportunity for the ship to demonstrate the accuracy and expertise of its gunnery operations. For a ship successfully to engage the enemy was typically sufficient for the awarding of some sort of commendation to the ship and its personnel, perhaps even the receipt of the Navy Unit Commendation Medal.

Upon arriving in the "battle zone" of Vietnam, a ship usually reported in to the task force commander. He controlled the movements and assignments of ships within a given geographical area; that is, within a subdivision of the battle zone. He was typically stationed aboard an aircraft carrier whose movements would revolve around a geographical point (such as "Point Yankee"), which, in reality, "moved" on a day-to-day basis to avoid enemy detection. On being detached by the task force commander for a shore bombardment assignment, a ship would steam to the designated area to report to the operational commanders located ashore in Vietnam. There were four areas designated in Vietnam: I Corps, II Corps, III Corps, IV Corps.

The officers and relevant gunnery personnel of the ship usually would meet with the various persons designated as "spotters" for that area on arrival. The spotters' task was to assign the ship an individual firing mission and to report to the ship the results of that mission. A spotter could be located on the ground, called a "ground spotter," or could be the pilot of a light single-engine aircraft, called "FACS." During this meeting, the spotters would inform shipboard personnel about the nature of their task, the kind and nature of targets to be fired on, and the nature of the geographical area (with special notes for any pertinent navigation information, any information about threats or contingencies one might expect while "on the gunline" in that area, and information pertaining to the coordination of the firing missions with other routines). Such routines included departing from an inland or off-shore station to an area further out at sea for the purposes of making water, dumping trash, or conducting underway replenishments with supply, fuel, or ammunition ships. These departures, necessary to maintain operational readiness, were often needed daily. Also, high ranking ship's officers informed spotters about the degree of training and experience of the shipboard personnel in fulfilling gunnery missions and perhaps about any special needs that the ship might have. The assignment of a ship to a shore bombardment mission was often strenuous for its personnel. They would be often required to remain at their battle stations for sixteen to twenty hours a day. The typical period of time a ship was assigned to firing missions was fourteen days.

Spotters usually informed the gunnery personnel that they would be firing on known enemy targets that were recorded in intelligence reports sometimes two to three weeks old. Such targets were usually designated as "base camps," "infiltration routes," "bunkers," "supply depots," "staging areas," "trails," "tree lines," and so on. Targets also were classified by several residual categories. One category was called an "area target," which meant the ship would fire into a specified area, but at no specific target. Another was a "target of opportunity," designed to include those rare occasions when an enemy unit may initiate some sort of firing action with a ship. With the exception of the Tonkin Gulf Incident and one other incident in 1966, destroyers rarely engaged fire with such targets of opportunity. But, as we shall see below, target of opportunity could be used for other purposes.

During the initial briefings, spotters would also inform shipboard personnel about the relevant linguistic categories to report "battle damage assessment" for the firing missions. For example, spotters would inform them that on completion of the firing of the specified number of "rounds" or "salvos" into a given area, spotters would indicate to the ship via radio transmission that one "infiltration route" had been "neutralized." Spotters would also inform the gunnery personnel about the current procedures for a "harassment and interdiction" mission. For these, the ship would receive a listing of targets during the latter part of a given afternoon and would be directed to fire on them during the night at the ship's discretion. Since "H & I" missions occurred at night, spotters informed them to report battle damage assessment as, for example, that one "infiltration route" had been "interdicted."

The procedures discussed below were usually followed for a typical firing mission. At the beginning of the day, ship's personnel would contact the shore-based director of the firing mission via radio-telephone transmission on a preestablished frequency. After assuring that radio-telephone contact was sufficiently established, the shore-based commander would then inform the ship when the spotter (who would direct the daily firing missions) would be airborne. When airborne, the spotter would establish voice radio contact with the ship on the same frequency and would transmit a listing of the geographical coordinates for the targets. The spotter would then direct the calls for fire at given targets. Calls for fire typically included the numerical designation of the target, a brief description (for example, a "base camp"), and its geographical coordinates. He would also instruct the ship about the type of ammunition to be used for a given target, for example, whether it was to be high explosive (HE), variable time fuse (VT), or "willy peter" (white phosphorous). The spotter then directed the ship to fire and also gave instructions regarding how many rounds of ammunition were appropriate to "neutralize" or "interdict" the target. Upon completion, the spotter would then fly over the target area and report the battle damage assessment. Battle damage assessment was then recorded, or "logged," and these records were accumulated throughout the day, or given period of firing, to construct the relevant reports. Such reports, detailing the successful completion and effectiveness of a ship's firing missions, were then transmitted to various task force, task group, and shore-based commanders.

REDEFINING BATTLE DAMAGE ASSESSMENT

For the most part, these procedures were sufficient for the practical purposes of completing a given firing mission. Ambiguities of the procedures or certain situations that emerged but were not yet covered by any of the formal rules were ironed out between the shipboard personnel and the spotters during informal meetings. The procedures allowed for the spotter to designate a given area as a target, to direct the movements of the ship in completing a call for fire, and to provide battle damage assessment.

In spite of the clarity and explicitness of these procedures, however, there were many occasions for which the spotter was unable to provide damage assessment for the firing. There were a variety of reasons for this: inability because of bad weather, the loss of the rounds fired (which could result from navigational difficulties of the ship, an error or misunderstanding in the transmission of target coordinates, and other factors), and especially the inability of the spotter to detect battle damage through the dense jungle foliage. Before illustrating how some of these practical contingencies were managed, the following comments by one of the *Walden's* officers (the officer responsible for submitting the official reports of the ship's gunnery missions) illustrate the general importance of battle damage assessment on missions such as these:

Au.: Where did you get the information for the reports? I mean, how did you get it from the spotter?

S: From CIC [the ship's Combat Information Center].

Au.: And where did they get it from?

S: From the spotters over the voice circuit. The firing was always controlled from CIC. For example, the spotter would say, "good shoot, you got four bunkers, two hamlets, and five grave stones." [laughs]

Au.: Well, here, let's take this. Assuming that what came over the voice circuit was accurate, then, ...

S: Now that's one thing you can't assume, you know. They didn't care, they'd say—you know we talked to those spotters at the briefings—they'd say, they'd give you six bunkers if you shot up a mile of beach.

Au.: Why? What did they. . . .

S: Why? Because they had to; it was written in the regulations that damage assessment will be given at the completion of each mission. So even if there wasn't any damage, they'd give you some, because they had to justify—eventually the ship had to justify sending 300 shells onto a beach only to come back with no damage. I mean, no damage? The Type Commander is going to want to know why am I spending 18,000 dollars a shell, or whatever it is, and why are you firing 300 of these shells against no target? So they had to justify their sending rounds in there by faking some damage assessment. You follow me? You understand this?

Au.: Yes.

S: They do the same thing with the aircraft carriers. Same thing. In other words, these planes take off at a monumental cost for an air strike, just like the B-52's from the shore facilities. They *have* to, they *have* to come back with significant damage. Otherwise their funds will be slashed. In other words, that's money. Damage is money. So, in order to get the money, if they don't have any real damage they gundeck it. Spotters do it; they do it all the time. In other words, take this. I fire a shell onto a beach. That shell makes a crater. The next shell hits that crater. That's one bunker destroyed. That's common; it's just accepted as common knowledge. It's common knowledge yet nobody ever says anything about it, right up through the Type Commander. It's the only way they can continue to fire shells and justify it. You read the news reports, don't you?

>   *Au.:*   Yes, I've gotten these. . . .
>
>   *S:*   Everyone knows it. He [the Type Commander] knows that it's
>   the only way he can continue to get money from the govern-
>   ment, from Congress. He can only justify it if he can show that
>   shells are being fired at lucrative targets.

This comment documents the following: (1) the perceived importance
attributed to battle damage assessment for recording one's success on a
given gunnery mission; and (2) the black-and-white (or dichotomous)
nature of the recording categories used by the members for ordering this
feature of their work.

The following comments document one example of an instance in
which the members' understandings of the formal procedures, even as
elaborated through the ironing out processes of the informal briefings, are
insufficient for preparing them for all of the contingent circumstances that
they encounter in actual occasions. A former Gunnery Officer of the *Walden*
comments:

>   *S:*   One time, I don't remember whether we had just arrived on
>   the gun line in a particular area, or whether we'd been firing
>   there for a couple of days, but anyway, this time we ran into
>   a green spotter. This was his first time out, although we didn't
>   find this out until a couple months later in [the Philippines].
>   It was our first mission of the day, I think, and he came over
>   the phone and said, due to the dense foliage, he couldn't give
>   us any [battle damage] assessment. The Old Man [the Cap-
>   tain] told me to ask him again, to tell him that we *had* to
>   have damage, but the spotter repeated the same thing again,
>   that he couldn't give us any. Well, the Captain got on the
>   circuit and gave a call to the spotter's CO [Commanding Offi-
>   cer] and said, very to the point I thought, no damage assess-
>   ment for our rounds, and we pick up our marbles and go
>   home. He didn't say it exactly that way, of course, but that
>   was the message. Following this, we could hear the spotter's
>   CO get on the same circuit, and he told him to fly a little
>   lower over the target once again, to see if he couldn't find a
>   few bunkers. The spotter could hear all of this, of course, and
>   by this time he knew what it was all about. He found some, too.

The formal rules and procedures typically used for a given shore
bombardment mission may not provide for all contingent circumstances.
Such constructions of the organization *not only* implicitly assume a fully
socialized organizational actor; they also assume that such organizational
socialization includes more than merely being able to perform a given
task. In this case, such competence includes knowing the various structures
of relevance of *others* situated at diverse points within the organization

and knowing exactly how one's specialized competence fits in with that of others. In this example, even if we assume that the airborne spotter had been competently trained to do the "spotting" aspects of his job, we can also see learning the expectations and structures of relevance of many others situated at other points, which is an equally crucial feature of organizational competence. As the construction of any large social order, such as that of the United States Navy or Vietnam conflict, depends necessarily on individuals' perceptions of the relevant features of the environment that constitute the social reality of that organization, such constructions are fundamentally problematic, even to people who are old hands at doing this sort of activity. Thus, when the Commanding Officer of the USS *Walden* redirected the attention of the spotter to the target area, we can see that competent members may use the procedures of the organization to indicate to others that such perceptions are "intended" or "called for" in the first place: their relevance is established reflexively by referring to the formal constructions of rules, procedures, and so on.

The following comments illustrate some of the features involved in an organizational education or competence and also some of the many problematics of generating the type of "knowledge" seen as relevant for successful gunnery missions. These are the comments of a navy officer who was stationed for one year with various United States Marines and ARVN (Army of the Republic of [South] Vietnam) forces as a *ground spotter*.

Au.: I've already had a number of talks with people on various ships about their side of shore bombardment, and now I'd like to get the story from the other side, so to speak. I'd like to hear about shorbom from a spotter's point of view.

S: The whole show was a charade, strictly an exercise in you-scratch-my-back-and-I'll-scratch-yours. I'd give calls for fire, the ship would throw out a few salvos, and I'd give them a couple of bunkers, or whatever. It wasn't only a case of *them* needing some justification for firing, but so does the spotter, that is *me*. Took me some time to realize that, couple of weeks or a month maybe, but I soon realized where our bread was buttered.

Au.: Now wait a minute, Bill, it doesn't even sound plausible that the whole thing was a charade. There's got to be more to it than that, I mean, what was the story with the targets? Were some of them erroneously plotted? Was the terrain so bad that you couldn't be sure of the coordinates? Were you always too far away to give an accurate assessment? I mean, there's got to be more to the story than that. . . .

S: Yeah, well, for one thing, well, I guess I was a bit oversimplifying with that first remark. It is much more complicated than that of course. Here, let me start at the beginning. Oh gee, okay, [pause] where did we get the targets in the first place? Now that makes a difference right off. First of all, all of the targets came from two places and were always two to three weeks old. Sometimes, every once in a while you'd get a target that was a couple of days old, that depending on what type of target it was. Well, it depended on a number of things, actually. Anyway, okay, we got our targets either from ARVN intelligence or reconnaissance units or patrols who'd stumbled across some VC bunkers or whatever, and they either didn't have the muscle to destroy it themselves, or didn't want to give their position away for some reason. So they'd give us the coordinates over the radio, or sometimes in a written report of some kind. The second source was the [indigent peasants on the payroll for supplying information for US or ARVN forces]. Now, in the case of the ARVN. Well, okay, I should say this. There were actually many more sources where we could get our targets: support planes flying over an area where they had been engaged by ground fire, gunboats, all sorts of sources. The ARVN and [the peasants] were the two major ones, though. Now, in the case of the ARVN—or any other military unit for that matter—the reports and coordinates were usually more or less accurate. By more or less I mean that they were as accurate as you could expect under the circumstances. In the case of [the peasants] you couldn't ever be sure of the exact location of the target; well, sometimes you could see them, but many times you couldn't, and we always wondered if about half the time whether there was anything there at all. Let's face it, that was their livelihood, at least for some of them.

Au.: You mean that some of the peasants could get away with faking their sightings of VC camps or whatever?

S: No, not exactly. Sometimes there would be some way to check out the reports; in other situations there wasn't. It depended on a number of things, such as what area you were in. There was one hell of a lot of difference between the hills of "eye corps" [I Corps] and all of that elephant grass in three-corps, you know what I mean?.... Anyway, none of the [peasants] could've gotten by with any kind of complete fake job, but it was possible every now and then, and I'm sure many of them knew it. Anyway, I'd go out for shorbom missions and, let's face it, half the time I couldn't see the damn target even when figuring out the coordinates wasn't any trouble. Like most of those so-called bunkers were underground, remember, and who in the hell can pick out what was called a quote infiltration route unquote in a four canopy jungle when you're perched on top of some damn hill? And, of course, that's even easier than down in three-corps where you don't even have that many hills. Almost none, in fact.

Au.: Now was it this way for all your spotting? I mean, is this peculiar to shore bombardment, or is the same thing true when you're spotting in company with some troops or ground forces?

S: Oh, that's different; that's a much different story altogether. No, it's not the same at all. I thought you just wanted to know about shore bombardment?

Au.: Yes, let's stay with shore bombardment for the moment. Let's see, so far you've mentioned that the geographical area makes a difference in the origin of the intelligence report. Anything else?

S: I guess I should've said that at the beginning. The situation is completely different when you are working with some troops. I was just talking about shore bombardment with the ships, and I personally never had any experiences where I directed a call-for-fire from a ship in support of ground troops. Good God, heaven forbid. Anyway, when I first got to Vietnam I'd only had my training, no previous experience. The spotting in [the Philippines] was the most realistic, but it still didn't prepare me for anything like Vietnam. In the Philippines all of our training was really more or less without difficulty. I mean, we worked on the major problem of trying to give the correct spots [recommendations to the ships for its fire control solution of the computer] to the ships, and it never even dawned on me that you'd ever have any trouble finding the target *in the first place!* In Vietnam, however, or in the real world, as they say, it was much different than firing at [an island off the coast of Southern California], or even in the Philippines. Most of the time I wasn't too sure where the target was, anyway, and not that they were all visible, anyway, understand, and so if the ship sent a couple of salvos in the general area of where *I thought* the target was, then I'd report back to them they'd destroyed the target. As I said before, that was the name of the game.... If a given ship got a lot of damage they'd send us a letter of commendation through the chain of command, and we'd do the same....[1]

REDEFINING THE TARGET

Although naval gunfire support is widely acclaimed for its accuracy among people in the various branches of the military, such accuracy is highly dependent on the capability of ascertaining one's navigational position while either at anchor or at sea. When a destroyer would conduct its naval gunfire support missions while at anchor, ascertaining one's true navigational position was usually no problem. An exception to this was when the firing missions were located at the western edge of the four corps area, where the shoreline appeared very ambiguously on one's navigational radar and where there were few other geographical markings (such as islands) that could be used for establishing one's position. When a ship conducted its missions while steaming at low speeds, usually off shore at a distance of two to four miles, the accurate acquisition of one's true navigational position was more difficult, especially when weather made radar readings ambiguous and vague. To some extent, at least, the difficulties of ascertaining one's navigational position were seasonal; positions were more difficult to establish during the monsoon season.

The formal procedures of naval gunfire support did not provide for the possibility that a ship would fire at a target and miss it. If a ship had indicated that it was on station and ready to respond to the spotter's call for fire, then it was presumed that the target at which one fired would be hit. Of course, there were many instances when the rounds fired did not hit the target exactly. At these moments, the spotter would inform the gunfire support vessel that they should check their solution (indicating that he desires certain recalculations of the inputs into the shipboard fire control computer—called a "spot"). Then the spotter would redirect the ship to fire additional rounds or salvos at the corrected target location. During those rare instances when a ship was firing in direct support of American or Allied ground forces, such recalculations were frequent and of great importance. It was understood by shipboard gunnery personnel that when firing in direct support of ground troops, it would be necessary to recalculate the computer solution several times for a given firing mission. This would mean that the ship's criterion of success for the battle efficiency awards, that is, the number of shells expended per target, would rise during these kinds of missions. But, on the other hand, this apparent cost was perceived to be offset by the greater importance of these missions in support of ground troops. On the more frequent indirect firing missions, which were not in direct support of ground troops, however, such recalculations were thought to constitute a self-labeling of one's command as lacking expertise in gunnery, or as incompetent. The reason for this was that shipboard personnel did not think that it was fair for the airborne spotter to request them to increase the number of shells expended per target when it could never be determined with certainty that the initial rounds' or salvos' inaccuracy had been due to a poor navigational fix, to inadequate computer inputs, or perhaps to inaccurate information supplied to the ship by the spotter himself.

Given such contingencies, there were often occasions when fired rounds of ammunition were "lost." This could happen for a variety of reasons, some of which have been listed above. This could also happen as a result of human error; for example, when a spotter was looking for the rounds to engage target #3 and the ship was still firing at target #2. During times such as these, the spotter then redirected the ship to fire on the target initially intended in the first place. On board the ship, to account for these rounds for one's battle efficiency, shipboard personnel routinely used the category "target of opportunity" to indicate that their rounds had indeed fallen on target. By using this category, the members of the USS *Walden* systematically avoided the necessity of averaging the lost rounds into the overall calculation that would indicate number of shells expended per target, the operative criterion of competition for the battle efficiency award vis-à-vis the other ships in the division or squadron. A former gunnery liaison officer of the USS *Walden* comments on this procedure:

> **S:** Here's what I mean by "lost rounds." Now this wasn't too common, understand, but it wasn't rare either. That is, this was common if you ran into bad weather in four-corps, but other than that it wasn't too common. What happened here was that nobody knew what happened. I mean, we might be firing one day, perhaps we'd fire off a couple of salvos at a given target, wait for a couple of minutes, and the spotter would report back that he hadn't seen a damn thing. If the weather was no problem that day, then my guess is that the spotter was looking at the wrong target, or maybe was doin' a little skylarking on the job. You have to understand this, though, that's only my side of the story. Jesus, I almost got into a fight over this one night in the Philippines. I was out drinking with a couple of spotters, and suggested that they were sometimes asleep at the switch, and one of them nearly clobbered me. From his opinion, he said [that when] such things like this happened it was all due to an incorrect input on board the ship. I must admit that's a possible answer, but it happened a little too often for me to accept it outright. . . . When we were in four-corps though, my God, the major problem was trying to figure out where we were. Sometimes the only definite navigational fix would be forty or fifty miles from where we'd end up anchoring, and you know damn well that you cannot rely on that type of fix for any accuracy, unless you're just enroute somewhere, of course. . . . Over there [IV Corps], we'd often fire off several salvos which couldn't be spotted. If it didn't happen too often we'd log 'em on the same target, but if we had a pretty good idea that the trouble was with the spotter, then we'd use the old stand-by, target-of-opportunity. Why in the hell should we log in fifty rounds to destroy some measley bunker when the problem is the spotter who can't see over the elephant grass . . . you can't use that target-of-opportunity stuff too often, though, the Commodore's staff is pretty wise in seeing through that kind of thing.

These comments indicate that in situations in which one is accountable to various sets of rules and regulations of a large organization that do not seem to fit, or in situations in which the various rules or procedures may be in conflict with one another, the routine use of procedures that are sufficient for practical purposes most of the time may have to be modified or compromised in order to sustain the sense that the activities taking place within an organization are indeed a part of its unified program of action. These modifications to the procedures are sometimes deemed necessary by competent members when, in their judgments and reasoning, the goals or objectives of the organization at one time are deemed more important than other goals or other objectives of the organization. In this light, then, the methodical use of the category "target of opportunity" is a kind of *minimax strategy* to construct the larger social order of the Vietnam conflict, one determined by the members' judgments of the priorities of the situation.

CREATING A TARGET

By using our commonsense notions of antecedent conditions, or cause and effect, the following reasoning might appear warranted. First, some feature of the environment socially defined as "a target" may be unproblematically perceived by competent organizational actors; that is, as an "objective feature" of that environment. Second, because of such an objective identification, and the concomitant member knowledge that such entities are sometimes worthy of destruction, harassment, or interdiction, ships (or other military units) direct their gunfire at them. Third, since it is a target that one fires on, the effectiveness or efficiency of such an activity (however recorded or categorized) thus "reports on" (or "indexes") that activity. The following discussion will illustrate the limited utility of such commonsense notions for understanding these activities and will suggest the plausibility of the opposite sequence. That is, by desiring the submission of a certain kind of report on one's actions, rounds of ammunition are expended, which then define "the target." Stated differently, a target may become a target because it has been fired at, rather than being fired at because it was a target.

On one of the USS *Walden's* deployments the following incident occurred. The *Walden* had been assigned shore bombardment missions for three or four periods of approximately two weeks each and had received many letters of commendation attesting to its expertise during these missions. It was commonly thought by many on the *Walden* that during this deployment the *Walden* had been assigned to more firing missions (than any other ship in the division or squadron), had successfully engaged more enemy targets, had expended fewer rounds of shells per target, and had generally gained a wide recognition as a "Can-Do-Tin-Can" among military forces within the area. Accounts of the *Walden's* successes had been heralded in various newspaper stories and press releases. Among those people who were interested in the competitive spirit of such activities, many thought the ship had demonstrated far greater expertise than two of the remaining three ships within the division. It was thought that there remained only one competition (at least within this division) for the squadron battle efficiency award, the USS *Huff*.

The USS *Huff* was reported to have expended 3,750 rounds of ammunition in support of American and allied forces in Vietnam as it departed from its final mission in the area. It had also established a reputable record for gunnery expertise. On the last day of its final assignment as a naval gunfire support ship, the USS *Walden* gunnery personnel determined that the ship had expended a total of 3,952 rounds of ammunition at the conclusion of its final mission. At the end of this firing, when he learned this, the Commanding Officer of the *Walden* radioed the shore-base commander of the II Corps area in which the ship was located and requested that he designate an "area target" into which the *Walden* could "unload" 49 additional rounds of ammunition. The *Walden's* Commanding Officer said to the II Corps Commander that such a designation was called for in order to "remove potential dangerous ammunition from the handling rooms." But he indicated to shipboard personnel that he wanted the *Walden* to be the only ship in the division to expend more than 4,000 rounds of ammunition for the deployment. The shore-based commander (or his representative) designated such an "area target," and 49 additional rounds were expended into this area. For accounting purposes, it was recorded that 49 rounds had been "on target" for this "area target," one of the officially recognized residual categories mentioned previously. The *Walden's* Gunnery Officer at the time commented on this occasion:

> S: ... So we unloaded the 49 rounds in some rice paddy or what-
> ever. It wasn't any big deal really, wasn't any more of a
> waste of ammunition than those H & I [Harassment and Inter-
> diction] missions, I'm sure. From my point of view, it saved
> Second [Division] a lot of work. That's when accidents hap-
> pen, having to strike below [return the shells to the maga-
> zines] ammunition after everyone is tired as hell and wants
> to rack it [go to bed]. So who knows, maybe unloading those
> rounds saved us from something that could've been worse.
> Anyway, the XO sure got a lot of mileage out of it in the
> plans of the day from then on, extolling the heroic feats of
> the so-called *Walden* Warriors, oh, my God, well, anyway, the
> XO had everyone thinking that we were the heroic warriors
> of Vietnam even though no one ever thought so before, when
> we were actually doing it. ...

In this situation, then, it can be seen that the formal organizational program can be used by the members as a sort of "secular canopy," or symbolic superstructure, under which the various activities taking place within the organization may be subsumed. In this illustration, the formal rules may be used in a systematic fashion to manage certain contingencies for which the formal schema could not possibly provide in its literal usage, such as the promotion and/or maintenance of the esprit de corps, or "collective consciousness" of the USS *Walden* as an integral fighting unit. In situations such as these, the creation of an additional target can be seen to promote the members' sense of accomplishment in their tasks and even a sense of pride in having done them well.

REDEFINING THE RELEVANCY OF A MISSION

The prescriptions of the formal rules and the everyday use of them deemed no considerations more important than the fulfillment of a battle-related mission. There could be exceptions to this, although they were infrequent. The only exceptions accorded any "legitimacy" included equipment casualties to the ship's battle capabilities of one sort or another, or a serious accident (such as a fire). On the other hand, it was also widely known that the Commanding Officer is charged with the overall responsibility for the safety of the ship's personnel. The imputed importance of battle-related missions and the general responsibility of the Commanding Officer typically involved no conflict. On one occasion, however, the Commanding Officer of the USS *Walden* broke off a gunfire support firing mission and ordered his ship to sea. From his perspective, the perceived threat endangering the ship possessed a greater priority than the gunnery mission to which the ship was then assigned. The officer who was the Public Affairs Officer at the time commented on this situation.

> S: ...We had one situation where we broke off a mission. We were anchored in the Saigon River where we had been firing for several days, between unreps [replenishments of supplies, fuel, etc.], that is. We, I'd say we were about three miles inland from Vung Tau [on the coast]. All of a sudden, and I had the watch at the time, the Old Man orders me to haul-in the anchor, and we steamed out of there all-ahead-full, you know, like twenty-seven knots. Broke off the mission just like that. Now the cause of all this, or supposedly, at least, was the Captain spotted a swimmer in the water. You know what that water's like? Like, man, first of all it's so damn muddy you couldn't see *anything* if you had to under the surface. And, second, there are so damn many jellyfish in that river no swimmer could ever survive it [intended as an exaggeration]. And not one person saw it other than the Captain, not one of the lookouts on the bridge, nobody on the main deck, the signal

bridge, nobody, anywhere. But the Captain says he saw a swimmer, and so we give it all-ahead-full and put out to sea. Not only that, here, get this, he furnished a complete description of him [the swimmer] right down to the black shorts and black web belt. You believe that, a black web belt! So I went ahead and wrote up all of the news releases on it, two copies to the, well, practically to everyone in the world, the full shot, including the black web belt. Since we'd broken off a mission, our primary mission over there, we really had to do a job in the releases. The whole thing was completely gundecked from my opinion. There just ain't no way you could convince me there could've been a swimmer in that water, especially since I was standing right there. I must say though, the Captain, I don't think he was lying or anything like that. I actually think he thought he saw a swimmer, really. . . .

Au.: How do you explain it then? Was he. . . .

S: I'm not really sure I can. [Pause] One thing that's related here, I think, oh hell, I don't know. Well, one thing, and I saw this with two different CO's, one thing is that that old saw about, you know, the general regulations, about the Commanding Officer being ultimately responsible for anything and everything that happens on the ship. I think it suddenly takes on a different slant when you're doing something like anchoring in the Saigon River, when the whole show could come to an end at any minute. It spooked me a couple of times, believe me. The only thing I know for sure is that I'm glad I didn't have that responsibility. If I'd been in his shoes, maybe I'd be seeing kamikazes . . . !

The above comments warrant our interest for several reasons. First, like the preceding illustration, they suggest that an assignment to a given mission is not one of the "givens" of the situation, but is fundamentally grounded in the members' choices, sometimes involving situated judgments related to other priorities or structures of relevance. Second, these comments raise the issue of "the public-affairs angle" of the Vietnam gunnery mission. This is a specific case of a more general point we made in chapter 7. Decontextualized information often becomes reified as reality when the public hears, sees, and reads it as news. In the same interview, this officer commented further on this aspect:

S: . . . now the Battle E, that's where you get it, in Vietnam, or at least the last couple of years that's the case. It's different than the Operations E, and the ASW E, and so forth. I think there are four possible E's all together which any given ship could win, depending on the readiness of each department. But the Battle E . . . that's only for one ship per squadron, and that's where my public affairs work came in. I wrote a story each day describing each day's missions. These weren't the same as the reports of the targets, rounds, and all that, though. I did usually glance at those to find out how many rounds we'd fired that day, and would usually begin with something about that. Not always, though. But the stories I wrote, the stories, they always left the ship at 1800 each evening in a message format and were always some kind of story about the firing that day. Here's an example, for example after telling what kind of mission it was, I might then go on to write a paragraph or two about some Seaman Deuce in Mount 53, and what he'd done that day to contribute to the day's mission.

Au.: Were these always cleared by the Captain?

  S: Oh, sure, anything leaving the ship in message form was approved by the Captain.

Au.: Did he ever tell you what to write? In the stories?

  S: No, never. He'd never tell me what to write, he'd just approve 'em. It was the XO. He'd completely....

Au.: Did he edit the stories?

  S: Sure. In fact, there were many stories that I couldn't recognize after he'd edit them and they went out. I'd see the....

Au.: What do you mean? In what ways did he edit them?

  S: Editing would be a euphemism for what he did to them. [Laughs] Completely rewrote them.

Au.: Like what?

  S: Well, in one case, let's say I'd write a perfectly good paragraph about Seaman Smith in Mount 53, what he'd done that day, what he said about it, stuff like that. What Seaman Smith would actually say about it, of course, would be unprintable. But I would create some statement that would make him out to be a nice guy, you know, a nice guy doing a dirty job in a gun mount, something like that. Usually pretty trite. Would've earned a flat F in any freshman composition class. [Laughs] And then, when I'd see the final draft of it after it would come out and I wouldn't be able to recognize any of it.

Au.: What do you mean? Was it just a matter of style?

  S: Well, to some extent. The XO would always begin by saying something like "The blazing guns of the Walden Warriors once again obliterated so many enemy targets...."—you know, bullshit like that. He'd rewrite the whole story; not one sentence I'd recognize.

Au.: You mean just a different style or the content?

  S: Both. You know, standard naval sentence structure, standard inflation. All of it was inflated, to play it up bigger....

Au.: But did he actually change any of the facts, I mean like the type of mission or number of rounds, anything like that?

S: Oh no, at least not that I remember. It wasn't that kind of story, it wasn't. . . .

Au.: Well, what was it used for? I mean, what was the use of writing them in the first place?

S: The use? Just publicity. Just publicity for the command, for the stateside papers. You've seen 'em, especially in [local paper].

These comments document another feature of many members' understandings within large-scale (or bureaucratic) organization; namely, even when the formal rules are combined with the various kinds of practical arrangements within a setting, these various combinations rarely define but one objective environment of objects (or meanings). That is, as the comments illustrate, many members are very aware that their organizational activities are relevant (and in different ways) to different audiences. What constitutes the "objective facts" for one audience (as in a report of battle effectiveness within the organization) are not necessarily the same "objective facts" for another audience or for a different report (as in a news release). The great difficulty in transcending these barriers between the public and private are perhaps appropriately illustrated by the comments of one officer (cited earlier), when he began his account with the term "charade," readily admitted this as an "oversimplification," and proceeded to talk for several hours about the various activities and contingencies to which "charade" had previously referred.

This raises another set of issues; the various attempts by many of the members to explain, justify, or bring any sort of other rational understanding to their own activities. Within several of the interviews conducted during this research, some of the members commented to the effect that some activities they had seen, witnessed, experienced, and so on, had rendered problematic the idea of "objective facticity." In two of the interviews, two different members tried to describe how they saw their own activities at the time they had accomplished them within the context of some practical activity and why they were subsequently led to "reinterpret" them in light of new knowledge or differing values. At one level, this is only to say that one's personal experiences (or personal biography) are continually renegotiable. But the members also experienced such events problematically themselves. They harbored uncertainty long after the practical accomplishment of their various tasks. A member comments:

S: I first arrived on the *Walden* in the fall of 1964. My first billet was Second Division [Gunnery Officer], where I spent my first twelve, maybe fifteen months. I'd never been to any one of the gunnery schools; a Boot Ensign in every sense of the word. During that first year, or however, I think it was a little over a year, actually, I became absolutely convinced that those guns couldn't hit the broadside of a barn under absolutely perfect conditions. I felt stupid as hell, but also thought it was quite a challenge to learn the system [the fire control system or various computer inputs, which controlled the movements of the guns]. I don't have to say that all during this time, however long it was, we never ran any of the really competitive exercises, had spent the whole first cruise without ever firing a shot. I really became quite fascinated with the whole system. . . . [At this point, a long discussion of the various complexities of determining the various inputs to the gunnery systems on the ship]. . . . Anyway, it wasn't until after I'd moved over to ASW [Officer] twelve or fifteen months later that [the guns] made a believer out of me. It happened one day during an air shoot; the first couple of rounds knocked off the sleeve [the metal target at the end of a long wire streamed behind a jet aircraft], and the rounds started to climb right up the wire towards the jet 'til he broke it off. Man, from my experiences as Weps I would have never even put a 100-to-one bet on anything like that happening; really made a believer out of me. . . . The entire second cruise [this officer made only two cruises on the *Walden*] when we did all of the firing I was just an observer. I just watched the whole show from ASW Control [adjacent to CIC] but didn't play any part myself. During the whole show, though, it never even entered my mind that those rounds might actually kill someone. I know that sounds stupid as hell to say, but it was true. I just didn't see it in those terms. Didn't see it, that is, until that last day, or at least it was on one of the last days, of our gunfire support missions, when the spotter reported three KIA's [killed-in-action] and four whiskeys [WIA, or wounded-in-action] among some other damage. God, I'll never forget that day. I was standing right there in the doorway to CIC when the message came over the circuit, and all of a sudden everyone in CIC broke into this incredible cheering and shouting. I was absolutely terrified, I mean absolutely terrified. All before in my life, or at least since college, I'd always thought of myself as an idealist, and here I was, I'd been there doing war without any sense that people were getting killed until that particular day. . . . Well, I won't bother you with all the gory details of all the agony I've gone through about that, but I must admit, I've become terribly cynical about the possibility of eliminating wars once and for all time. . . .[2]

BATTLE EFFICIENCY REPORTS AS PROPAGANDA

Battle efficiency reports do not reflect the reality they claim to; but they do tell us about the reality of official reports, and especially the practical and meaningful context that informs the activities of making war a rational endeavor. There is no reason to assume that these reports are atypical of all other military reports (cf. Wilensky, 1965), although we do not claim that this is actually the case. Other researches will either support or reject these findings. What is more important is how war appears when viewed from the perspective of the officers and men of the USS *Walden*. Their war was inextricably anchored in a context broader than the murky waters of Vietnam, although their activities were very much influenced by this context. They had to account for their warfaring skills and to document, in a form acceptable to superiors, that they were not only doing their jobs, but also were being successful, and helping the war effort. This was what counted, even if it meant dumping thousands of rounds of ordnance on targetable areas. It was irrelevant whether an independent observer might or might not confirm that there was a stockpile of enemy supplies, and that the target might or might not have actually been destroyed. That is only one reality. From the perspective of the *Walden*, however, the targets existed because there were good reasons for them to be there.

From these illustrations, we have seen that "battle damage assessment" may be defined as a social phenomenon for the purposes of constructing an account of it. Such definitions are fundamentally problematic due to the adult socialization processes on which they depend, processes that are necessarily open ended. From the second example present here, we have seen that a "target" as a social definition may be redefined when, as a product of members' judgments of the priorities or relevancies of the situation, such as a reinterpretation is conceived as following the *intent* of the organizational rules in the first place. In the third example, it was argued that an alternative to the commonsense understandings of antecedent and consequential conditions (or cause and effect) provides a more plausible understanding of the definition and redefinition of "a target" as a social phenomenon. In this example, it was asserted that the formal schema of the organization may be used for *symbolic purposes* for which no conceivable set of rules could possibly provide in any adequate fashion, independently of how such constructions were "interpreted" or "strictly enforced." And in the final example, we have seen that the very presence of the organizational personnel at the scene of a given mission is itself a product of commonsense situations of choice (Garfinkel, 1967) and may be changed or revoked by the use of different rules, understandings, or features of the formal organizational program seen as relevant for the situation at hand. This is not to imply that all parties are equally powerful to realize their own individual choices within a given situation, but merely to indicate the fundamental datum for any empirically adequate sociological theorizing.

In the situations analyzed here, the practical tasks of completing accounts of battle efficiency were seen to require the cooperation and/or co-ordination of many variously situated persons, although such co-ordinations are rarely unproblematic. Since such accounts are as much a function of the various audiences who receive them as of those who initiate them, it makes little sense to argue that such accounts are "structurally determined." Moreover, competent organizational members may use differing conceptions of the "objective facts" relevant for a given audience. Constructing such accounts, as we have seen, involves presenting the appearance of orderly organizational situations (presumably, what the report is taken to stand for) by the members. But such accounts may also gloss over certain situated contingencies of action that could not possibly be provided for in any formal program of rules and regulations. Any given account, therefore, is necessarily problematic to those constructing it because of their *incomplete knowledge* of the reactions of the audiences (or various persons to whom a given account is sent). The people making the report can never be sure that its recipients will understand such situated contingencies in a similar manner to the members' understandings at the time the report was made.

The significance of reports cannot be divorced from the context and meanings of those who will learn of them. Military personnel, for example, who are not on the scene and who are unfamiliar with the practicalities of off-shore bombardment and its relevance for personal and group recognition, competition, and the practical "way to do your job," will not look beyond the statistical and rhetorical "data." If so, they may interpret such reports in terms of their understanding of what hitting a target means. If this interpretation is not informed by the considerations noted throughout this chapter, the recipients will be deceived. However, this is not likely to happen since the career route and experience of most military superordinates likely to receive and assess such information readily informs them about what happened. This is useful since it means that they can then use the reports to reward their subordinates off the coast of Vietnam. The reports also can be used to compete with other representatives of the armed services and to join their colleagues in arms by citing objective evidence that "we're giving them hell." To this extent, everybody benefits—except the public.

Passing versions of reports on to the news media further distorts the original context. Now the public, and especially persons unfamiliar with the relationship between shelling and spotting procedures, career mobility, and military public relations efforts, are likely to deduce that a target in the *Walden's* terms is a target in his or her terms; that a hit from one perspective is a hit from all perspectives. Such misinformation cannot be construed as a lie; it is more correctly regarded as reports without context. This is why we claim that the context of the information process must be clearly delineated.

The implications of all this for warfare and citizen involvement are perhaps evident. For one thing, fighting the war is less a result of overt feelings of "genocide," "racism," and "capitalistic exploitation," although such notions may account for its early history, definition, and public acceptance of it. There are good organizational reasons for carrying on the war in a certain way; simply defeating the enemy does not guarantee positive recognition of performance and does not ensure career and professional awards. Only record keeping based on rational procedures and assumptions can do these things. Beating one's competition and documenting it may encourage accidental killings of both soldiers and civilians who find themselves in officially sanctioned target areas. This will be inevitable when war is waged for good organizational reasons.

NOTES

1. Harold Wilensky (1967: 25–28) has noted that similar problems occurred with the identification of targets during World War II, especially when "area bombing" was involved.
2. Because of the rather limited interests of the research, a disproportionate number of commissioned officers were interviewed during the research. This comment, then, is not intended as being representative.

9

The Future of
Bureaucratic Propaganda

This book has shown how bureaucratic propaganda operates in a variety of organizational settings and how this operation depends on the honoring of certain accounts by various audiences. It is also apparent that the form and logic of bureaucratic propaganda are self-perpetuating. Once accepted, such propaganda will be repeated because it works; eventually it takes on the appearance of factual and objective appraisals. Moreover, once established, the form of bureaucratic propaganda relies on, and indeed demands, certain kinds of data. This process has helped establish the bizarre situation we find ourselves in today, whereby the most fundamental goals and issues are tied to the guidelines and practical logics that themselves focus attention on only certain "facts" to the exclusion of all others.

We have also seen how such selective interpretations and verification of certain claims are legitimized by being patterned after similar approaches in other organizations, while at the same time, the organization's unique focus is legitimized by appealing to an audience that also accepts a certain form. Since the operation of bureaucratically oriented activities depends on the selective perception by a target audience of a "bottom line," it is no surprise that much artful impression-management is involved in providing proper conclusions· as well as claiming the rigorous pursuit of scientifically valid procedures and standards.

SOCIAL IMPLICATIONS

The major problem posed by bureaucratic propaganda for the future of our society is that it pervades most aspects of social life, including commerce, religion, politics, education, and we suspect, even science. Such deep rootedness makes it exceedingly difficult for one institutional framework to be critical of another, especially if new options, values, and procedures for validation are proposed. Rather, the appropriateness of one institution—and any organization within that framework—to scrutinize and assess the implications of a particular course of action by a member agent is itself limited by the extent to which the evaluating outside agent meets the specifications and philosophy of knowledge adopted by the members. As aspiring members strive to receive the legitimation from their would-be-peer institutions (and organizations), they will increasingly adopt many of the same procedures for legitimizing their interests; we refer to impression-management, as well as to sanctioned questions and methods of study. For this reason, higher education in American society is rapidly adopting the same kinds of bureaucratic cost-accounting methods to justify offering particular courses of study. When academic departments hire and fire faculty on the basis of "full-time student equivalents," and when entire programs of study are erected and wiped out on the same basis, it is no surprise that a lot of university energy is devoted to surviving through official reports.

Impression-management dominates the organizational culture because it has been elevated to a higher practical purpose than the day-to-day reality within a particular scene may warrant. The commitment to this kind of symbolic survival played no small role in the development and continuation of the Vietnam conflict, the world energy outlook, and even the political fate of Bert Lance, a Georgia banker and short-time Director of the Office of Management and the Budget in the early days of the Carter administration.

Vietnam survived partly because organizational reports kept it "successful." The energy "crisis" will take an awesome toll not only because of particular shortages, but also because current—as well as past—information about supplies is enmeshed in bureaucratic propaganda. The plausible energy options are also hopelessly tied to organizationally-mandated-information-made-to-appear-in-the-public-interest; who really knows the various economic, social, political, and health benefits—and costs—of nuclear power vs. solar power, for example.

Can the reports from organizations, and a government that derives most of its information from the same source, be relied on to provide the "objective" facts? This is the problem of bureaucratic propaganda. The fate of Bert Lance tells us even more about the significance of sound impression-management. Lance was forced to leave office after an unprecedented three appearances before the Senate Governmental Affairs Committee in 1976 and 1977. Despite many charges of "illegalities" and "improprieties" during his earlier life as a Georgia banker, and despite the repeated demand by reporters and a handful of powerful politicians skilled at media presentations, Lance was never found to be guilty of any serious offense. Indeed, it became clear throughout the confirmation process that regardless of the outcome of his "defense" before the committee, he would be asked to resign. The reason was perfectly clear: he had been accused of "having the appearance of a conflict of interest," the "appearance of impropriety"; in an age of extreme political front-work, Lance became tarnished goods. This, too, is a problem, as well as a crucial implication for bureaucratic propaganda.

The major significance of bureaucratic propaganda is that it is part of a new form of discourse that is infused with rationality and scientific appearances. It is a dominant cultural form that, like television ratings, continues to be used and grows more common and more legitimate precisely because it is already so wide-spread, and so taken-for-granted. It is hard to penetrate and delegitimize because so many people work very hard to hold up the walls of respectability. When certain events like Vietnam and the energy problem are set before us, cracks in this symbolic structure appear, but are quickly repaired. How much repair work can be done remains to be seen, but it is clear to us that the future of our social order is inextricably tied to bureaucratic propaganda.

THE FUTURE

The future of bureaucratic propaganda will be shaped by the same influences that led to its original development: the interaction between organizations, relevant audiences, and communication channels. The "right" messages delivered to the "right" audiences constitute the significant perception and definition of an organization's character, purpose, and legitimacy. Not surprisingly, the role of organizations in our society has expanded with the communications explosion, particularly the electronic media. Not only have bureaucracies grown, but their acceptance as normal parts of the social landscape should be regarded as a significant accomplishment in its own right. As the communications media have become bureaucracies interested in packaging and disseminating imagery, the production of favorable public impressions of all kinds has become a business; organizational products and perspectives are marketable.

The growth of the mass media as a significant definer of reality in an increasingly pluralistic society led to broader demands among various groups to obtain the public recognition that others were receiving. As the number of organizations has increased, the relative availability of social and economic support—and legitimacy—have become more scarce. The developing communications technology and its skilled applications contributed a means for competing organizations to justify their existence and to demonstrate how well they were doing a particular job. The overall effects were increasingly to focus part of an organization's efforts at generating "public relations" messages and to encourage officials to edit reports about activities and efficiency in order to promote further an organization's legitimacy. As we have stressed throughout this book, accounts are produced for a particular audience. Just as nation-states have historically used emotional appeals to rally (manipulate) the population to support a cause, bureaucratic propaganda couches its phraseology in terms more familiar to sophisticated and educated people. Edelman (1977: 45) lucidly describes the former process as "The Labeling of Crises":

> The word 'crisis' connotes a threat of emergency people must face together. More powerfully, perhaps, than any other political term, it suggests a need for unity and for common sacrifice. . . . As is often the case with controversial political issues, the language conventionally used to describe a crisis helps people to adapt to it by evoking a problematic picture of the issue. . . . While political rhetoric evokes a belief in a critical threat to a common 'national interest,' the impacts of each crisis inevitably reflect internal conflicts of interests and inequality of sacrifice.

However, what the various interests are and what is "really" being promoted are clear only to "insiders," not the "outsiders" whom the message is intended to mobilize for support.

Even though the essentially manipulative character of propaganda has remained the same throughout history, major social and economic changes that promoted bureaucratic forms in particular, and logical-rational coordination in general, have altered the nature of topic, form of argumentation, and audience addressed. Now "crises" are usually quite specific and may be relevant for only a particular organization, rather than for all citizens. Also, with the pursuit of rationality in an effort to insure efficiency by removing the personal bias of individuals, positivistic logic was combined with quantitative techniques to forge new forms of accounting and justification, which were embraced by technically educated people who respected the new forms of evidence as valid mirrors of real behavior, and even of intentions. Many of these people accepted jobs in organizations. The relevant audiences they had to contend with were not only superiors, but also people in other organizations and agencies who could evaluate their individual work, as well as make general assessments of organizational performance.

One result of the encroaching bureaucratic forms on social life was to transform workers into co-conspirators. How well an individual would do within an organization, and how well an organization would do compared to competitors, would depend on official assessments of performance. Personal considerations were to have no "official" part in any evaluation of individuals or organizational goal attainment. In this context, rules and regulations continued to increase, and in the process, more dimensions of work and other goal-related phenomena became rationally definable; competence was systematically operationalized according to rules.

The eventual institutionalization of rule-dominated legitimacy and competence had to coexist with an unwielding fact of human social life— people's feelings and the nonrational pursuit of dominance (Douglas and Johnson, 1977). No one liked to be defined as a failure, and no one liked to have his or her organization declared unnecessary, illegitimate, and inefficient. These concerns continued to be primary in human affairs, although they were increasingly masked as bureaucratic impression management increased to comply with the norms of legitimate appearances. Ultimately, the forms that were intended to mark the passing of feeling and irrationality in favor of impersonal logic fulfilled an important role in the bureaucratic drama. As we have stressed throughout this book, personal interests in the outcome of "objective" assessments inevitably produce a victory for the former, but in the guise of the latter. Thus, bureaucratic impression management by laundering official information has become the rule in our society because: (1) bureaucratic-rational organizational forms dominate our occupational and political realities; these images comprise an important part of our conception of and belief in order; and (2) more people become involved in these organizations, and in so doing, their individual identities and futures become fused with their job status; ego protection and job security inevitably lead people to do what they "feel" is best, and "best" is almost always viewed in terms of self-definitions.

The fusion of feeling with the appearance of objectivity transformed official information from some "really objective" assessment to having a dual meaning: one meaning for the insiders, who knew how feelings had found their way into a report and even influenced what would be included; and one meaning for the outsiders, who, knowing nothing specifically about the career of the report, would be likely to assume that only rational considerations led to the assessment of the facts, trends, and so forth, thus producing an "objective" appraisal. Whether or not such discrepancies between the insider and the outsider perspective would ever become obvious to the outsider depended on the subject matter of the report and on the outsiders' ability to cut through the organizational smoke-screen that will continue to be presented in the event that certain "facts" become questioned. Molotch and Lester (1974) argue that only when accidents occur will the largely bogus information contained in such reports be more evident, and therefore questionable. They also show, however, that interested parties will perform a variety of public relations and media tricks to repair the image, including defining the apparent discrepancy as a "deviant case" or as "one of those things." Such organized front work makes it exceedingly difficult for any true outsider successfully to challenge the truth status of organizational claims while simultaneously reinforcing the organizational confidence in defining the world for its own purposes. For example, Stockfish (1971) has shown that financial considerations inform how information is used. Whereas private business organizations are financed by selling products in the marketplace, and thereby depend to a great extent on consumers' outside of the organization contributing to its overall budget, this is less true of government bureaucracy. In the latter case, financing is carried out through taxation and/or inflationary monetary techniques, both of which operate on the basis of the state's ability to coerce tax dollars from citizens. In short, the consumer of government programs—the taxpayer—has little direct say about the budget, or "organizational product," and is therefore largely irrelevant in the funding process. What does count, however, are the preferences of such powerful interest groups such as elected officials and career bureaucrats whose lifeblood depends on the public support of numerous programs. Not surprisingly, these are the same people who have access to the information essential in evaluating these projects, and they are also the people who promote these projects to legislative bodies in the "public interest." The potential dilemma for thorough evaluation and for especially painstaking care to assess critically the extent and quality of relevant data is obvious. As Stockfish notes (1971: 473),

> It can be properly argued that the problem of the public bureaucracy is actually the problem of the democratic political process, including policy evaluation and policy making, public administration, and social conflict in its broadest sense. . . . But it should also be forcibly emphasized that this broader problem and the conflict it entails have a very high information content. *And for many purposes, they can be fruitfully approached as information and statistical production problems.* [Italics added]

The significance of one's perspective and practical purpose at hand in influencing assessments of organizational work has also been well stated by Edelman (1977: 80).

> When organizational objectives are stated in concrete terms, many studies find them strikingly ineffective, though articles in the administrators' professional journals almost always see success. It is hard for anyone who reviews evaluations of organizational effectiveness to avoid the conclusion that what such studies 'find' hinges upon how they define organizational goals and how they define the policy outcomes they assess. Definition, perception, and interpretation are crucial, for the same results mean very different things to different administrators and to outsiders who examine their policies.

The practical circumstances surrounding any organizational effort to "find out" and then "present" what is going on in regard to a specific problem, issue, or program are central to the work that produces a "reasonable" job of evaluation. This is why the meaningful environment in which organizational reports take place must be understood and carefully considered when reaching such reports. Failure to place such reports in their proper context produces "pathologies of information," in which the "truth" is presented for certain practical purposes—usually maintaining a particular program and image of an organization—but will prove to be less valid for other purposes, such as implementing policy. This results in organizational failures that are direct by-products of intelligence failures (cf. Wilensky, 1967). The upshot is that maintaining the organization may be good in its own right, but not necessarily useful in carrying out its avowed and publicly sanctioned purpose.

The capacity to promote organizational purposes through official information implies that perhaps some other purpose is not being served, and may even be negated. We believe this does occur. Bureaucratic propaganda, as we have presented it, defines and maintains power differences throughout our society. Obviously, not everyone's perception of reality is accorded official status, but rather, only the ones generated by certain organizations. Moreover, within any organization, there is a tendency for administrators who maintain the appearance of efficiency and equity for their relevant audiences—usually subordinate workers—situationally to accept and reject the limits put on them by their superiors' use and interpretation of rules that will be accepted in order to justify or deny a course of action or request made by one of their own charges. The use of rules by officials establishes the legitimacy of their own decision making; it also provides a virtually unassailable account, namely, placing the blame on the people "up above." Indeed, one's own administrator may even attack his superior, blaming him for the plight and the rules that must be followed. Of course, when the same administrator confronts the superiors, he or she is cooled out in precisely the same way. The denial of responsibility is also a way of avoiding a challenge to the symbolic legitimacy that all of the parties cooperate in maintaining. But as noted above, each party will also promote its own official information, which in turn will be used by the people to whom they pass it on for their own purposes. This is how conflicting interests within an organization are masked in order to present the grandiose impression of a functioning organization that shares the same goals. Official accounts thus obliterate the impression of bureaucratic feudalism, in favor of consensus. Outsiders will then conceive of the organization as a whole rather than as an array of diverse and even conflicting units.

In previous chapters, we have presented evidence about the significance of impression management; it is important to stress the role that such impressions have in sustaining the idea of legitimacy in the face of change. The relationship between subordinates and superordinates within an organization is, to say the least, quite problematic. Each individual soon becomes aware of the vested interests at stake in keeping things pretty much the way they are, in form if not content. By this we mean that, for example, a department's budget in a university tends to be regarded as an obdurate fact by administrators at all levels, although the amount in that budget and for certain items may fluctuate from one year to the next. However, some of the legitimate enforcers of this bureaucratic form will willingly confront the authority—and respective symbolism—of those above them who can, presumably, alter it because in "exceptional" cases (if one's friends are involved) more money can be found and rules can be rather easily modified. But in regarding these as exceptions, the underlying myth in "objective" limits is maintained. And the alternative explanation that "they always have more than they tell us; all we must do is find a way to get it from them," is seldom invoked. Indeed, routinely to pursue this course of action would necessarily create problems for an administrator who was selected by those above him precisely because he or she could be relied on to "maintain the myth." Not only do many administrators accept these conditions of their status, but they also learn to see their former colleagues and friends as the "enemy" who want more than can easily be delivered. Thus, good workers are increasingly defined in terms of their ability not to cause trouble; good work is "hassle free" for those above them, who in turn resolve the majority of problems before they reach their superiors.

All this fosters the great myth of consensus and legitimacy, but most importantly, it is all created and protected by the various actors in the scenario, who will in turn blame "budget problems" on "the system." To this extent, bureaucratic propaganda and its related justificatory accounts divert attention toward an "enemy out there," rather than the "enemy within."

TOWARD A DISCOVERY OF BUREAUCRATIC TRUTH

What, then, becomes of truth? How are we to know what is going on in organizations if their accounts cannot be completely trusted? Does this mean, for example, that all organizational activities and goals are fraudulent and that no organization is effective or efficient?

Such questions strike to the core of the dilemma of bureaucratic propaganda. How truth is regarded depends, of course, on what one wants the truth to do (Bensman and Lilienfeld, 1973). Truth, like everything else, has a practical context—usually the concern motivating us to ask the question in the first place. In regard to organizations, the truth of their respective official reports is adequate to achieve the various goals, such as obtaining funding, legitimacy, and perhaps even giving some impression about what is being done, and how it is being accomplished. This book has been devoted to clarifying the rationale and perspective of official information; we have not claimed that we really know the truth and that "they" do not, but we have been concerned with "how they go about constructing and using their information."

Of course, once the practical dimensions of "truth work" are laid out, then we may be increasingly skeptical about related reports; we again are likely to ask, "But what is the real truth," about, say, battle efficiency and military preparedness? Our only response is that this question can be answered partially, but *not solely,* from the self-promotive information generated by the various branches of the military. But does this mean that our military is totally unable to defend the country? Not necessarily. It may suggest that our ability to defend ourselves against attack cannot be adequately encompassed within existing parameters—and uses—of official information. Stated differently, the "battle efficiency" reports discussed in chapter 8 may have little actual bearing on what a naval destroyer is likely to do—or not do—under "real" combat conditions. The entire paper war and practice wars that are routinely being waged once peace breaks out may best be regarded as a way to give troops something to do, to give military commanders something to command and direct, to give congressional overseers, mass media people, the public, and our "enemies" a dramatization that we have an army, navy, and air force that are "really prepared" and are indeed "standing by" capable of going into action at a moment's notice.

We suspect that, given this interpretation, we *may* be relatively safe from attack, but since we have not as yet carefully examined how such a state of preparedness would look, and compared to what, the question remains unanswered. But it is important to note that the categories contained in the official reports may have little relationship to other assessments of military preparedness; and that is our point—that the reports have a purpose, a career, and a meaning in their own right. In other words, the *work of being* battle ready is not necessarily in accord with the *work of showing* certain audiences in rational and quantitative terms that we are battle ready. The failure to make that distinction has obfuscated the essential qualitative differences between appearance and reality, even as the cultural forms of bureaucratic impression management become more sophisticated. Thus, the most creative work in organizations, including news bureaucracies, has been directed to improving appearances and rhetoric rather than substance; indeed, the appearance and front work have become the "real substance," what really counts for all practical purposes.

Ironically, the useful criterion for truth is not in itself bad. We believe the problem rests in what the uses are, who is defining them, and our capacity to recognize this. As long as bureaucratic propaganda gets results, organizations will continue to use it. As we have stressed, their main concern will be practical, and not philosophical or scientific. However, as long as this information is directed at certain audiences who assume that the reports reflect an "objective reality," the appearance of science will continue to be used because it gets results. The expanding use of the appearance of systematic research, evaluation, and so forth has produced an information war. Entire occupations and industries, for example, are tied to the peril of attack and another shooting, "hot" war. This connection will continue to exist whether or not "there is really" such a threat. Rather, the threat is at least partially construed from the capacity to do something about it, and the vested interests in doing something, thus prevent a war from breaking out. Clarifying the nature of information as an "invisible weapon" joins our concern about propaganda with Ellul's (1965: 257):

> The only truly serious attitude . . . is to show people the extreme effectiveness of the weapon used against them, to rouse them to defend themselves by making them aware of their frailty and their vulnerability, instead of soothing them with the worst illusion, that of a security that neither man's nature nor the techniques of propaganda permit him to possess. It is merely convenient to realize that the side of freedom and truth for man has not yet lost, but that it may well lose—and that in this game propaganda is undoubtedly the most formidable power, acting in only one direction (toward the destruction of truth and freedom), no matter what the good intentions or the good will may be of those who manipulate it.

With each of the above cases, and countless others as well, the perception of information and truth as useful is evident. Our long-standing commitment to truth as an ideal has rendered us vulnerable to its sophisticated use against us. Only when individual members of the various audiences susceptible to efforts at bureaucratic impression-management become more knowledgeable of this information war, and of the weapons used, will the organizational context of such information become more identifiable, and therefore less susceptible of manipulation.

We offer but a few rules of thumb for self-defense. The first thing is to be aware of the character of organizational information and to realize that the context of any report will necessarily infuse its meaning. The real question becomes trying to estimate the extent of distortion. In practical terms, this means that a report should not simply be accepted, but that it should be held up against a template of potentially significant sources of bias such as, *what* do the people involved have to gain, *who* did the study and provided the information, and *how* will the study be used. The most basic question to ask of a report is, What would the consequences be if the opposite findings were claimed? What would happen if, say, welfare officials demanded that their subordinate workers "tell the truth" and fill in the "time study" forms with only numbers they were certain were accurate? By the same token, what would the consequences be if a naval destroyer did not "gundeck" reports and artfully construct "battle efficiency reports," but rather made every effort literally to follow the rules, even if it meant admitting that procedures were breached, bent, and reinterpreted within practical guidelines? And, what would members of a television audience do if newscasters prefaced their remarks by saying: "Due to scheduling pressures, we cannot spend much time on a particular event, and in order to make it interesting (especially since you viewers are not really very bright), we will now tell you in thirty second about the great crime problem in our city." Asking such questions makes one aware of the practical incentives for selectively considering data, screening interpretations, and artfully presenting the "findings."

The best guideline, however, is to check reports for their completeness, including some statements about the broader context. The more detailed reports are, and the more we know about the actual procedures used in data collection, analysis, and interpretation, the more carefully we can assess the findings. By the same token, one's own experience on a job within an organization, and especially familiarity with an official report, can provide a useful framework for assessing the quality of information. This is no doubt why more and more people correctly believe that "you can do anything with statistics"; most people in our scientifically and quantitatively oriented society have had direct experience with the absurdity of applying fixed categories that are essentially incompatible with the complexities and nuances of most work situations. This is true of riveters in an airplane assembly line, and it is true of university professors who routinely must fill out "faculty service reports." Both workers "tell the organizational truth" for practical reasons even though it usually has little correspondence to what they actually do. Thus, if the riveter wants to know if faculty members really spend as much time working as these official reports claim, he can gain some insight by drawing on his own experience in filling out work-related reports.

The implications of modern propaganda generated by both private and government organizations are enormous. The studies reported in the previous chapters make it clear that human lives, tax dollars, and adequate public information can fall victim to organizational practicalities and routines. Our own research, plus reviews of the literature and informal interviews with dozens of workers and officials at all levels of government and business, suggest that propaganda is ubiquitous in contemporary life. Indeed, we have not discovered *one case* in which knowledge of the broader context of information processing and awareness of the procedures used in collecting, categorizing, interpreting, and presenting data in reports has not significantly altered the meaning and confidence in those reports. This leads us to conclude that such distortions are part and parcel of organized work informed by practical goals and purposes. It also directs our attention to assessing the potential impact of information compromised by promotive efforts on our society.

We can only hope, with Douglas (1971: 78), that citizens, particularly the social scientists who routinely use official information in their assessments of social trends and other such phenomena, will develop the reflection necessary to prevent the further encroachment of bureaucratic propaganda.

Unless great care is taken to investigate systematically the data one is using, organizational intelligence will infect the findings of scholars dedicated to finding the truth and not merely promotive activities. If scientists avoid asking such questions, science becomes but an extension of bureaucratic propaganda, and this we fear.

References

Adams, Sam
    1975   "Playing War With Numbers," *Harper's Magazine* (May): 21–51.

Albig, John W.
    1956   *Modern Public Opinion*. New York: McGraw–Hill.

Allport, Gordon W., and Leo Postman
    1947   *The Psychology of Rumor*. New York: Henry Holt.

Altheide, David L.
    1975   "The Irony of Security," *Urban Life*, 4 (July): 179–196.
    1976   *Creating Reality: How TV News Distorts Events*. Beverly Hills, Ca.: Sage Publications, Inc.
    1977   "Mental Illness and the News: The Eagleton Story," *Sociology and Social Research*, Vol. 61 (January): 138–155.

Altheide, David L., and Robert P. Gilmore
    1972   "The Credibility of Protest," *American Sociological Review*, 36 (February): 99–108.

Altheide, David L., and Paul K. Rasmussen
    1976   "Becoming News: A Study of Two Newsrooms," *Sociology of Work and Occupations*, Vol. 3 (May): 223–246.

Altheide, David L., Patricia A. Adler, Peter Adler, and Duane A. Altheide
    1978   "The Social Meanings of Employee Theft," pp. 90–124 in John M. Johnson and Jack D. Douglas (eds.), *Crime at the Top*, Philadelphia: J. B. Lippincott Co.

Argyle, Michael
    1959   *Religious Behavior*. Glencoe, Ill.: Free Press.

Aronson, James
    1970   *The Press and the Cold War*. Boston: Beacon Press.

Bagdakian, Ben H.
    1971   *The Information Machines*. New York: Harper and Row.
    1974   "Congress and the Media: Partners in Propaganda," *Columbia Journalism Review*, 12 (Jan./Feb.): 3–10.

Baird, Jay W.
 1974 *The Mythical World of Nazi War Propaganda*. Minneapolis: University of Minnesota Press.
Bartlett, Fred Charles
 1940 *Political Propaganda*. Cambridge, Eng.: Cambridge University Press.
Batscha, Robert M.
 1975 *Foreign Affairs News and the Broadcast Journalist*. New York: Praeger.
Bechtel, Robert B., Roger Akers, and Clark Achelphl
 1972 "Correlates Between Observed Behavior and Questionnaire Responses on Television Viewing," pp. 257–273 in Eli A. Rubinstein, George A. Comstock, and John P. Murray (eds.), *Television and Social Behavior: Television in Day-to-Day Life: Patterns of Use*. Washington, D.C.: U.S. Government Printing Office.
Beharrell, Peter, Howard Davis, John Eldridge, John Hewitt, Jean Oddie, Greg Philo, Paul Walton, and Brian Winston.
 1976 *Bad News*. London: Routledge and Kegan Paul.
Bendix, Reinhard
 1968 "The Cultural and Political Selling of Economic Rationality in Western and Eastern Europe," pp. 335–351 in Reinhard Bendix (ed.), *State and Society*. Boston: Little, Brown.
Bensman, Joseph, and Robert Lilienfeld
 1973 *Craft and Consciousness: Occupational Techniques and the Development of World Images*. New York: John Wiley & Sons.
Berger, Peter L.
 1961 *The Noise of Solemn Assemblies*. Garden City, N.Y.: Doubleday and Company, Inc.
Berger, Peter L., and Thomas Luckmann
 1966 *The Social Construction of Reality*. Garden City, N.Y.: Doubleday and Company, Inc.
Bernstein, Carl
 1977 "The C.I.A. and the Media," *Rolling Stone*, 20 (Oct.): 55–67.
Bittner, Egon
 1965 "The Concept of Organization," *Social Research*, 32 (August): 239–255.
 1967 "The Police on Skid Row," *American Sociological Review*, 32 (Oct.): 699–715.
Blumer, Herbert
 1948 "Public Opinion and Public Opinion Polling," *American Sociological Review*, 13: 542–554.
Bogart, Leo
 1976 *Premises for Propaganda: The United States Information Agency's Operating Assumptions in the Cold War*. New York: Free Press.
Boulding, Kenneth E.
 1956 *The Image: Knowledge in Life and Society*. Ann Arbor: University of Michigan Press.

Braestrup, Peter
1978 *Big Story.* New York: Anchor.

Broom, Leonard, and Philip Selznick
1963 *Sociology.* New York: Harper and Row.

Burns, Tom
1969 "Public Service and Private World," pp. 53–74 in J. D. Halloran (ed.), *The Sociology of Mass-Media Communicators.* Sociological Review Monograph, 13.
1977 *The BBC: Public Institution and Private World.* London: Macmillan.

Calhoun, D. C.
1957 "The Illusion of Rationality," pp. 155–167 in Richard W. Taylor (ed.), *Life, Language, Law: Essays in Honor of Arthur Bentley.* Yellow Springs, Ohio: Antioch Press.

Cantril, Hadley
1953 "Educational and Economic Composition of Religious Groups," *American Journal of Sociology,* 47 (March): 574–579.

Childs, Howard L.
1965 *Public Opinion: Nature, Formation and Role.* Princeton, N.J.: Van Nostrand.

Cicourel, Aaron V.
1968 *The Social Organization of Juvenile Justice.* New York: Wiley.

Cicourel, Aaron V., and John I. Kitsuse
1963 *Educational Decision Makers.* Indianapolis: Bobbs-Merrill.

Cicourel, Aaron V., K. H. Jennings, S. H. M. Jennings, K. C. W. Leiter, Robert Mackay, Hugh Mehan, and D. R. Roth
1974 *Language Use and School Performance.* New York: Academic Press.

Cohen, Stanley and Jack Young (eds.)
1973 *The Manufacture of News.* Beverly Hills, Ca.: Sage Publications, Inc.

Collins, Randall
1975 *Conflict Sociology: Toward an Explanatory Science.* New York: Academic Press.

Dalton, Melville
1959 *Men Who Manage.* New York: John Wiley and Sons.

Davis, Arthur K.
1948 "Bureaucratic Patterns in the Navy Officer Corps," *Social Forces,* 27: 143–153.

Davis, Nanette J.
1975 *Sociological Constructions of Deviance.* Dubuque, Iowa: Wm. C. Brown.

DeFleur, Melvin
1970 *Theories of Mass Communication.* New York: David McKay.

Denisoff, R. Serge
1975 *Solid Gold: The Popular Record Industry.* New Brunswick, N.J.: Transaction Books.

Dike, S. W.
 1909 "Church Membership in England," *American Journal of Sociology*, 15 (1909): 361–368.

Douglas, Jack D.
 1967 *The Social Meanings of Suicide*. Princeton, N.J.: Princeton University Press.
 1971 *American Social Order*. New York: Free Press.

Douglas, Jack D., and John M. Johnson (eds.)
 1977 *Official Deviance*. Philadelphia: J. B. Lippincott Co.

Durkheim, Emile
 1951 *Suicide*. New York: Free Press.

Edelman, Murray
 1964 *The Symbolic Uses of Politics*. Urbana, Ill.: University of Illinois Press.
 1971 *Politics and Symbolic Action*. Chicago: Markham.
 1977 *Political Language: Words that Succeed and Policies that Fail*. New York: Academic Press.

Elliott, Phillip
 1972 *The Making of a Television Series*. London: Constable.

Ellul, Jacques
 1965 *Propaganda: The Formation of Men's Attitudes*. New York: Knopf.

Epstein, Edward J.
 1973 *News from Nowhere*. New York: Random House.
 1977 *Agency of Fear: Opiates and Political Power in America*. New York: G. P. Putnam's Sons.

Fathi, A.
 1978 "Public Communication in Medieval Islam," paper presented at the annual meeting of the Pacific Sociological Association in Spokane, Washington, April.

Frank, Jerome D.
 1961 *Persuasion and Healing*. New York: Schocken Books.

Freidson, Eliot
 1953 "Communications Research and the Concept of the Mass," *American Sociological Review*, Vol. 18: 313–317.

Garfinkel, Harold
 1967 *Studies in Ethnomethodology*. Englewood Cliffs, N.J.: Prentice-Hall.

Garfinkel, Harold, and Harvey Sacks
 1970 "On Formal Structures of Practical Actions," pp. 338–366 in John C. McKinney and Edward A. Tiryakian (eds.), *Theoretical Sociology*. New York: Appleton-Century-Crofts.

George, Alexander L.
 1959 *Propaganda Analysis: A Study of Inferences made from Nazi Propaganda in World War II*. Westport, Conn.: Greenwood Press.

Goebbels, Joseph
 1948 *The Goebbels Diaries, 1942–1943*. Garden City, N.Y.: Doubleday and Company, Inc.

Goffman, Erving
  1959   *The Presentation of Self in Everyday Life.* N.Y.: Doubleday and Company, Inc.
Goldenberg, Edie N.
  1975   *Making the Papers.* Lexington, Mass.: D. C. Heath.
Gusfield, Joseph R.
  1963   *Symbolic Crusade.* Champaign, Ill.: University of Illinois Press.
Halberstam, David
  1978   "Time, Inc.'s Internal War Over Vietnam," *Esquire,* January, 94ff.
Hardy, Alexander
  1967   *Hitler's Weapon: The Managed Press and Propaganda Machine of Nazi Germany.* New York: Vantage Press.
Homans, George C.
  1950   *The Human Group.* New York: Harcourt, Brace, and World.
Hughes, Helen MacGill
  1940   *News and the Human Interest Story.* Chicago: The University of Chicago Press.
Irwin, Will
  1936   *Propaganda and the News.* New York: McGraw-Hill.
Jacobs, Jerry
  1967   "A Phenomenological Study of Suicide Notes," *Social Problems,* 15: 60–72.
Johnson, John M.
  1972   "The Practical Use of Rules," pp. 215–249 in Robert A. Scott and Jack D. Douglas (eds.), *Theoretical Perspectives on Deviance.* New York: Basic Books.
  1973   The Social Construction of Official Information. Unpublished Ph.D. Dissertation, Department of Sociology, University of California, San Diego.
  1975   *Doing Field Research.* New York: Free Press.
Katz, Daniel, Dorwin Cartwright, Samuel J. Eldersveld, and Alfred McClung Lee (eds.)
  1954   *Public Opinion and Propaganda.* New York: Dryden Press.
Katz, E., and Paul F. Lazarsfeld
  1955   *Personal Influence.* New York: Free Press.
Kitsuse, John I., and Aaron V. Cicourel
  1963   "A Note on the Use of Official Statistics," *Social Problems,* 11 (Fall): 131–139.
Kuhn, Thomas S.
  1970   *The Structure of Scientific Revolutions.* Chicago: The University of Chicago Press, second edition.
Lang, Kurt, and Gladys E. Lang
  1960   "Decisions for Christ: Billy Graham in New York City," pp. 415–427 in Maurice R. Stein, Arthur J. Vidich, and David M. White (eds.), *Identity and Anxiety.* Glencoe, Ill.: Free Press.

Lasswell, Harold D.
1927   *Propaganda Techniques in World War I.* Cambridge, Mass.: M.I.T. Press. (Reprinted 1971).
1950   "Propaganda and Mass Insecurity," *Psychiatry,* 13, 3(August): 284–285.

Lasswell, Harold D., *et al.*
1935   *Propaganda Promotional Activities, An Annotated Bibliography.* Minneapolis: University of Minnesota Press.

Lazarsfeld, Paul F., Bernard Berelson, and Hazel Gandet
1948   *The People's Choice.* New York: Columbia University Press.

Lee, Alfred McClung
1952   *How to Understand Propaganda.* New York: Rinehart.

Lerner, Daniel (ed.)
1951   *Propaganda in War and Crisis.* New York: George W. Stewart.

Lippmann, Walter
1922   *Public Opinion.* New York: Free Press.
1926   *The Phantom Public.* New York: Harcourt, Brace and Co.

Lyman, Stanford M., and Marvin B. Scott
1970   *A Sociology of the Absurd.* New York: Appleton-Century-Crofts.

McLoughlin, William G., Jr.
1955   *Billy Sunday Was His Real Name.* Chicago: University of Chicago Press.
1959   *Modern Revivalism.* New York: The Ronald Press.
1960   *Billy Graham: Revivalist in a Secular Age.* New York: The Ronald Press.

McQuail, Denis
1969   *Towards A Sociology of Mass Communications.* London: Collier Macmillan.

Machiavelli, Niccolò
1963   *The Prince.* New York: Washington Square Press.

Manning, Peter K.
1977   "Rules in Organizational Context: Narcotics Law Enforcement in Two Settings," *The Sociological Quarterly,* 18 (Winter): 44–61.

Manning, Peter K., and Laurence John Redlinger
1977   "Invitational Edges of Corruption: Some Consequences of Narcotic Law Enforcement," pp. 284–305 in Douglas and Johnson (eds.), *Official Deviance.* Philadelphia: J. B. Lippincott. (Originally published in Paul Rock (ed.), *Politics and Drugs.* New York: Dutton/ Society Books, 1976).

Merton, Robert K.
1946   *Mass Persuasion: The Social Psychology of a War Bond Drive.* New York: Harper.

Meyer, John W., and Brian Rowan
1977   "Institutionalized Organizations: Formal Structure as Myth and Ceremony," *American Journal of Sociology,* 83 (Sept.): 340–363.

Michels, Robert
   1949   *Political Parties*. Glencoe, Ill.: Free Press. (Originally published 1911).
Miller, James Nathan
   1977   "They're Giving Us Gas, All Right," *New Republic*, Feb. 12: 15–17.
Molotch, Harvey, and Marilyn Lester
   1974   "News as Purposive Behavior," *American Sociological Review*, 39 (February): 101–112.
Neumann, Franz
   1942   *Behemoth*. New York: Oxford.
Niebuhr, H. Richard
   1959   *The Social Sources of Denominationalism*. New York: Meridian Books.
Nielsen Co., A. C.
   1964   *What the Ratings Really Mean*. Los Angeles: A. C. Nielsen Co.
Palmer, Paul A.
   1936   "The Concept of Public Opinion in Political Theory," pp. 230–257 in Carl Wittke (ed.), *Essays in History and Political Theory*. N.Y.: Russell and Russell.
Park, Robert E.
   1923   "Natural History of The News Paper," *American Journal of Sociology*, 45 (March): 664–686.
Pepinsky, Harold E.
   1978   "Despotism in the Quest for Valid U.S. Crime Statistics," in Robert J. Meier (ed.), *Criminological Theory*. Beverly Hills, Ca.: Sage Publications, Inc.
Pirenne, Henri
   1956   *A History of Europe.*, New York: University Books.
Piven, Frances Fox, and Richard A. Cloward
   1971   *Regulating the Poor*. New York: Pantheon.
Pollner, Melvin
   1970   *On the Foundations of Mundane Reasoning*. Unpublished Ph.D. Dissertation, Department of Sociology, University of. California, Santa Barbara.
President's Commission on Federal Statistics
   1971   *Federal Statistics: Report of the President's Commission*, 2 Vols. Washington, D.C.: U.S. Government Printing Office.
Presthus, Robert
   1978   *The Organizational Society (revised)*. New York: St. Martin's Press.
Qualter, Terrence H.
   1962   *Propaganda and Psychological Warfare*. New York: Random House.
Rehberg, Angus Wilhelm
   1809   *Über die Staats verwaltung deutscher Ländes*. Hanover, Germany.
Riesman, David
   1950   *The Lonely Crowd*. New Haven: Yale University Press.

Riess, Curt
 1948   *Joseph Goebbels: A Biography.* Garden City, N.Y.: Doubleday and Company, Inc.

Rivers, William
 1965   *The Opinionmakers.* Boston: Beacon Press.
 1970   *The Adversaries: Politics and the Press.* Boston: Beacon Press.

Roper, Elmo
 1971   "An Extended View of Public Attitudes Toward Television and Other Mass Media." New York: Television Information Office.

Rosengren, Karl Erik
 1974   "International News: Four Types of Tables," Paper presented to the VIII Nordic Congress of Sociology, Geilo, Norway.

Rosengren, Karl Erik, Peter Arvidsson, and Dahn Sturesson
 1978   "The Bärseback 'Panic'; A Case of Media Deviance," pp. 131–49 in Charles Winick (ed.), *Deviance and Mass Media,* Beverly Hills, CA.: Sage Publications, Inc.

Roshco, Bernard
 1973   *Newsmaking.* Chicago: The University of Chicago Press.

Roth, Guenther
 1968   "Personal Rulership, Paternalism, and Empire-Building in the New States," pp. 581–591 in Reinhard Bendix (ed.), *State and Society.* Boston: Little, Brown.

Roth, Julius A.
 1963   *Timetables.* Indianapolis: Bobbs-Merrill.

Roy, Donald F.
 1952   "Quota Restriction and Goldbricking in a Machine Shop," *American Journal of Sociology,* 62: 427–442.

Schandler, Herbert Y.
 1977   *The Unmaking of a President: Lyndon Johnson and Vietnam.* Princeton, N.J.: Princeton University Press.

Schorr, Daniel
 1977   *Clearing the Air.* Boston: Houghton Mifflin.

Schutz, Alfred
 1967   *The Phenomenology of the Social World.* Translated by George Walsh and Frederick Lehnert. Evanston, Ill.: Northwestern University Press.

Schwartz, Barry
 1975   *Queuing and Waiting.* Chicago: The University of Chicago Press.

Schwartz, Tony
 1975   *The Responsive Chord.* New York: Anchor.

Scott, James C.
 1972   *Comparative Political Corruption.* Englewood Cliffs, N.J.: Prentice-Hall.

Selznick, Philip
 1948   "Foundations of the Theory of Organization," *American Sociological Review,* 13: 25–35.

Shaw, Donald L., and Maxwell E. McCombs
    1977   *The Emergence of American Political Issues: The Agenda-Setting Function of the Press.* St. Paul, Minn.: West Publishing Co.

Skornia, Harry J.
    1965   *Television and Society.* New York: McGraw-Hill.

Smigel, Erwin O., and H. Lawrence Ross
    1970   *Crime Against Bureaucracy.* New York: Van Nostrand Reinhold.

Smith, Bruce L.
    1968   "Propaganda," Vol. 12, pp. 579ff, *International Encyclopedia of the Social Sciences*, David L. Sills (ed.). New York: Macmillan.

Smith, Ronald W., and Bruce P. Asher
    1977   "Organizational Accounts." Unpublished paper, Department of Sociology, University of Nevada, Las Vegas.

Speier, Hans
    1950   "The Historical Development of Public Opinion," *American Journal of Sociology*, 55 (Jan.): 376–388.

Stockfish, Jacob A.
    1971   "The Bureaucratic Pathology," pp. 455–476 in Report of President's Commission on Federal Statistics. Washington, D.C.: U.S. Government Printing Office.

Sudnow, David
    1965   "Normal Crimes," *Social Problems*, 12 (Winter): 255–276.

Szulc, Tad
    1976   "Freezing Out the C.I.A.," *New Republic*, (July, 24): 12–14.

Tracey, Michael
    1977   *The Production of Political Television.* London: Routledge and Kegan Paul.

Tuchman, Gaye
    1969   News, the Newsman's Reality. Unpublished Ph.D. Dissertation, Department of Sociology, Brandeis University, Waltham, Mass.
    1974   *The TV Establishment.* Englewood Cliffs, N.J.: Prentice-Hall.
    1976   "What is News? Telling Stories," *Journal of Communication*, Vol. 26, (Autumn): 93–97.
    1978   *Making News: A Study in the Construction of Reality.* New York: The Free Press.

Tunstall, Jeremy
    1977   *The Media are American.* New York: Columbia University Press.

Turner, Ralph H.
    1969   "The Public Perception of Protest," *American Sociological Review*, 34 (December): 815–830.

Vidich, Arthur J.
    1975   "Political Legitimacy in Bureaucratic Society: An Analysis of Watergate," *Social Research*, 42 (Winter): 778–811.
    forthcoming   "Legitimacy, Capital, Accumulation, Imperialism in the Third World," in Vidich and Ronald Glassman (eds.), *The Crisis of Legitimacy in Modern Society.* Beverly Hills, Ca.: Sage Publications, Inc.

Weber, Max
    1958   *The Protestant Ethic and The Spirit of Capitalism.* Translated by
           Talcott Parsons. New York: Charles Scribner's Sons. (Originally
           published in 1904).
    1968   *Economy and Society.* New York: Bedminister Press. (Originally
           published in 1922).

Wheeler, Michael
    1976   *Lies, Damn Lies, and Statistics.* New York: Liveright.

Whitam, Frederick L.
    1968   "Revivalism as Institutionalized Behavior: An Analysis of the Social
           Base of a Billy Graham Crusade," *The Southwestern Social Science
           Quarterly,* (June): 115–127.

Whyte, William H.
    1956   *The Organization Man.* New York: Simon and Schuster.

Wilensky, Harold
    1967   *Organizational Intelligence.* New York: Basic Books.

Wilensky, Harold, and Charles N. Lebeaux
    1965   *Industrial Society and Social Welfare.* New York: Free Press.

Wise, David
    1973   *The Politics of Lying: Government Deception, Secrecy, and Power.*
           New York: Vintage Books.

Zeman, Z. A. B.
    1973   *Nazi Propaganda.* London: Oxford University Press.

Index